Ways Ahead:
Proceedings of the First International Csound Conference

Edited by

Joachim Heintz, Alex Hofmann
and Iain McCurdy

CAMBRIDGE
SCHOLARS
PUBLISHING

Ways Ahead: Proceedings of the First International Csound Conference,
Edited by Joachim Heintz, Alex Hofmann and Iain McCurdy

This book first published 2013

Cambridge Scholars Publishing

12 Back Chapman Street, Newcastle upon Tyne, NE6 2XX, UK

British Library Cataloguing in Publication Data
A catalogue record for this book is available from the British Library

ISBN (10): 1-4438-4758-5, ISBN (13): 978-1-4438-4758-2

TABLE OF CONTENTS

FOREWORD

The First International Csound Conference, held at the Hanover University of Music, Drama and Media (HMTMH) between the 30th September and the 2nd October 2011, marked the first time that the principle people involved with Csound—in existence since 1986—met in person. Contacts and relationships had long been established through discussion lists and publications, but meeting together in one location felt like the Csound community had drawn closer together—it finally felt like a real community.

I. The Conference

It is surprising to note that it took 25 years for the first Csound conference to come about, but sometimes an unexpected event can be fortuitous, someone simply asking the right question at the right time. It was whilst involved in a research project at the HMTMH that Alex Hofmann, who was at the time more familiar with MaxMSP and SuperCollider, listed what he regarded as the pros and cons of Csound in its current state. Based on his conclusions, one of the proposals he made was: a Csound conference!

When this idea was pitched towards the Csound community it prompted many enthusiastic reactions. With the kind support of the HMTMH, Joachim Heintz, head of the electronic studio in the Institute for New Music *Incontri,* was able to host this conference. It is a measure of the conviction and dedication of many within the Csound community that so many travelled so far in order to attend. The conference welcomed people from Ireland, UK, Norway, France, Italy, Switzerland, Germany and from as far afield as Estonia, Russia, Iran, USA and Japan.

II. ...And Its Proceedings

Some documentation pertaining to the conference already exists at www.cs-conf.de. This was the original website for the conference and it contains an outline of the events that took place, papers presented, workshop overviews and concert programmes. Videos from round tables, paper sessions and workshops are available at www.youtube.com/user/csconf2011 but it is thanks to the initiative of Cambridge Scholars Publishing that the proceedings of the conference are now published as a book. The three authors of this foreword had already worked closely together on The Csound FLOSS Manual so it felt appropriate to share this new challenge together.

This *was* a real challenge because this book is not simply a documentation of the conference. It was our publisher who encouraged us to take the opportunity to work on a book that contained a lot of new material. Of course, the conference papers and workshop descriptions are all represented—and in many cases updated and expanded—but the reader will find a lot more.

III. Content of this Book

The first part is dedicated to Csound's history, a history that goes back to the very origins of computer music. This publication opens with Csound legend Richard Boulanger's original conference keynote, *Csound Past, Present and Future,* which is followed by an interview with Csound's chief maintainer John ffitch, *How to Become a Csound Root.* This part of the book concludes with an interview with Richard Boulanger in which he discusses the process and reason for moving Csound's licence to LGPL.

The second part of the book showcases various aspects of Csound's development. Victor Lazzarini's article, *The Technology of Csound*, is not just a summary of the conference's first user-developer round table discussion, it is an in-depth "snapshot 2012" of Csound's internals, from the implementation of the new parser to the porting of Csound to mobile devices. There is a new interview with Michael Gogins about The Csound API as well as his article about writing Csound opcodes in Lua, another of his innovations as a Csound core developer. Reza Payami's discussion about Csound and object-orientation documents a paper he presented at the conference while the last three texts in this chapter are completely new: Partikkel Audio's Øyvind Brandtsegg is interviewed about his Csound powered granular synthesis plug-in "Hadron". Rory Walsh has written a comprehensive explanation of his front-end for Csound, "Cabbage", which offers new ways of exporting Csound instruments as plug-ins. Gleb Rogozinsky describes his implementation of a new Csound GEN routine in *Wavelets in Csound.*

Csound is principally used for the creation of music and accordingly the central part of this book is dedicated to the music featured at the conference. Not every piece that was performed at the conference could be featured in this book but the reader will find interviews with many of the contributing composers, which will provide an insight into the myriad of ways in which Csound can be used as a compositional tool.

The fourth part, *Usage*, showcases different ways of using Csound. *The Csound Journal,* edited by James Hearon and Steven Yi, can be considered the major platform for users to present and discuss different aspects of Csound usage, so an interview with both editors seemed timely here. For most Csound users, Andrés Cabrera's "CsoundQt" front-end is their main way of interacting with Csound, so both an interview with him about this project and his original conference contribution about Python scripting in CsoundQt are presented here. Peiman Khosravi describes a method of using Csound's famous streaming phase vocoder opcodes for multichannel work in his article, *Composing Circumspectral Sounds*. This is a new and extended version of the original conference paper, as is Kim Ervik and Øyvind Brandtsegg's contribution, *Creating Reverb Effects Using Granular Synthesis.* Two more of the conference's workshops appear also in a new light in this part: Steven Yi introduces his own Csound front-end in *Composing with Blue,* providing a thorough explanation of design and usage, and Richard Boulanger explains *CsoundForLive,* which connects Csound with two of the most extensively used audio applications: Ableton Live and MaxMSP. The ever-expanding User Defined Opcodes Database, established and maintained by Steven Yi, is the focus of the last interview in this part of the book with Steven and Joachim Heintz.

Because of its history and its simple signal flow language, Csound is well known as a tool for teaching audio programming and digital sound processing. For this reason, the final part provides an overview of Csound within various aspects of education. Iain McCurdy contributes a summary of the second round table discussion, which used the theme: *Learning and Teaching Csound.* Gleb Rogozinsky describes his experiences of teaching Csound in Saint-Petersburg State University of Film and Television in *A Personal View on Teaching Csound.* Massimo Avantaggiato outlines his use of the programming language PWGL for composition in *PWGL: a Score Editor for Csound.* Maximilan Marcoll describes his program "quince" in the chapter: *A Modular Approach to Music Editing.* Alex Hofmann and Joachim Heintz talk about the role of Csound at the HMTM Hannover from the perspectives of former student and lecturer respectively. Iain McCurdy introduces his popular collection of real-time Csound examples in another chapter and interviews Peiman Khosravi and Rory Walsh about their experiences in teaching with Csound in England and Ireland. At the end of this final part of the book, the three editors introduce "The Csound FLOSS Manual", Csound's collaboratively written textbook.

IV. Ways Ahead

We hope that the publication of these articles and interviews will suitably mark the momentous occasion that was the first Csound Conference and afford people, who were unable to attend the conference in person, the opportunity to benefit from the wealth of intellect, experience and talent that was present during those three days. We believe that this book is also a documentation of the many different activities within the Csound community—developers and users, musicians and programmers, students and teachers—at this time, 25 years after its creation by Barry Vercoe at MIT.

Csound has come a long way from demanding to be invoked from a terminal window. Now users have the choice of a variety of front-ends, such as *CsoundQt*, *WinXsound*, *Blue* and *Cabbage*, with which to interact with Csound. Even further abstraction is evidenced in the seamless use of Csound within *PD*, *MaxMSP*, *Ableton Live* and other software via its API or as a plug-in.

It seems that Csound's forward thinking design has facilitated a wide diversity of musical applications. Whilst most music software focusses on one or two applications and styles, Csound is equally adept at producing Electroacoustic music, techno, imitations of conventional musical instruments, live electronics, sound installations, self-generating musical processes... the list goes on.

Csound defies its age through the living work of musicians, researchers and teachers. We hope that this book can contribute to these "Ways Ahead", as the conference certainly has done.

We would like to thank all the contributors for their efforts and their willingness to publish their thoughts here. Thanks are also due to Anna Heintz-Buschart for her help in completing the manuscript, and to Carol Koulikourdi and Amanda Millar from Cambridge Scholars Publishing for their patience and kindness.

Hanover, Belfast, Vienna. January 2013.
Joachim Heintz, Iain McCurdy, Alex Hofmann.

HISTORY

CSOUND PAST, PRESENT AND FUTURE: KEYNOTE FOR THE OPENING OF THE FIRST INTERNATIONAL CSOUND CONFERENCE

RICHARD BOULANGER

It is a great honor to have been asked to present the keynote at this, the *First* International Csound Conference.

Thank you so much to Joachim Heintz and Alex Hofmann for inviting me, for inviting all of us, and thanks to the Hanover University of Music, Drama and Media for supporting them and helping them to host this historic gathering.... a gathering that points to the future—The Ways Ahead—for Csounders and for Csound.

I am so humbled to be here in the company of so many brilliant Csounders from all around the world. For years now, we have known each other through our email, our code, our music, but to finally meet in person—face to face—is absolutely incredible. I will start my greeting with extreme gratitude. Your work, your research, your questions, your feedback, your suggestions, and most importantly your sounds, your instruments and your music have so inspired me, have so enlightened me, and have given me so much to share with my students and to explore in my music. Truly, your work, your questions, your suggestions, and your *sometimes* frustrations - all served to guide and propel Csound into the future - making it *always* current and always relevant - making it the "go-to" synth.

To those developers here among us - John ffitch, Michael Gogins, Victor Lazzarini, Andrés Cabrera, and Steven Yi, I offer my deepest gratitude. You kept Csound alive; and as a result, you kept our musical creations, our dreams... alive.

Thanks to you, Csound is "Future-Proof". New hardware comes along. New operating systems come along. New protocols. New sensors and interfaces. And you have made sure that Csound keeps on "rendering" the classics while taking advantage of all of these new possibilities.

The "prime directive" for Csound has been "100% backward compatibility". We will not allow new technology to trash yesterday's music. We will not throw away the music when we upgrade the machinery—the baby with the bath water. And thanks to you, this is truly the case. This is a unique quality of Csound. It still works. It *all* still works! The earliest pieces. The first tutorials. They all still run. As we all know, Csound carries on the tradition of the Music-N languages developed by Max Mathews at Bell Labs in 1956/57. And, in Csound much of his code and examples still work too! With Csound, we have all been able to stand on the shoulders of giants and learn from the masters who have come before us. This is possible because of the selfless dedication of these amazing developers.

It all started at MIT where Barry Vercoe wrote the earliest versions of Csound. They were based on the *MusicV* language of Max Mathews as manifested first in his *Music360* language (for the IBM360 mainframe), and then in his *music11* language (for the PDP11 MiniComputer). Adding opcodes and functionality, composing original works, hosting conferences, offering workshops, commissioning composers, and delivering papers, Barry Vercoe carried the Csound torch from 1986-1996. (It could be argued that Csound was born in 1977, and called *music11* after the PDP11 computer on which it ran, and was then rewritten in the new "portable" C Programming Language in 1986 with an appropriate name change to Csound). In fact, I composed Trapped in Convert (in *music11*) at Barry's 1979 summer workshop and, in 1986, came back to MIT after my Ph.D. (in Cmusic ironically) to work again with Barry as he was moving from the PDP11 to the VAX 11780. During that period, we were revising and using "Trapped in Convert" as the main test suite for his new port of *music11* - Csound.

In 1995 or so, Barry went off to develop a proprietary version of Csound for Analog Devices and passed the torch for "public Csound" to John ffitch and myself. (Actually John and I were there working with him at Analog Devices too; and it was exciting to have Csound running on the ADI SHARC DSP (we called this version SharCsound) and, for that time period, Csound was doing unheard-of real-time, multi-channel signal processing and synthesis! (In fact, Barry added some amazing opcodes to SharCsound, which, sadly, have never made it into "public Csound" as they are the proprietary property of Analog Devices.)

From the fall of 1989, John ffitch had been working on PC, Linux, and Mac versions of Csound and he and I were communicating quite regularly over the Internet. But it was the Analog Devices project that brought us to work together in the same lab; sent us off to deliver papers and demos at conferences together; and got us "performing" together - playing Csound live! (Something that we will do again here at this conference in tonight's concert.)

Barry always said that passing Csound on to John gave him the time to follow his muse. And thanks to John's indefatigable work on Csound, we were all able to follow our muse. Because of John's work, we could use Csound on virtually any and every computer that we could get our hands on. John ffitch's work on Csound opened the doors of the MIT Media Lab to students, composers and musicians around the world. The Csound mailing list, which he started and managed, was our way to communicate, with him, and with each other. From its very inception, this has been a respectful and insightful dialog; a rare exchange between musicians, researchers, scholars, students—experts and beginners—of all ages, and from the broadest range of technical and musical experience, aesthetic, and perspectives. Some of us liked MIDI, some of us liked note lists (OK, that's pushing it—none of us liked note-lists), some of us liked Techno, some of us liked Disco, some of us liked Xenakis (Xenakis and Disco in the same sentence - pretty good right!). All kidding aside, this rich conversation continues to this day, and it serves as a model to all creative online communities. In the Csound community, which John ffitch so fundamentally helped to build—everyone is welcome, everyone is heard, everyone's questions are answered, and everyone's suggestions and ideas seem to get implemented!

I have been working with Csound for more than 30 years now, and I am still discovering new things, new sounds, new ways of working, new ways of thinking, and new ways of performing and interacting. It is thanks to the developers here, and to those who could not make it, but whose contributions are sited in the Csound manual, that we can all continue to grow with Csound. In particular, I would like to extend a special thanks to: John ffitch for Csound, Csound5, Csound6, and WinSound; to Gabriel Maldonado for CsoundAV; to Matt Ingalls for MacCsound and csound~; to Davis Pyon for csound~; to Øyvind Brandtsegg for Hadron; to Peiman Khosravi for FFTools; and to Jinku Kim, Enrico De Trizio, and Colman O'Reilly for CsoundForLive; to Richard Dobson for CDP (and all the streaming vocoder opcodes); to Victor Lazzarini for the Csound API; to Michael Goggins for CsoundAC and Silence; to Steven Yi for Blue; to Jean Piché and Olivier Bélanger for Cecilia and the OLPCsound apps TamTam and SynthBuilder; to Rory Walsh for Lettuce; to Stefano Bonetti for WinXound; and especially to Andrés Cabrera for his award-winning QuteCsound (now called CsoundQt). Their intuitive, brilliant and powerful "front-ends" to Csound, with all sorts of built-in "features", "short cuts", and "assets" (including GUI tools, Multi-channel output and support for all sorts of hardware, expanded MIDI and OSC, Python, and so much more), have made Csound a tool for education, composition, research, concert performance, and commercial production, and as such, have helped to introduce Csound to a wider audience of creative musicians—have brought Csound from the "media lab" to the independent media artists around the world.

In addition to the inspiring front-ends that have been developed by these fantastic Csounders, the work on the Csound manual has been incredibly important to the longevity of the program and to the education of the community. It was because of the fact that Barry's original *music11* manual was so terse and difficult to understand that I was inspired to write The Csound Book. I had read it dozens of times, from cover to cover; filling every margin with notes and comments, but there was so much that I still did not get. Sure, it was heralded (by Barry at least) for its "concise technical descriptions" of *all* the *music11* opcodes; but the language, and the code fragments were completely alien (to me at least, and I suspected that they would not totally "click" for many other composers and practicing electronic musicians). And so, in an indirect, but quite literal way, it was Barry Vercoe's *music11* and subsequent Csound manual that inspired me to write "The Csound Book" (for the rest of us!), which explained how things worked and, as a rule, contained *complete* working instruments in every tutorial chapter. According to Barry, the *music11* and Csound Manuals were "reminders", for experts, about the working parameters for the opcodes, "not tutorials" on how the opcodes actually worked—to know that, "read the code". Well, electronic musicians and composers (like me!) needed more. And so, I insisted that "The Csound Book"... WORKED! Through it, we learn by hearing, touching, tweaking, revising, remixing and composing. In fact, as I was getting started writing it, and I had already signed the contract with MIT Press, I quickly realized that I didn't actually know enough to write such a comprehensive text on my own, and so, I reached out to the Csound community and invited the subject specialists to write working tutorial chapters on each of their specific areas of expertise. The "Csound Book" teaches computer music, software synthesis, and digital signal processing - through Csound, and the best computer music professors from around the world are on the faculty. I am truly grateful to each and every one of them, and I think that you might be too!

The Csound Book took five years to write and was published in 2000. Since then, things have changed in the world of Csound and especially in the Csound Manual department. The current Csound Manual (over 1500 opcodes covered in over 3000 pages!) has come a long way with the help of some dedicated Csounders - Jean Piché, David M. Boothe, Kevin Conder, John ffitch, Michael Gogins, Steven Yi, and many others who labored to get the words right, but most importantly, through the efforts of Menno Knevel, who has invested years into making sure that *every* opcode has a working *musical* example - he strove to get the *sounds* right. The addition of his musical models to the manual, and those that he collected, edited, and curated, has been huge. Thank you to everyone who has contributed to this important document, and to those who continue to breathe life into it with new words, new instruments, and new opcodes every day.

But wait, there is another. Another Csound manual (as if 3000 pages is not enough)! In fact it is not. And to coincide with this First International Csound Conference, a team of three - Joachim Heintz, Alex Hofmann, and Iain McCurdy are releasing a new, collaboratively written, Csound Manual/Book - called the Csound FLOSS Manual (It's really the 2010 Csound Book but they were being polite). It is amazing and incredibly inspiring. There have been so many new things added to Csound over the years, and there are so many powerful new ways of working with Csound. This book, filled with working *instruments* and examples, connects yesterday's Csound with tomorrow's Csound - TODAY! It is a "must read" for every Csounder.

It turns out, in fact, that these are not the only two Csound books by any means. There have been a number of significant texts written on the language and they all bring something special to our understanding and appreciation of it. Riccardo Bianchini and Alessandro Cipriani wrote "Virtual Sound" around the same time as The Csound Book; Andrew Horner and Lydia Ayers wrote "Cooking with Csound" a couple years later. Jim Aikin has just released "Csound Power"; And Giorgio Zucco just released Digital Synthesis: A Practical Laboratory in Csound.

Between the years that separated the publication of these fantastic books, there have been two online magazines, distributed quarterly, whose articles and instruments have helped beginner and expert alike share their work, introduce unique approaches, and discover new algorithmic, compositional, and production possibilities. Starting in around 2000, Hans Mikelson pretty much single-handedly wrote the "Csound Ezine". It appeared for several years and totals about 10 issues. A great and inspiring read to this day. Carrying the torch from Hans was James Hearon and Steven Yi with "The Csound Journal" which is up to about 17 issues now. They release four issues a year and the articles range from the practical to the esoteric, from a new look at the basics, to the exposition of the most cutting edge topics. If there is something new that is possible with Csound, The Csound Journal is the place to find out about it.

There have been some important websites that give this international community a home. Our Csound page at SourceForge, managed by John ffitch is pretty important and continues to grow; and I have been maintaining *Csounds.com* for 20+ years now with the help of some fantastic Csounders and Berklee College of Music Students - Jacob Joaquin, Young Choi, Juno Kang, Greg Thompson, David Akbari, John Clements and Christopher Konopka. A few years back, a Csounder came forward, Cesare Marilungo, and helped to totally renovate and revitalize the site. His dedication and that of these Berklee alumni, have helped to make it a real "home-base" for Csounders everywhere.

We can't forget to mention the inspiration and insight that we have been able to draw from those great Csound instrument libraries and instrument collections. I had been collecting things since literally "day one", and many of them appeared first in "The Csound Catalog" (which has been updated this year by Christopher Konopka and Tito Latini and now contains over 14GB of categorized and organized working instruments in .csd format!) Some of my favorite "Classics" are the huge and diverse libraries created by: Josep Comanjuncosas, Steven Cook, and Hans Mikelson; and the Csound version of all the instruments from "The Computer Music Book" by Charles Dodge and Thomas Jerse; and, of course, the gem of the collection - Jean Claude Risset's "Instrument Catalog" from MusicV that was converted to Csound - this is truly an example of being able to stand on the shoulders of giants! Today's top Csound sound designers are: Joachim Heintz, whose examples in CsoundQt are incredible; and Iain McCurdy, who's "Real-time Instrument Collection" is so comprehensive and inspiring that it takes your breath away; Iain shows you how to do "everything"! And... it all sounds amazing! We owe these great sound designers so much, because it is their work that teaches each of us how "it" works.

And so... we have the tool (arguably the finest and most powerful synthesizer in the world). We have the instruments! We have the knowledge. We have the books, the journals, the papers, the research, the teachers and the curriculum. We have this amazing community. But... what we don't have... is enough music. If there is any *one* challenge that I would like to pass along to all of you here today, and to the entire Csound community, it is that we need to push ourselves to make more music with Csound. We need to use Csound in more of our compositions; (it doesn't have to *all* be Csound, but it *always* sounds better when you have added *some* Csound); we need to use Csound in more of our productions (add a

Csound reverb or ring modulation, or EQ); we need to use Csound in more of our game audio and sci-fi TV spots (I want to hear more background ambience, explosions, and alien voices created with Csound); we need to use more Csound in our installations (come on... Csound is the ultimate sonification tool); and we need to add Csound to our love songs (that's right, I want to hear Madonna, and Rhiana, and Prince, and Beiber, and Ringo, and Bono, and Janet, and Sting, and Usher using Csound on their next CDs). We all need to do more to turn our Csounds into Cmusic - to move from sound design to musical design.

The future of Csound is in the *music* that we make with Csound.

For me, Csound has always been the place that I could turn to for answers. The answers were in the instruments, in the code, in the emails, in the generous gifts of time and knowledge that this community has shared with me and with each other. In the beginning, I was fortunate enough to hang out with Barry Vercoe at the MIT Media Lab and when I had a question, I would walk into his office and ask him. I can't possibly tell you everything that I learned from him; but I have tried to pass along much of what he taught me through "The Csound Book", "The Audio Programming Book", “Csounds.com”, "The Csound Catalog", and most importantly, through my students.

In a way, Barry Vercoe trusted us with his "baby", and I think that we have raised a "child" that would make him proud.

Csound has brought us all together, and I am incredibly honored and proud to be associated with each and every one of you, and truly grateful for all that you have taught me. Thank you, for giving me this great opportunity to thank you.

HOW TO BECOME A CSOUND ROOT?

INTERVIEW WITH JOHN FFITCH

John ffitch has been at the forefront of Csound development for about twenty years. Despite long hair and beard, was never a hippie, he says in his biography. In this interview he talks about his way to Csound, and his view on the different periods of its development, including the ways for the developers to collaborate, before and after the Sourceforge platform brought a new standard.

How did you come in contact with Csound?

First a little background. I started writing (bad) music way back, but got very serious about it in the early 1960s, when I wrote a piano concerto late at night, every night after I was supposed to be in bed, and other works, like pieces for girls at school. However not being a pianist and only a self-taught recorder player, I could only hear my music in imagination. About 1970 as a research computer geek I thought about getting a computer to play some of it for me, but cosmology and astronomy took my time outside computer algebra and LISP.

When I got my chair in Bath and having done a lot of administration I returned to thinking about music again. So I lurked on net-news systems reading music material. As a result I took the sources of Csound from MIT. I had a Unix computer as my home machine so building it was reasonably easy. Never managed to work out how to use it but it was there. Must have been late 1980s or 1990. All this introduced me to a world I did not know, and led me to a conference in Greece celebrating Xenakis, and then to ICMCs.

What was your first participation in the development of the Csound code?

My general interest in music led me to lurk on newsgroups; really cannot remember which one it was but possibly comp.music. After some time with little understanding someone asked if Csound ran on a PC. As I said I had downloaded the Csound sources from MIT earlier, but it was a wet weekend and my software company (the owner of my unix computers) was developing and selling algebra software on a range of systems, including PCs, and so I had a C compiler for it, and time, so I tried to build Csound. Actually was not very hard. I announced this to the news group and that was all. A short time later the same question was asked so I replied along the lines of "yeah did that a few weeks ago". I then started getting emails asking me for it. I think the majority of the messages came from Dennis Miller at Northeastern University. I started looking into realtime output from a soundblaster and fixing compilation problems. All I did was on PCs/DOS at this time, but I did expand to Acorn and Atari over time. Perhaps I should add that my main job at this time was researching and teaching software, especially LISP and event simulation, with a small sideline in music software, like Rosegarden.

How did you become the main responsible developer?

By mistake? Out of the blue I got a phone call at home from Barry Vercoe (who I only knew by name) introducing me to Mike Haidar of Analog Devices. They had heard of what I had been doing on PCs and invited me at short notice to Boston and Norwood, just before Christmas 1994. This was the Extended Csound project, using a DSP processor to get real-time synthesis. I had a great time, and as well as Barry I met Richard Boulanger (DrB, Rick,...). I flew home on Dec 23, arriving (late) at Gatwick on Christmas Eve just in time for the last train home.

From this I visited Analog Devices Inc on a number of occasions, and increasingly I was working at weekends (and sometimes all night) with Rick, and making changes as he suggested. Over time I moved the code to ANSI C, added some opcodes, etc. I never consciously ``become the main responsible developer" but it sort of emerged that Barry was happy to let me deal with users, and he was working on Extended Csound; I suppose Rick pushed me into it. I invented things like version numbers, changelogs etc., and I was now working on Unix, Mac, PC/Windows, Acorn and Atari. At this time *de facto* I had complete control over sources, and what went in.

Who else has been on board at this time? How did development work without platforms like Sourceforge?

People sent revised code or patches, or complete opcodes and I checked them, ANSIfied them and incorporated in the next release. Releases happened when I wanted, or a major bug was fixed or on demand. There were a number of other contributors whose names can be found in the current sources and manuals, but I did the incorporation. Many people proposed many changes, and I tried to act as liberally as I could.

I have checked the files and there were 49 people credited in the sources before we went open source as contributing (list naturally available). Of those about eight stand out in my memory as contributing to the core (Richard Dobson, me, Michael Gogins, Matt Ingalls, Victor Lazzarini a little later, Gabriel Maldonado, Istvan Varga and of course Barry Vercoe) but this list is not complete. For example a student of DrB asked me for a feature in the score -- he contributed but his name is buried in a comment I think. DrB himself did not write a line of code but was active in pushing for improvements and developments. And there were others like Maurizio Umberto Puxeddu who was very active for a while, did a great deal and then vanished from our world. The breadth of actions can be seen in the mailing list, which was run from University of Exeter by a local user for many years. Too many people to catalog!

When did the Csound development move to Sourceforge and what were the resulting changes for you and the other developers?

We registered for SF on 2003 May 25 as Csound 5 was taking true shape. Apart of the licence change we had to have an accessible base and Sourceforge was the obvious solution at that time. Naturally the changes in work process was major. Personally I had never used any source control system, and not having the master sources directly on my computer was initially hard. But I quickly found it useful even between working on my desk machine, laptop or university desk machine. One had, on the other hand, to take care about submitting non-working code. But a good discipline.

I have over the years worked on many software projects from about 1970, but usually with one or two friends with whom I shared an office, or later a close relationship. Not seeing the co-workers was a change. But one learns. At least in Sourceforge I controlled who had what access!

As you mentioned before, you have a liberal way of retaining control. Do you believe in Csound as a pluralistic or even anarchic project?

I had not thought of labelling it, but I suspect anarchy is close to the truth. The main developers were/are all composers and that tends to influence what gets developed. Sometimes I get into less popular areas tweaking code and adding system-like things, but we are a mutual community driven by users' requirements. Personally I like writing code, and implementing other people's ideas is an entertainment for me; and I enjoy the dynamics of working with musicians.

Interview: Joachim Heintz

LICENSING CSOUND TO LGPL

INTERVIEW WITH RICHARD BOULANGER

Richard Boulanger, editor of the famous *Csound Book* (MIT Press, 2000) and host of the main Csound community site *www.csounds.com*, has not just accompanied every step of Csound since its „birth" in 1986. In this interview, he describes both, the years before this first release of Csound, and the complicated process of moving Csound to the GNU Lesser General Public Licence.

Richard, you actually worked with Csound before its first main release in 1986. Your piece "Trapped in Convert" was written in 1979. Please describe working with Csound at this time?

The spring and summer of 1979 were life-changing for me. So many things were coming together in my studies, my composing, and my career. I was working on my Masters Degree at Virginia Commonwealth University where I was the teaching assistant in Electronic Music and had 24-hour access to several labs filled with some incredible analog modular synthesizers. In the fall, I had a symphony for large acoustic orchestra and 2 Arp 2600 synthesizers commissioned and premiered by two different orchestras (I was one of the synthesizer soloists).

That spring, I was invited by Dexter Morrill, to spend a few weeks at the computer music lab at Colgate University. (At the time, this was one of the few places in the US with high-end digital-to-analog converters; and with a mainframe that had any sort of MusicN language installed on it. It was a DEC PDP10.) Not only did I have weeks of unlimited access to this incredible machine; but I had the great fortune to be working there together with another visiting artist—a recent Stanford/CCRMA graduate Bruce Pennycook. Bruce spent hours teaching me Stanford's Music10 program. He helped me to create the most amazing sounds I had ever heard, and he laid the foundation for my deep understanding of how computers actually make music. With him, I was able to make the connection, translation, and transition from my experience and work with analog modular synthesizers to their digital counterparts. And later that same summer, I was invited to return to Colgate, and to work there as the "Studio Assistant" for Dexter's Computer Music Workshop. There I met, helped, and learned from a number of legendary electronic music composers; guys I had been reading about, and whose records I had been buying and devouring for years.

Dexter Morrill was not the only person offering computer music workshops in the summer of 1979. Barry Vercoe was also running a highly publicized and coveted set of workshops at The MIT Experimental Music Studio. They attracted engineers, programmers, and composers from around the world who would come for a month to learn about these new possibilities and work on systems developed at MIT to digitally transform sound and make computer music. There were about 20 of us in the class, but only 10 were composers and only these 10 would stay for the full four weeks. The first two weeks were focused on theory, hardware, and software (this was mainly for the engineers, but the composers were there too). Every morning, from 9am until noon, Barry Vercoe, (mostly from memory), would fill the walls (literally "fill" the walls - they were all "white-boards") of a very large MIT classroom, (we all sat side by side at long white tables in the center of the room), with equations, block diagrams, circuit diagrams, instruments, opcodes, algorithms, and code. We were literally surrounded with his work. And when he ran out of space, the walls would slide from side to side to reveal additional white-boards on which to write. It was breath-taking how much information, knowledge, and experience was pouring out of him. And I was doing my best to absorb as much as I possibly could! Each afternoon, we would have a distinguished guest like Marvin Minsky (the father of AI), or Max Mathews (the father of computer music), or Mario Davidovsky (pulitzer prize winning electroacoustic composer) to name but a few, present their research and creative work. During the second two weeks, most of the engineers went back to work, and the composers stuck around and applied their new found knowledge and understanding to the creation of new pieces that were premiered on the final day in a major, sold out, concert (yes, this was really "new" back then, and quite rare, and so there was a huge public audience interested in what we were doing at MIT, what the future of music would be). The concert was held in Boston's famous and beautiful sounding Kresge Auditorium. It was reviewed in all the Boston papers as well.

Along with some promising (and now quite famous) young composers, and some already established celebrities, I was accepted into this 1979 summer class. It was very inspiring to work with, live with, and hang out with this group. Strong and lasting friendships developed. We all lived in the MIT dorms, and we worked around the clock - five of us on the computers during the night shift, and five of us on the computer during the day shift. My twelve hour time slot was from 6pm to 6am. What was so great about the late-night shift was that most of the morning shift composers didn't usually show until about 9am or later, and so, I would always get at least 3 or 4 more hours of pretty much solo computer time each day. In fact, most in my group would drop off to sleep between 1am and 6am and the load on the CPU would lighten then too.

We were all sharing time and CPU cycles on the Digital Equipment Corporation (DEC) PDP11 Minicomputer (about the size of a refrigerator) on which Barry Vercoe had written music11, a newly revised, optimized, and significantly expanded version of his former, MUSIC 360 language (a language based on Max Mathews' MUSIC V) in RT11 Assembler. It was fast for those times (in fact it could do real-time computation of simple oscillators and envelopes), but with five or more of us rendering audio at the same time, (most of us would leave our jobs running for days because that's what it took to make even simple sounds back then), and even running our jobs at a 16k sampling rate, to lighten the load and speed up the turnaround, one waited a long, long, long, long time to hear a few seconds of often very bad, very loud, very weird, very nasty, totally unruly, and absolutely unexpected "garbage". A *long long* time. For most... too long. But for me... well…

I loved it.

This was "composer's time". Time to study. Time to read the manuals. Time to listen again to the Vercoe lectures (I had recorded them all on my portable "cassette tape" recorder). This was time to dream. And time to talk about new music with each other, and about each other's music. Time to learn from each other. Time to explore all those amazing new opcodes. Barry Vercoe's music11 was an infinitely large synthesizer, and I went through the manual trying to make sense, and sound, of every module (opcode) he offered.

I would use this time to design instruments (on paper), type them in from the DEC terminal (click, click, click, click - green phosphor), and imagine how they would sound when rendered. There was no mouse. I forget what editor I used - probably VI.

Barry called his software synthesis language "music11", naming it after the PDP11 computer on which it ran. His personal interest in the

PDP11 was to do cutting-edge research on computer-based real-time synthesis and signal processing. He demonstrated these systems for us. His visionary "RTSKED" program not only rendered in real-time, but supported a Common Practice Music Notation display, and a visual instrument design language, that looked and worked very much like Max/MSP or PD, with which one could design "instruments" graphically by "patching" together icons representing music11 opcodes on the screen. Yes, the future. And more, there was an electronic piano keyboard attached, so that one could actually play the computer!

All of this was at least 10 years ahead of its time, and was so incredibly exciting to all of us; but the quality of the real-time synthesis and the limited number of algorithms and opcodes that one could run, in real-time, served to shift my focus to music11 proper because I wanted to make *huge* and *complex* sounds. For years, I had been working with my Arp 2600 analog synthesizer, my Arp Sequencer, my Oberheim Expander, some PAIA and Aries modules, and a Sony 4-track tape recorder and TASCAM mixer (a pretty nice set up really), and I *loved* designing sounds, creating evolving textures, and delicate ambiences; but there wasn't a day that went by that I didn't wish I had a few more oscillators, a few more filters, some additional envelope generators, more voltage processors, modulators, attenuators, patch cords and mults. With music11, my prayers had been answered. I finally had all the filters, oscillators, and envelope generators that I could imagine - and then some! And not only did I have more "modules", but with music11, I could automate all of their parameters using Barry's line, expon, linseg, and expseg opcodes.

On the Arp I would use envelope generators (2) and oscillators (3) to apply dynamic qualities to my patches; but here at MIT and with music11, I was thinking in terms of time and space - auditory space, spectral space, physical space - clock time, musical time, and psychological time. Instead of patches that I would trigger and play from a keyboard, I began to think of sound objects, spectral mutation, complex contrapuntal textures, radiant new timbres, and the most acrobatic melodic and rhythmic gestures - all moving, morphing, evolving, breathing, and living. All of my instruments in "Trapped" were conceived as unique expansions of what I might have done if I had an unlimited Arp2600 synthesizer at my disposal. Well, in fact... I did.

"Trapped in Convert" was the musical result of that summer in paradise. OK, well it wasn't always paradise, in fact, that's how the piece got it's curious name. At MIT, they were incredibly proud of their floating-point Digital to Analog converters custom built by Analog Devices. And as I had stated earlier, high-quality DACs were pretty rare in

1979. Given that we were sharing this computer, and we were not all too clear about what exactly we were asking it to sing or play; there were many "crashes". When the computer crashed, there was always a printout on the huge (and noisy) line-printer/mechanical typewriter in the machine room. This printout read: "trapped 0 in convert...".

I think that filters were blowing up because we were "dividing by 0 all over the place". As you might imagine, by the end of the summer, as I was desperately waiting (always hours and sometimes days) for the final sections and sounds to render, praying that it would all run without a crash, and praying that what came out would be good enough for the concert, I began to feel like "I" was "trapped in convert". I remember walking over to the printer one evening, reading the printout, and saying to everyone - there's the title for my piece - "Trapped in Convert!"

As the days and nights passed, it seemed an even more fitting title, and I made adjustments to sounds and structure of the piece to make it an even better fit. For instance, the finals section of the piece was particularly composed to have a sense of being "chased" and, after a short silence (possibly caught?), and then breaking free. In the middle of the piece, I added a section where there were "samples out of range" that distort and sound like the speakers were tearing, all to enhance the sense of "struggle" with the machine. Audiences seem to get it, and have been getting into it for many years now. It is quite gratifying and humbling - that such a simple piece could have such a long life and inspire so many generations.

When I came back to MIT in 1986, after completing a PhD in Computer Music at the University of California in San Diego doing "Cmusic" with F. Richard Moore, Barry showed me a new project that he was working on - rewriting music11 in C. He invited me to join him at the newly opened Media Lab, to help with the testing and especially to use "Trapped" as a measure. I would meet him at the Media Lab at 6am every day (which meant leaving my house at 4:30am.) We would start downstairs on the 4th floor with a coffee (he taught me how to double-up the filters to make it even "stronger"), and then we would get to work. He would add new opcodes, give me a new version of the program, and I would design instruments to test each of the opcodes. It was so exciting.

We did this for several months, until all the opcodes were there and all sounded the same. We worked until "Trapped" worked and sounded identical.

To the user, Csound looked, rendered, and sounded exactly the same as music11. In fact, many of the manual pages for the Csound manual were taken from the music11 manual. In the fall of 1986, all of the music11 opcodes were rewritten in C and became the core set of Barry's new computer music language - Csound. I was happy to be there at the dawn of a new era and to have been able to suggest some additional opcodes, like "loscil" that he added at my request. I am still suggesting new opcodes to this day.

I was happy to have been able to continue working on Trapped at the dawn of Csound. I fixed some things here, balanced some things there, tweaked the ending a bit. In fact, I will admit it now, for the 1979 premiere of Trapped, the ending was "spliced", but in the Csound version it is not. Back then, the entire concert was played from analog tape. (Quite ironic don't you think?) There had been a few too many "trapped 0's in convert" the days leading up to the concert, and we could not get a complete render of the piece done without one of my "colleagues" crashing the PDP. (It actually took days to compute the four minutes back then.) We had a clean render of most of the piece from a week earlier already on tape, but we did not have the *whole* piece. Time was short. We decided to just compute the ending (which took a night), and then bounce that to tape and splice it, just minutes before the start of the concert. In fact, the silence prior to the last set of sounds was something we added from the "cutting room floor" to give it a little "breath".

Now you know the story of Trapped in Convert, how it got it's name and how it came to be. The "Trapped" that everyone knows today. The one that most Csounders use to benchmark their CPU, or test the latest build of Csound, was indeed the very first "Csound" piece, but for sure... it will not be the last!

Csound can be considered to be "Open Source" at that time. But was it legal for anyone to distribute and use copies of Csound?

The story of The Csound License is quite convoluted. As I understood it, there was initial funding from an NSF grant that helped to support Barry Vercoe's original work on Csound. And this grant stated that the results of this work should be open for "educational and research use". That's nice, but this "distinction" left quite a number of us, those who actually "used" Csound, quite confused. What made it worse was the fact that the copyright also stated that one needed "permission" from MIT to do anything else with Csound. Not particularly "open" right? Many of us wondered if we were allowed to "compose" with Csound or "perform" with Csound, or "process recordings" with Csound, and we were very concerned when we thought to make and release records and CDs using Csound. These all seemed to be "commercial" uses of the program that might not fall under the "education and research" label.

Even back then, in the early days of Csound, I am happy to report that Barry Vercoe gave permission to me and to John ffitch and allowed us to distribute the program. MIT Press and I distributed it on the CDs included with The Csound Book. I was using it in my teaching and research, but I was also using it on stage and in my compositions, and I was helping to get it into computer games, and TV shows, and into major hollywood films. In fact, I brought Barry Vercoe to see the premiere of Sony Pictures sci-fi/AI BlockBuster "Stealth" directed by Rob Cohen and featuring Josh Lucas, Jessica Biel, Jamie Foxx, and Sam Shepard. The score was done by a Berklee alumni, collaborator, student, and friend - Brian Transeau (aka. BT). The film opens with the Csound grain opcode producing a glorious granular texture as this intelligent, pilotless, stealth bomber is flying overhead. The movie is filled with Csound and I got to do some of the sound design too! (I processed David Bowie's voice with the sndwarp and schedkwhen opcodes in one of the "club" scenes.) Barry wanted Csound to be free, and often said this in the lectures that he gave, but he felt that his hands were tied somewhat given the stipulation of the original funding source.

In April of 2003, Barry Vercoe and I met with the lawyers at the MIT Licensing Office and, to our surprise, they were very interested in helping us to change the license to an open-source license like the GLP or LPGL. On May 1, I was there to witness the signing.

For sure I was pushing for this. For years I had been pushing for this. But the real push came from the developers on the Csound mailing list who were becoming more and more "concerned" (and more and more vocal) about the fact that they were adding their opcodes to a program that "theoretically" was preventing others—even them—from doing what they wanted with the program—creatively, professionally, or commercially. What they were saying, and rightfully so, was that essentially, once they added an opcode to Csound, it became the property of MIT and its use was constrained by the Csound copyright—for education and research only. Top developers, individuals who were making a huge difference to Csound, were leaving Csound behind because they were donating their time and their code, and they wanted their code to be free. I made the case to Barry that we were losing the top Csound developers because of this "technicality", the "mixed message", free, but not free. Barry wanted Csound for everyone and so, off the record, the NSF wording was something that he himself did not truly support—he never wanted to restrict its use in any way.

On May 1st 2003, Csound went LGPL and was "at last... free"!

You said "Signed the Contract" ... who actually signed the contract about Csound's Licence at MIT? With whom?

Quite near the Media Lab at MIT, there is an office dedicated to intellectual property - The MIT Technology Licensing Office. If you go to their website, you will see that they have a large staff of lawyers working there who advise and help to develop, patent, and license the creative work of students and faculty. (I think that we met with Jack Turner, the Associate Director in charge of the Media Lab, and with several others in our first meeting.) Barry arranged for he and I to go over and meet with them to discuss the current Csound license and, essentially, to ask their permission to change it. In some ways, I think that he wanted me there to hear exactly what they had to say. My fingers were crossed, but I was thinking inside that they were going to tell us that there was "no way" that this license could be changed, particularly since it had been established, in part, from a very high-level National Science Foundation grant whose "charter" was to support "education and research".

We met there with two of their top attorneys. I told them the Csound story. I spoke for "the users" and the community. Barry then told him of his "original" intention that the software be free and open. I asked about the Creative Commons model and if it were possible to go with a more clearly "open" license such as the GPL. Clearly they had prepared for the meeting well in advance because they both had reviewed the license and had some background on both the program and our concerns. I told them of my work on the manual and asked if we could open up the license on this as well. They told us that they thought that a GPL or LGPL and FDL license "made more sense" for Csound and that they saw no issues with changing the license. They asked us to come back in a week when they would have all the legal documents drawn up for Barry and them, on behalf of MIT, to sign. We left that meeting pretty excited. I don't remember my feet actually touching the ground as I walked back across the bridge from Cambridge to Boston and went in to teach my Csound class that day. A few days later, Barry and I were back in the licensing office. They asked us to decide if we wanted to go GPL or LGPL. We made the case for LGPL. They approved of our reasoning; made a few corrections to the document; came back with a final printout, and Barry signed it. "Can I tell the world that Csound is... at last free?", I asked. They smiled and said yes. We walked back to Barry's office and celebrated (with a cup of coffee) and decided how to tell the Csound community this great news. As I sat there in Barry's office, looking over his library of books and dissertations and happily spotted his copy of The Csound Book,

I knew that this day was "the" day for Csound. He typed away and after what seemed like no time at all, jumped up from his seat, ran across the hall to the printer and popped back in with the following... and said - "send that!"

Dear all

Each time I have developed a major system for Musical Sound Synthesis I have tried to make the sources freely available to the musical community. With MUSIC 360 in 1968 that meant running to the post office every day to mail off a bulky 300 ft reel of 9-track digital tape, but I really did enjoy the many hundreds of pieces this caused during the late 60's and 70's. With my MUSIC -11 for the ubiquitous and less costly PDP-11, I chose to pass the maintenance and distribution task off to a third party. This was easier on me, and led to even more pieces in the community during the late 70's and early 80's. At the time I wrote Csound in 1985 the net had now made it possible for would-be users to simply copy the sources from my MIT site, so I put my time into writing a Makefile that would compile those sources along with the sound analysis programs and the Scot and Cscore utilities. And though this was initially Unix, I worked with others to port it to Apple machines as well. After I was awarded an NSF grant in 1986, it became necessary to add a copyright and permission paragraph to the sources and the accompanying manual. The spirit of my contribution however remained unchanged, that I wished all who would use it, extend it, and do creative things with it be given ready access with minimal hassle. Today the original wording of the permission no longer conveys that spirit, and the dozens of developers to whom I paid tribute in my foreword to Rick Boulanger's The Csound Book have felt it a deterrent to making the best extensions they can. So with the graceful consent of MIT's Technology Licensing Office, I am declaring my part of Public Csound to be Open Source, as defined by the LGPL standard. This does not compromise the work of others, nor does it make the whole of Public Csound into free software. But it does create a more realistic basis upon which others can build their own brand of Csound extensions, in the spirit of my efforts over the years.

I am indebted to John ffitch for having protected me from the enormous task of daily maintenance in recent years. His spirit is even greater than mine, and I trust you will continue to accord him that recognition as you go forward.

Sincerely,

Barry Vercoe

Why did you choose the Lesser General Public License?

At the time, we were trying to decide between the GPL and LPGL license for Csound. Barry and I chose the LGPL license because we felt that it made Csound even more "open" and "useful". LGPL allowed Csound to be used as a "library" in other applications that did not necessarily need to be totally open. Just the Csound part needed to be open. Since we could link Csound with proprietary software, and not be required to give out the proprietary part, we felt that this would allow Csound to become a part of any and every music program and project - educational software, research software, open-source software, plug-ins, commercial audio editors and DAWs. Csound could now run on any and every operating system, on tablets and embedded systems - and it does! We wanted... "Csound Inside". And thanks to the developers, the Csound community, and the LGPL license… it is.

Interview: Joachim Heintz

DEVELOPMENT

USER-DEVELOPER ROUND TABLE I: THE TECHNOLOGY OF CSOUND

VICTOR LAZZARINI

This chapter reports on the current status and prospective development of the technologies in Csound. It is based on the discussion at the technology round table of the Csound Conference. Speakers at this event included: John ffitch, Michael Gogins, Richard Boulanger, Francois Pinot, Steven Yi, Andrés Cabrera and the author, who chaired the session.

I. New Parser

The new parser for Csound, which has been developed for several years by John ffitch and Steven Yi is an essential piece of technology for the continued development of the system. As ffitch explains, the existing parser ('old parser'), written by Barry Vercoe, was appropriate for Csound until the need for further development of the language became clear. Its monolithic state and ad-hoc design is a good example of 1970s code design, which has served its purpose well, but is very difficult to extend and maintain.

For this reason, a new parser, written using up-to-date tools and concepts, is absolutely essential. A parser is a piece of software that translates the code written by the user into data structures that are used by Csound to run. The new parser is written using the flex lexical analyser and the bison parser generator. These two tools allow a much simpler maintenance and debugging of the software, compared to the old parser code, which is coded directly into C and thus more opaque to developers. It also allows means of enabling new language elements or features more easily.

The new parser has been present in Csound for a number of years, and could be employed with the *–new-parser* option. By version 5.14, at the time of the conference, it was almost complete, but not ready for production. Its development required three final steps: testing (debugging), intelligible error reporting and optimisation of code. These steps were completed in the three months that followed, and version 5.16, released in February 2012, switched to the new parser as default (and the old parser was made available through the *–old-parser* option). The new parser produces faster code, compiles it at a faster speed and produces better error messaging with correct line reporting (which was a recurrent bug in the old parser).

Linked to development of the new parser is the parallel processing option for Csound. Using the -j N option, it is now possible to run Csound in a multithreaded form for N processing cores. This is only possible in the new parser as it depends on a semantic analysis code that was designed to work with it. John ffitch explains that the principles behind multicore Csound are that users should not need to use any special syntax to take advantage of the process. It is left to the system to automatically allocate the processing. Of course, some ways of organising the way orchestras are designed might be more suited to multicore processing, but in general, the operation is completely transparent. At the time of the conference, there were a few elements of Csound programming, such as channels and zak opcodes, that were not supported by the multicore code, but these were resolved in the subsequent versions of the software.

II. Language Developments

Parallel operation is an essential aspect to future systems and the code for this in Csound is in constant development so that it can utilise the computing resources at its disposal in the most efficient way. The system must be prepared to embrace the possibilities afforded by multicore processors, as these increase in the number of cores and complexity. As pointed out by the Csound developer Michael Gogins, computing platforms are continuing to develop, not only in terms of hardware, but also in terms of what is possible with software, as well as access/mobility.

The programming environment for audio and Music is also constantly changing. He cites the example of dynamic typed languages such as Lua, which are increasingly capable of delivering performance at the level of implementation languages, C and C++. It is now possible to envisage a moment where the use of higher-level environments would not require a compromise in terms of computing capacity. Opening up Csound for integration with a variety of programming languages would allow us to seize these possibilities. Gogins' work with the Lua opcodes, which allow for fast implementation of signal processing algorithms inside a Csound orchestra, is an example of these developments. These types of possibilities are so useful that Gogins envisages a mechanism for *pluggable* embedding of languages in the Csound orchestra, which would then facilitate the use of a variety of them, not only Python or Lua. The evolution of the Csound language is guided by what its users require and by what developers can implement. Sometimes the requirements that users have, do not map into what it is possible to deliver. One example is the question of arrays, which on the surface appears to be a simple one, but which involves some difficult semantics issues. Arrays of values, vectors or matrixes, are not problematic at all, and traditionally, in Csound there are ways to use create and manipulate them, tables or the linear algebra opcodes being two obvious examples of this.

However, arrays in general might imply something else, which could be described as *arrays of unit generators*. This is more difficult because of the fact that unit generators, opcodes, are in fact objects. In normal use, this does offer any issues, because opcodes are defined *singly* in a code line. For instance,

```
a1 oscil k1, k2, i1
```

defines one object *oscil* that has two internal, hidden, methods, one to initialise it and the other to run it and produce a ksmps vector each k-cycle (stored in the a1 variable). The object is actually nameless, as there is no syntax to name individual instances of the oscillator opcode. When we then include a syntax for arrays, then this becomes muddled, because there can be more than one interpretation to the line:

```
a1[kN] oscil k1, k2, i1
```

Do we mean the same *oscil* object, or do we have different ones, and if so, how do we treat its inputs, and each object's initialization? This, of course, is not a problem that cannot be resolved, but it is more complex than just introducing a square brackets syntax. In fact, for those wanting to create arrays of oscillators, there is already an unambiguous way of doing just that, via recursive user-defined opcodes (UDOs). This is clearly outlined in the reference manual and can be used very effectively for spawning parallel or serial opcode graphs.

Some users, nevertheless, would like to have a square brackets syntax for arrays of values and that is reasonably straightforward. We have introduced, following the Csound Conference, a new t-type that allows for vectors of any size, as well as a number of operations on them. This is, in fact, an example of the usefulness of the new parser. Following user requests, this author and John ffitch were able to design and implement the new type in a matter of a few hours, but of course, only in the bison/flex parser, with the old parser remaining very opaque and immutable with regards to these types of additions. The new t-type is fully documented in the Csound reference manual.

Another two aspects of language/system development could be very useful to ensure the continued development of Csound. The first one is an internal one: the separation of the parsing and compilation and the runtime signal processing-graph synthesis engine. This would disentangle the connection between the Csound language as it stands, its opcodes and the actual running synthesiser. It would allow the possibility of plugging new language translators to create the graphs for the engine, so at some point users would eventually not require the original Csound language itself, but could employ another one designed for the task.

This internal development would also allow the second addition to the system that has been a constant user request: dynamic loading and unloading of instruments. In other words, instead of relying on a compile-once-run cycle, we would be able to compile many times whilst Csound is running, adding or substituting instruments that are available to the engine. This would allow a more flexible real-time operation for Csound, which is the kind of facility that is offered by other comparable systems. These two changes have been deemed sufficient to trigger the development of a major new revision of Csound, its version 6, currently under way. Some other requests and ideas for Csound 6 will be discussed later on in this chapter.

III. The Csound API

The Csound API, introduced in its early form in version 4.21, is one of the main features of Csound 5. It allows a complete programmatic control of the operation of the system, enabling it to be embedded in a variety of environments, and for it to function as a generic synthesis engine for multiple applications. Its existence sparked the development of several front-ends for the system, and its use in new platforms, such as the XO-One Laptop per Child, mobile phones and tablets.

The Csound API is an object-oriented interface, based on the Csound class, and is divided into a number of sections:

- Initialisation and compilation: functions to initialise and create instances of Csound, compile orchestras and preprocess scores. Any number of individual objects can be created and used; the library is fully re-entrant.

- Performance: functions to run the Csound engine, which can be controlled at the ksmps, input/output buffer, or full-score interrupts.
- Software bus: functions to get input and output control, audio and spectral data from Csound.
- Score transport: functions to control the score playback.
- Text messages: functions to retrieve Csound messages.
- Modules: functions to initialise audio and MIDI modules.
- Graphs: functions to get graphical data for display from Csound.
- Table access: functions for accessing tables.

The API is written in ANSI C, but it has a thin wrapper in C++, so it can be used directly from these two languages. In addition to the basic API, extra functionality is offered by the Csound interfaces API, which extends the Csound class (in C++), adding the manipulation of orchestras and score in memory, plus some composition facilities and pthread-based performance support for running Csound on its own separate thread. All of these have been wrapped programmatically with the Simplified Wrapper and Interface Generator (SWIG) in Python, Java and Lua, as well as manually in Tcl. Other third-party developers have also wrapped these APIs in languages such as Haskell, Common Lisp. Francois Pinot reported at the Csound Conference, his efforts in developing an OCaml version of the API.

A simple example of a minimal Csound host, written in Python using the Csound API is shown below:

```
import csnd
import sys

cs = csnd.Csound()
args = csnd.CsoundArgVList()
for arg in sys.argv:
  args.Append(arg)
err = cs.Compile(args.argc(), args.argv())
while(err == 0):
  err = cs.PerformKsmps()
```

The API is the central technology that allows the system to become more flexibly employed in a variety of situations. At the conference, Richard Boulanger explained how important it would be to enable Csound to be deployed in mobile platforms. At the time, two issues were preventing this from happening. In iOS, the problem was that dynamic linking of libraries and loading of modules was not supported. Csound has always been built as a dynamic-link library, as expected by modern operating systems standards. Making it a static-link library was not a major difficulty, but its opcodes were mostly lying in dynamic-loadable modules, not permitted in iOS. After some proof-of-concept in terms of creating static Csound libraries for ARM and testing simple applications based on this on mobile phones and tablets, we made the decision to move all opcodes with no external dependencies to the main Csound library. Now most of the opcode collection (about 1500 of them), do not require to be loaded from dynamic libraries. This allowed an iOS build to be released in early 2012.

The second issue that was problematic in Android has to do with its substantial audio latency, preventing a reactive real-time audio system to be provided. Whilst some work by the operating system developers is encouraging, there is still a lot of ground to be covered to achieve the same latencies as in iOS. Nevertheless, we have developed and released a Csound version for Android, simultaneous with the iOS release. Collectively, these efforts have been called the *Mobile Csound Platform*, and they also envisage the support of other systems and environments, including web deployment and cloud computing.

The Csound API has evolved slowly and constantly since the release of version 5.00 in 2006. Currently, there are a number of user requests for additions of functionality. For instance, one such call discussed at the conference was for better support for function table reading. The major difficulty found by API users was that, while complete access to tables is granted, there is no signaling of table modification by the Csound engine. This is required whenever new displays are to be produced, refreshing of data as it gets changed in Csound. A solution for this is to provide a callback mechanism that notifies the host when new data is written to a table. This is one of the issues concerning the API that is currently under review.

IV. Csound's Design Philosophy

Over the twenty-five years since its first public release, Csound has received a significant amount of code, contributed by a great variety of people. This contrasts with the original, single-vision, development by Barry Vercoe at the MIT, which evolved from his MUSIC11 and MUSIC360 experiences. The continued existence of the system is probably both a tribute to his original ideas and to the effort of the many developers involved in the project. Comparing the fate of Csound with another comparable system of the same time, Cmusic, is revealing. We have gathered at this Conference to celebrate Csound in 2011 as a powerful tool for music making, whereas Cmusic has been, for almost fifteen years, a museum piece. Some of the reasons for this were put forward by some people as an example of how a large worldwide development group has been working together in making it a flexible and comprehensive audio and music software. An interesting feature of this community of developers is their real interest in using the system for their own musical activities. This is possibly what connects most of its members together into a cohesive group. Of course, along the way the evolution of the system has gone through peaks and troughs. Also, the downside of this plurality of the development group is a diffusion of objectives and some degree of duplication, as well as a less focussed approach. However, as Steven Yi notes, recently, the development goals have been more unified and the coordination for the future of the language has been shared within the core development group. This has allowed more room for planning and user-directed development. The path towards Csound 6 has been made clear through this coordinated effort.

Finally, it is important to note that, the central tenet of our development philosophy for Csound is to preserve backwards compatibility. This means that a wealth of instrument designs, compositions, examples, didactical material, etc that has been gathered since the release of the first version, is preserved. In fact, this compatibility stretches, in many cases, to before the existence of Csound, with some MUSIC 11 orchestras and scores being fully compatible with Csound 5. At the Conference, this principle has been reiterated and agreed between users and developers. While it can lead to some issues to be tackled by the developers and an increase in the size of the language/system, its justification is completely sound.

V. Towards Csound 6

Whilst Csound 5 is now a mature and comprehensive system, plans for the future are at the forefront of its development. At the same time that bug-fix and small-improvement versions of Csound 5 are regularly released (5.18 is the current at the time of writing), the main development has moved to Csound 6. In addition to what has already been said in previous sections, a number of other ideas and goals for its development have been summarised by Andrés Cabrera:

- A Wiki is being setup to gather ideas from users and developers
- Encapsulation and reusability are increasingly important aspects of

the use and development of Csound code. Facilities for users to share code should be provided, possibly in the form of online repositories, as in the ones used for LATeX. This would be an evolution of the idea already embodied by the UDO database.

- Real-time safety in memory allocation and other blocking operations: this is an aspect of Csound that has been very seldom discussed and will require a complete assessment.
- More effort should be placed in code optimisation, for instance the use of vector operations can be explored more fully.
- The support for debugging should be enabled, allowing, for instance, the setting of breakpoints and step-by-step running of Csound code.
- Code re-factoring and reorganisation should be considered.
- The cleanup of the Csound API would also be desirable, and with version 6, there is a good opportunity for it, as API backwards compatibility is not necessary.
- Functional programming support might be useful.
- Maintenance of backwards compatibility is a must.

Cabrera also stresses, in complement to this, that he sees the traditional Csound syntax as a highlight of the system, as it is very simple when compared to other languages for music. In his opinion, maintaining this simplicity should an important consideration for the newer versions of the software.

VI. Conclusions

The technologies employed in Csound are varied and quite complex. However, it is a feature of the software that it can integrate and present these in a form that is very intelligible for musicians. In doing so, it represents an invaluable resource for Computer Music, which allows anyone wanting to engage with the field, the possibility of learning and developing his/her own creativity. In this chapter, we hope to have outlined the main elements of the technology of Csound and the shape of the future for the system.

Writing Csound Opcodes in Lua

Michael Gogins

Abstract

Lua is a lightweight dynamic language designed for embedding; LuaJIT is its just-in-time compiler. Csound's API has long had a Lua interface. Now, the `luaopcode` and `luacall` opcodes enable writing Csound opcodes using LuaJIT, and `lua_exec` runs Lua code during Csound performance. Lua code is embedded in the Csound orchestra, compiled at run time, and can call the running Csound *via* its API. Users can write Csound code in a modern language, with lexical scoping, classes, and lambdas, that can call any third party shared library. I timed Csound's Moog ladder filter written in native C, as a user-defined opcode, and in Lua. The Lua opcode runs in 125% of C's time, and 48% of the UDO's time. I also show writing a Lua score generator in a Csound orchestra using `lua_exec`.

I. Introduction

Csound (Vercoe *et al.*, 2011) is a programmable software synthesizer with a powerful library of signal processing routines, or "opcodes." Csound is written in C, but users write instruments in Csound "orchestra language" and notes in "score language." Csound computes audio in float samples, at any rate, for any number of channels. It automatically creates instruments for polyphony and handles variant tunings, tied notes, tempo changes, *etc*.

Csound's orchestra language was designed for musical usefulness, speed, and to simplify implementing Csound – *not* for easy coding! The assembler-style syntax mixes operations on control-rate variables with audio-rate variables. There's no lexical scoping or user-defined structures. So, Csound code is hard to write. Solutions to date are plugin opcodes, Python opcodes, and user-defined opcodes (UDOs). None is entirely successful. The Lua opcodes overcome some of their limitations.

Alternatives to Orchestra Code

Csound has always been extensible. In the past, users who wrote opcodes had to recompile Csound itself. Now, plugin opcodes can be compiled independently. I wrote a C++ library to simplify plugins; *e.g.*, these Lua opcodes. But most users aren't coders, and debugging C or C++ is hard.

The Python opcodes call into Python from Csound. Python code can be embedded in the orchestra, Csound can call any Python function, and Python is expressive. But it's too slow for audio, and can't define opcodes.

User-defined opcodes are written in orchestra language, like instruments. Unlike plugins or Python opcodes, UDOs are popular. They're faster than Python. But they obviously can't be used in place of orchestra language!

II. Defining Opcodes in Lua

The Lua opcodes' goals are (1) enable writing opcodes and orchestra code in a user-friendly language, (2) need no external compiler, and (3) run *fast*.

What is Lua?

Lua (Portuguese "moon") is a dynamic programming language designed for embedding and extending with C/C++ (Lua.org, 2011; Ierusalimschy *et al.* 2003; Ierusalimschy 2006). Lua has a stack-based calling mechanism, tables, metatables, lambdas, and closures, enabling object-oriented or functional coding. Lua is fast – LuaJIT (Pall 2011) is yet faster. It's a just-in-time optimizing compiler for Intel and ARM CPUs with a built-in foreign function interface (FFI). LuaJIT/FFI can be faster than C.

How It Works

The `luaopcode` opcode (Listing 1) defines Lua opcodes. The user gives an opcode name and writes a block of Lua code inside double braces (Listing 3). `luaopcode`'s `init` function retrieves the name of the Lua opcode, then executes the block of Lua using `luaL_dostring`. The Lua code first uses a LuaJIT/FFI `cdef` to declare an opcode structure in C, then defines the Lua opcode subroutines (Listing 3). `luaopcode` stores Lua references to these because it's faster to call Lua functions from C by reference than by name. LuaJIT is single-threaded, so the Lua opcodes keep a separate LuaJIT state for each Csound thread, using the thread-safe `manageLuaState` and `manageLuaReferenceKeys` functions.

Listing 1.

```
class LuaOpcode : public OpcodeBase<LuaOpcode>
{
public:
    MYFLT *opcodename_;
    MYFLT *luacode_;
public:
    int init(CSOUND *csound)
    {
        int result = OK;
        lua_State *L = manageLuaState();
        const char *opcodename =  csound->strarg2name(csound,
                                   (char *) 0, opcodename_,
                                   (char *)"default",
                       (int) csound->GetInputArgSMask(this));
        const char *luacode =  csound->strarg2name(csound,
                                (char *) 0, luacode_,
                                (char *)"default",
                       (int) csound->GetInputArgSMask(this));
        log(csound, "Executing Lua code:\n%s\n", luacode);
        result = luaL_dostring(L, luacode);
        if (result == 0) {
            keys_t &keys =
                       manageLuaReferenceKeys(L, opcodename);
            log(csound, "Opcode: %s\n", opcodename);
            log(csound, "Result: %d\n", result);
            char init_function[0x100];
            std::snprintf(init_function, 0x100,
               "%s_init", opcodename);
            lua_getglobal(L, init_function);
            if (!lua_isnil(L, 1)) {
                keys.init_key =
                       luaL_ref(L, LUA_REGISTRYINDEX);
                lua_pop(L, 1);
            }
            char kontrol_function[0x100];
            std::snprintf(kontrol_function,
                       0x100, "%s_kontrol", opcodename);
            lua_getglobal(L, kontrol_function);
            if (!lua_isnil(L, 1)) {
                keys.kontrol_key =
                              luaL_ref(L, LUA_REGISTRYINDEX);
                lua_pop(L, 1);
            }
            char audio_function[0x100];
            std::snprintf(audio_function,
                              0x100, "%s_audio", opcodename);
            lua_getglobal(L, audio_function);
            if (!lua_isnil(L, 1)) {
                keys.audio_key = luaL_ref(L,
LUA_REGISTRYINDEX);
                lua_pop(L, 1);
```

```
            }
            char noteoff_function[0x100];
            std::snprintf(noteoff_function,
                         0x100, "%s_noteoff", opcodename);
            lua_getglobal(L, noteoff_function);
            if (!lua_isnil(L, 1)) {
                keys.noteoff_key =
                         luaL_ref(L, LUA_REGISTRYINDEX);
                lua_pop(L, 1);
            }
        } else {
            log(csound, "Failed with: %d\n", result);
        }
        return result;
    }
};
```

The opcode subroutine signatures (opname is the opcode name) are:

function opname_init(csound, opcode, carguments) … end
function opname_kontrol(csound, opcode, carguments) … end
function opname_audio(csound, opcode, carguments) … end
function opname_noteoff(csound, opcode, carguments)… end

csound is a C pointer (Lua lightuserdata) to the running Csound; opcode points to the luacall structure; carguments points to luacall's arguments array of pointers to MYFLT, which holds not only out and in parameters, but also all opcode state.

In performance, the luacall opcodes (Listing 2) call the Lua opcodes. Out and in parameters (any number or type) go on the right hand side of the opcode name (Listing 4). Return values go back to Csound in the arguments. luacall1 is called at i-rate and calls opname_init; luacall3 is called at i-rate and k-rate and calls opname_init and opname_kontrol; luacall5 is called at i-rate and a-rate and calls opname_init and opname_audio. luacall_off1, luacall_off3, and luacall_off5 are similar but need opname_noteoff, which Csound calls at instrument turn-off. These subroutines retrieve the calling thread's LuaJIT state and the Lua opcode subroutine reference, push the opcode parameters on LuaJIT's stack, execute a protected Lua call, and pop the return value off the stack.

Listing 2.

```
class LuaCall: public OpcodeBase<LuaCall>
{
public:
    MYFLT *opcodename_;
    MYFLT *arguments[0x3000];
    const char *opcodename;
```

```
public:
    int init(CSOUND *csound)
    {
        int result = OK;
        opcodename = csound->strarg2name(csound, (char *) 0,
                                          opcodename_,
                                          (char *)"default",
                     (int) csound->GetInputArgSMask(this));
        lua_State *L = manageLuaState();
        keys_t &keys = manageLuaReferenceKeys(L, opcodename);
        lua_rawgeti(L, LUA_REGISTRYINDEX, keys.init_key);
        lua_pushlightuserdata(L, csound);
        lua_pushlightuserdata(L, this);
        lua_pushlightuserdata(L, &arguments);
        if (lua_pcall(L, 3, 1, 0) != 0) {
            log(csound, "Lua error in \"%s_init\": %s.\n",
             opcodename, lua_tostring(L, -1));
        }
        result = lua_tonumber(L, -1);
        lua_pop(L, 1);
        return OK;
    }
    int kontrol(CSOUND *csound)
    {
        int result = OK;
        lua_State *L = manageLuaState();
        keys_t &keys = manageLuaReferenceKeys(L, opcodename);
        lua_rawgeti(L, LUA_REGISTRYINDEX, keys.kontrol_key);
        lua_pushlightuserdata(L, csound);
        lua_pushlightuserdata(L, this);
        lua_pushlightuserdata(L, &arguments);
        if (lua_pcall(L, 3, 1, 0) != 0) {
            log(csound, "Lua error in \"%s_kontrol\": %s.\n",
             opcodename, lua_tostring(L, -1));
        }
        result = lua_tonumber(L, -1);
        lua_pop(L, 1);
        return result;
    }
    int audio(CSOUND *csound)
    {
        int result = OK;
        lua_State *L = manageLuaState();
        keys_t &keys = manageLuaReferenceKeys(L, opcodename);
        lua_rawgeti(L, LUA_REGISTRYINDEX, keys.audio_key);
        lua_pushlightuserdata(L, csound);
        lua_pushlightuserdata(L, this);
        lua_pushlightuserdata(L, arguments);
        if (lua_pcall(L, 3, 1, 0) != 0) {
            log(csound, "Lua error in \"%s_audio\": %s.\n",
            opcodename, lua_tostring(L, -1));
        }
        result = lua_tonumber(L, -1);
        lua_pop(L, 1);
        return result;
    }
};
```

luacall's arguments are Csound type N (any number or type), so Csound copies each argument's address into a slot of the arguments array without type checking. The Lua opcode casts the carguments address as a pointer to the opcode structure defined by the cdef (Listing 3). The arguments array and opcode structure are a union; array slots match structure fields, so arguments can be efficiently accessed *via* fields.

III. Results

The proof of concept is a port of Csound's moogladder filter opcode, written in C by Victor Lazzarini, to LuaJIT/FFI. The Lua opcode is defined in Listing 3. An instrument that uses it is shown in Listing 4.

Listing 3.

```
luaopcode "moogladder", {{
local ffi = require("ffi")
local math = require("math")
local string = require("string")
local csoundApi = ffi.load('csound64.dll.5.2')
ffi.cdef[[
    int csoundGetKsmps(void *);
    double csoundGetSr(void *);
    struct moogladder_t {
      double *out;
      double *inp,
      double *freq;
      double *res;
      double *istor;
      double sr;
      double ksmps;
      double thermal;
      double f;
      double fc;
      double fc2;
      double fc3;
      double fcr;
      double acr;
      double tune;
      double res4;
      double input;
      double i, j, k;
      double kk;
      double stg[6];
      double delay[6];
      double tanhstg[6];
    };
]]

local moogladder_ct = ffi.typeof('struct moogladder_t *')

function moogladder_init(csound, opcode, carguments)
    local p = ffi.cast(moogladder_ct, carguments)
```

```
    p.sr = csoundApi.csoundGetSr(csound)
    p.ksmps = csoundApi.csoundGetKsmps(csound)
    if p.istor[0] == 0 then
        for i = 0, 5 do
            p.delay[i] = 0.0
            p.tanhstg[i] = 0.0
        end
    end
    return 0
end

function moogladder_kontrol(csound, opcode, carguments)
    local p = ffi.cast(moogladder_ct, carguments)
    -- transistor thermal voltage
    p.thermal = 1.0 / 40000.0
    if p.res[0] < 0.0 then
        p.res[0] = 0.0
    end
    -- sr is half the actual filter sampling rate
    p.fc = p.freq[0] / p.sr
    p.f = p.fc / 2.0
    p.fc2 = p.fc * p.fc
    p.fc3 = p.fc2 * p.fc
    -- frequency & amplitude correction
    p.fcr = 1.873 * p.fc3 + 0.4955 * p.fc2 - 0.6490 * p.fc +
           0.9988
    p.acr = -3.9364 * p.fc2 + 1.8409 * p.fc + 0.9968
    -- filter tuning
    p.tune = (1.0 - math.exp(-(2.0 * math.pi * p.f * p.fcr)))
             / p.thermal
    p.res4 = 4.0 * p.res[0] * p.acr
    -- Nested 'for' loops crash, not sure why.
    -- Local loop variables also are problematic.
    -- Lower-level loop constructs don't crash.
    p.i = 0
    while p.i < p.ksmps do
        p.j = 0
        while p.j < 2 do
            p.k = 0
            while p.k < 4 do
                if p.k == 0 then
                    p.input = p.inp[p.i] - p.res4 * p.delay[5]
                    p.stg[p.k] = p.delay[p.k] + p.tune *
                                 (math.tanh(p.input * p.thermal)
                                 - p.tanhstg[p.k])
                else
                    p.input = p.stg[p.k - 1]
                    p.tanhstg[p.k - 1] = math.tanh(p.input *
                                         p.thermal)
                    if p.k < 3 then
                        p.kk = p.tanhstg[p.k]
                    else
                        p.kk = math.tanh(p.delay[p.k] *
                               p.thermal)
                    end
                    p.stg[p.k] = p.delay[p.k] + p.tune *
                                   (p.tanhstg[p.k - 1] - p.kk)
                end
                p.delay[p.k] = p.stg[p.k]
                p.k = p.k + 1
```

```
            end
            -- 1/2-sample delay for phase compensation
            p.delay[5] = (p.stg[3] + p.delay[4]) * 0.5
            p.delay[4] = p.stg[3]
            p.j = p.j + 1
        end
        p.out[p.i] = p.delay[5]
        p.i = p.i + 1
    end
    return 0
end
}}
```

Listing 4.

```
instr 4
kres        init        1
istor       init        0
kfe         expseg      500, p3*0.9, 1800, p3*0.1,
3000
kenv        linen       10000, 0.05, p3, 0.05
asig        buzz        kenv, 100, sr/(200), 1
afil        init        0
luacall3    "moogladder", afil, asig, kfe, kres,
istor
out         afil
endin
```

Getting this to run took experimentation! Nested for loops simply crashed. Fortunately, while can be used to create nested loops. Results of using moogladder with a moving center frequency to filter a buzz instrument are shown in Table 1. All implementations sound the same.

Table 1.

Implementation	Note 1	Note 2	Average	% of "C"	% of UDO
Native "C" by Lazzarini	5.787	5.775	5.781	100.0%	38.6%
UDO also by Lazzarini	14.939	15.029	14.984	259.2%	100.0%
LuaJIT port of native "C"	7.274	7.176	7.225	125.0%	48.2%

LuaJIT/FFI code runs almost as fast as C, twice as fast as Csound code.

IV. Score Generation

The `lua_exec` opcode executes any Lua code at any time during performance, acessing the running Csound's API *via* LuaJIT's FFI. `lua_exec` may be called in the orchestra header, in instruments, or in UDOs. It's simpler to do score generation in the header after sample rate, kperiod, and number of channels have been assigned, but before defining instruments. The APIs for inserting score events during performance are:

> PUBLIC void csoundInputMessage(CSOUND *csound, const char *message) Input a null-terminated string (as if from a console). Messages are streamed into a buffer of fixed size, then converted to score events, so only so many events can be scheduled at the same performance time.
>
> PUBLIC int csoundScoreEvent(CSOUND *csound, char opcode, const MYFLT *pfields, long pfieldCount) Insert a regular score event directly into the performance list, so there is no limit to the number of events that can be scheduled at the same performance time.

I use csoundScoreEvent so I can create any number of events.

The Score Generator

luajit_score_generator.csd (Gogins 2012a) has three sections, each generated by a chaotic dynamical system (the logistic equation) with its own attractor, tempo, dynamics, and arrangement of instruments.

The `lua_exec` call (line 16) first stores the address of the running Csound in a csound pointer in LuaJIT's global namespace, then executes the large block of Lua code inside the Csound literal quotation marks ({{ and }}).

First, the Lua code imports required Lua libraries (lines 18-20). The ChordSpace library (Gogins 2012b) makes some recent work in mathematical music theory available for use in algorithmic composition. Chords are represented as points in Euclidean spaces with one dimension per voice (Tymoczko 2006). ChordSpace implements neo-Riemannian operations on chords of any arity (Fiore and Satyendra 2005). These operations generate chord progressions that are applied to the notes generated by the logistic equation. LuaJIT's ffi library is used to access and control the running Csound. Lua's math library is also required. Lines 22 through 26 read Csound's API functions into the FFI tables.

Lines 27-29 are an FFI cdef, *i.e.* a C definition, which declares Csound's inputScoreEvent function for calling from Lua. Argument types aren't quite the same as in csound.h, *e.g.* I need no members of the CSOUND object, so it's declared as pointer to void. Similarly, Lua lacks char, so the char parameter for the event function is declared as int.

Line 31 calls LuaJIT's ffi.new to create a C array of 11 doubles for passing generated notes to Csound. Line 32 defines the ChordSpace.Chord object used to generate chord progressions, starting with B major 7th. Line 33 copies this chord to use as the piece's base "modality," required by the neo-Riemannian Q transformation to perform contextual transposition. Lines 34-36 define other variables.

In Section A, I define the starting time (line 38), and an arrangement (line 40), which re-maps instruments in the range [1, 4] generated by the code to a more pleasing choice from the orchestra. The velocity, d_velocity, and dd_velocity variables apply a difference equation to the notes' loudnesses, creating a dynamic envelope. The inc variable (line 44) determines the orbit of the logistic equation. Lower values iterate to a single fixed point, intermediate values (as here) cause a periodic orbit, and higher values (used later) cause a chaotic orbit. The iterations, interval, and duration variables defined in lines 45-47 define the count of notes to be generated, the interval in seconds between notes which determines tempo, and the duration of each note which determines its overlap with previous notes.

Lines 48-70 iterate the logistic equation (line 57). But first, the chord progression is advanced if sufficient iterations have occurred. Every 20th note the Q transformation performs contextual transposition on the chord by 7 semitones, and every 60th note the K transformation performs interchange by inversion. After the equation is iterated, its value (y1) is mapped to pitch, which is conformed to the chord. Then the pfields of the Csound event are filled in (lines 59-68). Instrument number is a round robin off the sequence of notes. Pan is a random number between -1 and 1. Lines 66 and 67 iterate the difference equation for dynamics. Finally, line 69 sends the note to Csound as a real-time i statement. The character i is passed to Csound as the integer 105, its ACII code.

Sections B (lines 71 through 104) and C (lines 105 through 138) are like A, except the number of notes, the tempo, the behavior of the logistic equation and/or its mapping to pitch, the chord progression, and the dynamic envelope all differ, as determined by trial and error.

Finally, at the end of the .csd file, I declare the length of the piece with an e event to keep Csound running for all the generated real-time events.

The Orchestra

I'll say only a little about the orchestra (lines 142 on). Each instrument is an independent block of text, some instruments apply effects, and instruments connect with effects using the signal flow graph opcodes. Each instrument has the same pfields: p1, instrument number; p2, time; p3, duration; p4, pitch (MIDI key); p5, loudness (MIDI velocity); p6, phase; p7, spatial pan; p8, height, p9, depth; p10, pitch-class set number (not used here); and p11, 1 to make the pfields a homogeneous vector.

Instruments and effects have graphical user interfaces. Widget settings are saved in a snapshot file associated with the .csd file by name. I use a GUI because it is faster and more precise to adjust parameters while a piece plays than to change a value, render the piece, listen to it, change the value, render the piece, *etc.*, *etc.*, *etc.*

References

Fiore, T.M. and R. Satyendra, "Generalized Contextual Groups," *Music Theory Online*, 11(3), 2005.

Gogins, Michael, "luajit_score_generator.csd," accessed October 13, 2012 (a), http://csound.git.sourceforge.net/git/gitweb.cgi?p=csound/csound5.git;a=summary.

Gogins, Michael, "Silencio," accessed August 31, 2012 (b), http://code.google.com/p/silencio/.

Ierusalimschy, R., L. H. de Figueiredo, and W. Celes. *Lua 5.1 Reference Manual*. August 2006. http://lua.org.

Ierusalimschy, R. *Programming in Lua*, 2nd edition. March 2006. http://lua.org.

"Lua.org," Pontifícia Universidade Católica do Rio de Janeiro. accessed August 18, 2011. *The Programming Language Lua*. http://www.lua.org.

Pall, Mike. "The LuaJIT Project," accessed August 23, 2012. http://luajit.org, 2012

Tymoczko, Dmitri, "The Geometry of Musical Chords," *Science* 313:72–74, 2006.

Vercoe, Barry, et al. "Canonical Csound Reference Manual," accessed December 21, 2012, http://www.csounds.com/manual/html/index.html.

THE CSOUND API

INTERVIEW WITH MICHAEL GOGINS

Michael Gogins has been one of Csound's core developers since more than two decades. Here he talks about one of the most important developments in Csound. The API (Application Programming Interface) provides access to the Csound engine from any external host („front-end“) or various programming languages like Java, C, C++, Lisp, Python or Lua.

How did you come across to see the necessity of an API for Csound?

My need for the Csound API arose out of my working methods as a composer. I pretty much exclusively do algorithmic composition, in which the computer both generates a score and renders a soundfile. Each piece is one program. I don't usually generate materials and assemble them in an editor. Instead, I write a process that generates a score and renders it with an orchestra embedded in a program, all in one go. In order to get good results, I edit the program, render the piece, listen to it, edit the program, render the piece, listen to it, etc., etc., etc., often for dozens or hundreds of times. Working speed is of the essence. I need the API so that once I have tweaked the score generating program, I can simply press a key to re-run the program to re-render the piece. In other words, the API permits me to embed Csound and an orchestra directly into my compositions. Automating this workflow not only saves time, but it keeps my musical thought processes flowing by preventing distraction by rendering tasks.

How did this working method evolve?

As I mentioned, my involvement in computer music was driven by my interest in algorithmic composition, which began with a desire to map fractals and other recursive and irreducible processes onto musical scores and sounds —both scores, and sounds. My very first computer compositions were maps from cellular automata onto MIDI files, done on an Apple IIe at Soundwork studio in Seattle in 1984 for a seminar in computer music that I was taking with John Rahn at the University of Washington. The sounds for these pieces were realized by a Yamaha DX7 synthesizer.

My very first piece using the computer for synthesis was 20 seconds of sound produced by a 1-dimensional rule 110 cellular automaton. Each cell in the automaton was mapped to one grain of sound at a specific pitch. Each time step of the automaton was therefore a different moment of sound. This piece was written in Fortran for a CDC mainframe. In this piece there was no distinction between "score" and "orchestra."

So how did you then actually come to Csound?

My interest in Csound came after I had graduated from college (with a BA in comparative religion, not music) and moved to New York in 1985, where I began experimenting with computer music on my own, pursing my interest in the use of fractals and irreducible processes. At that time, I was hanging out with the woof group, a "users group" for the computer music center at the Columbia-Princeton Electronic Music Studio that thanks to Brad Garton was welcoming to non-Columbia musicians and put on occasional concerts. I used the CMIX program at Columbia, but I was aware of Csound, and when the Columbia computer music center became less accessible to me, I switched to using Csound because I could run it on my own personal computer. Immediately, I felt the need for an API, because of my working methods.

Not only did I not like having to switch to a console window and execute a command to render my piece, I didn't like the score, the orchestra, and the piece itself being separate files. Too many times, I went back to a piece I had done in the past and wanted to re-work it, only to find that some file was missing.

So, I designed the Csound API to support not only an efficient compositional workflow, but also a truly archival format for computer compositions.

How was the process of working on this project? Who else took part? What were the main issues?

I was the first developer of the API. At first, I worked completely on my own. Later on, many people contributed, especially Istvan Varga but also the other Csound developers such as John ffitch, Victor Lazzarini, and Steven Yi.

Initially, the API was a Java class that simply stored the generated score, the orchestra, and the Csound command line, and "shelled out" to execute the Csound command. But I was not happy with my Java system. Too many moving parts.

Then Barry Vercoe, the author of Csound, was engaged by Analog Devices Incorporated to develop Extended Csound for embedded systems running on ADI DSP boards. Richard Boulanger, who was aware of my work with Csound, and Barry got ADI to hire me to develop a "launcher" with a graphical user interface for Extended Csound. I wrote it in C++ to use both Extended Csound and regular Csound. The API took its first usable form in this launcher.

Shortly after that, Gabriel Maldonado contacted me for advice on how to write a VST plugin based on Csound. In response I wrote CsoundVST, which permits Csound to run as an effect or an instrument inside a VST host program.

I adapted my "launcher" to become the graphical user interface for CsoundVST. I also had to add a class for storing Csound scores and orchestras in the API, because VST plugins need to store "presets" in song files saved by the VST host program. This class is the CsoundFile class, and the form of the Csound API used by CsoundVST is the CppSound class.

Istvan Varga was involved with Csound development at this time, and he took an interest in the API. He changed some things, and added many things. One thing he added was a pure header file C++ API wrapper for the basic Csound "C" API, csound.hpp.

There have been a number of issues with the Csound API. To begin with, not many Csound developers, at least as far as I could see, felt a need for such an API. They seemed to be content "shelling out" to run Csound. Then, once other developers did become interested, they had a tendency to not see the need for some features that I had added. Some people took things out that I needed, or broke them, and I was always patching it back up again.

Another issue is the layering of the API. I don't think it has been clear to some users and developers what the different parts of the API are or what they are for. It might have been wiser to stick with one single "C" API, even for score management, and to adopt Istvan Varga's header-file-only approach to the C++ form of the API.

What were the main decisions about the design?

- To create an API using Csound as a shared library, rather than "shelling out" to call the Csound command. (Me)
- To make the lowest, most basic level of the API a "C" language shared library with a clean "C" header file. (Me)
- NOT to make many changes to the internals of Csound to support the API, but to add new features in the API itself. A major exception to this was to make the Csound kernel re-entrant (nbxt item). (Me)
- To make Csound re-entrant, by creating a CSOUND structure to contain all state for a running instance of Csound. Of course, this DID end up greatly modifying the internals of Csound and even of the opcodes! (Me, Istvan Varga, John ffitch)
- To add plugin opcodes to Csound and to the API, to enable independent developers to create their own opcodes without having to re-compile Csound itself. (Me)
- To provide a C++ API on top of the C API. (Me, Istvan Varga)
- To add a score and orchestra storage and management facility to the C++ API. (Me)
- To add SWIG-generated wrappers for the C++ API for Python, Java, and Lua. (Me)
- To add pointers to all functions of the Csound API to the CSOUND structure, essentially creating a Csound class in C. This is so that opcodes will receive a pointer to the host instance of Csound and can call any function in the Csound API. (Me)
- To add a facility for managing control channels to the API for use in host applications. This has become a very important part of the API. (Istvan Varga, Victor Lazzarini)
- To add facilities for creating global variables to the API, and for getting and setting their values. (Istvan Varga)
- To add the "module loading" facility to Csound, and API functions for it, to generalize the ability of Csound to load plugins. (Istvan Varga)
- To add the CsoundPerformanceThread class to enable smoother integration of the API with host programs such as CsoundQt. (Istvan Varga)

Michael, thank you very much for these detailed answers!

Interview: Joachim Heintz

CSOUND AND OBJECT-ORIENTATION: DESIGNING AND IMPLEMENTING CELLULAR AUTOMATA FOR ALGORITHMIC COMPOSITION

REZA PAYAMI

Abstract

Although object-oriented design and implementation may not seem to be necessary when working with computer music languages and environments such as Csound, it provides with more strongly-typed facilities and well-structured reusable opcode libraries. Moreover, an object-oriented design is a result of a so-called real world point of view to a problem. In this article the problem of designing and implementing Cellular Automata, as an algorithmic composition component, as used by some composers like Xenakis in Horos, or Synthesizers like Chaosynth (Miranda, 2003), will be described. The currently existing Csound programming style is compared with the alternative object-oriented approach.

I. Introduction

Cellular Automata

A cellular automaton, or simply CA, consists of:

- A matrix, or grid, of cells, each of which can be in one of a finite number of states
- A rule that defines how the states of the cells are updated over time

The matrix of cells can have any specific number of dimensions and maximum number of states. Given the state of a cell and its neighbors at time t, the rule determines the cell state at time t + 1.

As an example, Game of Life CA is a cellular automaton which has a maximum number of two states, dead (0 or black) and alive (1 or white). From one so-called tick of the clock to the next, its cells can be either alive or dead, according to the following rules devised by Conway (Conway, 1970):

- Birth : If a cell is dead at time *t*, it comes alive at time *t*+1 if it has exactly 3 neighbors alive
- Death : If a cell is alive at time *t*, it comes dead at time *t*+1 if it has:
    - Loneliness: Fewer than 2 neighbors alive
    - Overpopulation: More than 3 neighbors alive

II. Design Overview

In an abstract way of thinking, a generic CA can be designed and implemented regardless of its specific values or behaviors such as maximum number of states (which is 2 for a non-generic CA like Game of Life) or the underlying rule for generating the next generation of cells.

In order to model the generic CA, we need a two dimensional matrix, or grid with a specific size. As there is no such a data structure in Csound, we have to implement a 2D array by using a one-dimensional table. The global variables "giSize", "giMaxState", "giStates" (using Csound function table: "giStates ftgen 1, 0, -giSize * giSize, -2, 0") are required for implementing CA data structure.

There should be a mapping from 2D indexes (row, column) to linear table indexes. The opcodes "ToLinearIndex" and "To2DIndex" provide this mapping between one-dimensional and two-dimensional matrices. Each CA can be represented by a matrix, each of which corresponds to a different Csound function table with a specific so-called "iCA" table index number. Some utility opcodes such as "GetCellState" and 'SetCellState' can also be implemented for reading and writing the cell states in a specific row and column. For instance, the following is the underlying code for "GetCellState" using the related CA function table and "ToLinearIndex" mapping opcode.

```
opcode GetCellState, i, iii
iRow, iColumn, iCA xin
   iIndex ToLinearIndex iRow, iColumn
   if iIndex < 0 || iIndex >= giSize * giSize then
      iCellState = 0
   else
      iCellState table iIndex, iCA
   endif
   xout iCellState
endop
```

A "CountNeighboursInState" opcode can be implemented to count the number of neighbors of a cell in a row and column which are in a certain state. A utility opcode for "CountNeighboursInState", named "AddCountIfInState", can be called for all the eight neighbors of each cell, to add the related counter when the cell is in the required state. As mentioned "iCA" specifies the specific CA, or its Csound function table index.

```
opcode AddCountIfInState, i, iiiii
iRow, iColumn, iState, iCount, iCA xin
   iNewCount = iCount
   iCellState GetCellState iRow, iColumn, iCA
   if iCellState == iState then ;IsAlive
      iNewCount = iCount + 1
   endif
   xout iNewCount
endop

opcode CountNeighboursInState, i, iiii
iRow, iColumn, iState, iCA xin
   iCount init 0

   iR = iRow - 1
   iC = iColumn - 1
   iCount AddCountIfInState iR, iC, iState, iCount,
iCA

   iC = iColumn
   iCount AddCountIfInState iR, iC, iState, iCount,
iCA
   ...

   xout iCount
endop
```

Specifically for Game of Life, the rule is implemented by specifying the next value for each state based on the number of alive or dead neighbors. An "AdvanceGeneration" opcode can generate the next generation by iterating over all the cells and calling "GetNextState" opcode for each, "GetNextState" can easily call the mentioned "CountNeighboursInState" to specify different cases such as birth, death, overpopulation or loneliness.

```
opcode GetNextState, i, iii
iRow, iColumn, iCA xin
   iCurrentState GetCellState iRow, iColumn, iCA
   iAliveNeighbours CountNeighboursInState iRow,
iColumn, 1, iCA
   iNextState = iCurrentState
   if iCurrentState == 0 then ;if is dead
      if iAliveNeighbours == 3 then
         iNextState = 1 ;become alive
      endif
```

```
    endif
    if iCurrentState > 0 then; else (is alive)
       if iAliveNeighbours < 2 || iAliveNeighbours > 3
then
          iNextState = 0
       endif
    endif
xout iNextState
endop
```

III. Object-Oriented Approach

Although the above Csound implementation provides the required functionality, the object-oriented approach suggests another interesting point of view to the problem design. The philosophy behind object-orientation approach divides the problem domain into some "Objects" instead of some separate opcodes and variables. This is really similar to the real world's life: there are some objects all around having some attributes and behavior. In addition to integrating attributes and behaviors, there are different advantages when using object-oriented programming and design like "Visibility", "Inheritance", "Method Overriding", "Abstract classes", "Hook methods" and "Instantiation" which are powerful tools comparing to the non-object-oriented Csound approach. These advantages are described in the following sections in more details.

Class: Member Variables + Methods

Using object-oriented concepts, instead of having data structures and opcodes as separate elements, a "Class" integrates these two as a whole. A "Class" contains two parts: attributes or member variables, and methods or operations. The former represents data while the latter represents the behavior. Translating this concept to Csound, global variables can be regarded as member variables, while opcodes can be considered as class methods.

So, the mentioned global variables like "giSize", "giStates", "giMaxState" will be some member variables of CA class. This sounds to be a proper translation of the first part of CA definition: ("A matrix, or grid, of cells, each of which can be in one of a finite number of states"). The second part of the definition ("A rule that defines how the states of the cells are updated over time") can be realized by its "AdvanceGeneration" method, instead of an opcode with an "iCA" parameter. In other words, instead of thinking of an opcode such as "AdvanceGeneration" and passing an "iCA" as a parameter, we can think of a "CA Object" as an instance of a a specific "CA Class" which can provide us with its next generation when its mentioned method is called.

Visibility

Member variables and methods may have different kinds of visibility. Taking "Car" as an example, its engine is not visible to a driver, while the steering wheel is visible and act as an interface for the driver. We name engine as a "private" and steering wheel as a "public" part of a car. Similarly, "AddCountIfInState" opcode is a proper example for a private method, while "AdvanceGeneration" can be a public method. The former opcode is only a helper method for the latter and is not called directly outside CA implementation. Moreover, to reach a higher level of encapsulation and security, one can define the entire member variables as private, and define some getter and setter methods for providing the access to them. All in all, by visibility the user of a class library will be clearly aware of how to apply the provided components: public methods are allowed to be called outside a class, while the private ones are related to the implementation aspects. This is not evident when looking at a non-object-oriented Csound code especially implemented as a kind of library to be used by many developers.

Inheritance

Inheritance is a certain relationship between different classes. For instance, we can regard "Elephant" as a sub-class of "Animal", which itself has different sub-classes like "AfricanElephant" and "IndianElephant". So, there is a hierarchy or tree like structure between the mentioned classes: "Animal" super-class (base class) as the top node, "Elephant" below, and "AfricanElephant" and "IndianElephant" at the bottom level. Each level inherits characteristics of the upper level and provides a more specialized type of class. This concept is exactly the same concerning generic "CA" super-class with more specific sub-classes, like "GameOfLifeCA", or "DemonCyclicSpaceCA" as another example. "Inheritance" is a prefect strongly-typed way of code reuse with so many benefits like "Methods Overriding", "Abstract classes" and "Hook methods" as described below.

Method Overriding

When a sub-class extends a super-class through "Inheritance", it can define some new attributes, and also add or modify some previously defined behaviors. In our CA example, to define the rule for the next generation of cells, each specific CA class like "GameOfLifeCA" can override some super-class generic CA methods. This is described more in the two sections below.

Abstract or concrete

Being abstract or concrete is another aspect related inheritance relationship and overriding methods. An "Abstract" class has at least one some abstract or undefined method. Abstract classes cannot get instantiated. As an example, we cannot have an instance of a generic "Animal" class; it should be an elephant, a lion, a cat, etc. In other words, the "Animal" class is abstract, while its sub-classes define the abstract behaviors and become concrete. In our example, generic CA is an abstract class and its rule definition method is an abstract method. The sub-classes should override it to define the behavior and declare some concrete classes such as "GameOfLifeCA".

Template Method, Hook Method

Considering a large method in the super-class which calls some different smaller methods, if we override the smaller methods in the sub-classes, the behavior of the large method gets changed without being directly overridden. The former type of methods is called "Template Method" and the latter is called "Hook Method". For instance, the implementation of "AdvanceGeneration" is always the same for all the CA sub-classes: it iterates over the states and calls "GetNextState" for each cell. "GetNextState" is an abstract method in "CA" base class, which is a slot for defining the rule. So, the sub-classes should not re-implement "AdvanceGeneration" method and "GetNextState" should only be overridden. In this case, "GetNextState" method is an example of a hook method.

Instantiation

Instantiation is the process of taking an instance of a class. When instantiating a class, an "Instance" or "Object" of that class will be created, and its attributes get concrete values. A "Constructor" is a method in each class which is called in the process of instantiation and the initialization logic of a class can be defined in its constructor. Each class can have different constructors with different number of parameters. The name of a constructor method may be a keyword like "Init" (In many object-oriented programming languages, the name of the constructor is the name of the class itself). In other words, using the "Init" keyword as a method name will change its type to a "Constructor" automatically by the compiler. To provide this feature in Csound, an object can be considered as a specific variable and Csound parser should change to know its class as a new variable types. The class member variables may be of different rates, e.g. i-rate or k-rate or a-rate, just like normal variables for each opcode.

Object-Oriented code

To sum up, the corresponding high level object-oriented Csound code may be something like the following. Some keywords are proposed to extend Csound to have an object-orientated kind of syntax.

```
class CA
   private iSize init 5
   private iStates ftgen 1, 0, -giSize * giSize, -2,
0
   private iMaxState init 15

   public opcode GetMaxState i, 0
      xout iMaxState
   endop

   public opcode GetSize i, 0
      xout iSize
   endop

   private opcode ToLinearIndex, i, ii
   ...
   private opcode To2DIndex, ii, i
   ...
   public opcode Init, 0, ii
   ...
   public opcode GetCellState, i, ii
   ...
   public opcode SetCellState, 0, iii
   ...
```

```
    private opcode AddCountIfInState, i, iiii
    …
    protected opcode CountNeighboursInState, i, iii
    …
    protected abstract opcode GetNextState, i, ii

    public opcode AdvanceGeneration, 0, i
    …
endclass

class GameOfLifeCA inherits CA
        protected abstract opcode GetNextState, i, iii
    …
endclass

class DemonCyclicSpaceCA inherits CA
    protected abstract opcode GetNextState, i, iii
    …
endclass

instr 1
    if p2 == 0 then
     ; Instantiation
DemonCyclicSpaceCA ADemonCyclicSpaceCA 5, 10, 1

        ;Calling method of an instance
ADemonCyclicSpaceCA.RepaintCA 1 ;
     …
    endif
endin
```

The above code and the proposed syntax show how some features like “Class” definition, “Visibility”, “Inheritance”, “Method overriding”, and object-oriented design patterns like “Hook methods” provide a strongly-typed way of design and implementation. In this way the problem domain, like real world’s life, can be decomposed into some well-designed “Objects” instead of having some opcodes and variables as separate concepts.

References

"Csound FLOSS Manual," accessed December 21, 2012, http://en.flossmanuals.net/csound/.

Miranda, Eduardo R., "On the Music of Emergent Behaviour: What can Evolutionary Computation Bring to the Musician?," Leonardo 36, no. 1, pp. 55–58, 2003.

Miranda, Eduardo R., "Granular Synthesis of Sounds by Means of a Cellular Automaton," *Leonardo* 28, no. 4, pp. 297–300, 1995.

Gardner, Martin, "Mathematical Games: The fantastic combinations of John Conway's new solitaire game 'life'", *Scientific American* 223, no. 10, pp. 120–123, 1970.

THE HADRON PLUGIN AND THE PARTIKKEL OPCODE

INTERVIEW WITH ØYVIND BRANDTSEGG

Øyvind Brandtsegg is a composer and performer working in the fields of algorithmic improvisation and sound installations. His main instrument as a musician is Hadron Particle Synthesizer, ImproSculpt and Marimba Lumina. Currently, he is a professor of music technology at NTNU, Trondheim, Norway. Øyvind Brandtsegg is the owner, concept designer, dsp programmer and presets designer of the Hadron audio plugin.

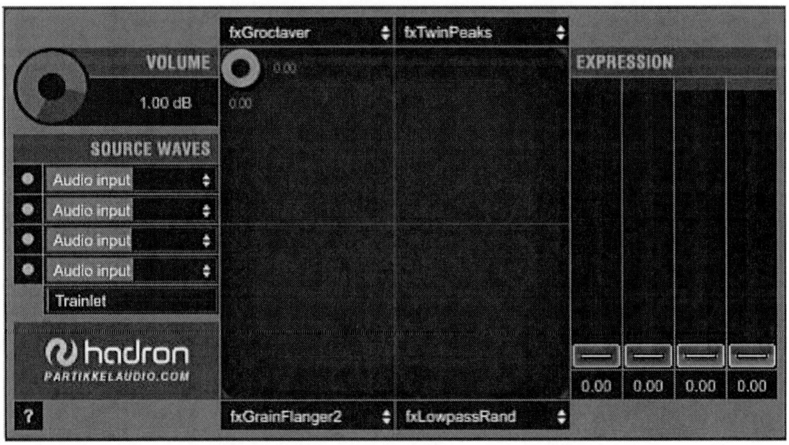

Figure: Screenshot of Hadron VST.

***Iain McCurdy:** Tell me a little about the origins of the Hadron plugin?*

Øyvind Brandtsegg: I'll have to take a few steps back in time, to around 2005, as there are some closely connected issues that initiated the development. During the artistic research project "New creative possibilities through improvisational use of compositional techniques, - a new computer instrument for the performing musician" (http://oeyvind.teks.no/results/) I realized I needed a very flexible sound generator. I wanted something that could do "everything" in one box, so that it could be used for free improvisation, controlled algorithmically, scripted, used for synthesis, sampling or audio processing. My idea was that the overall software design would be simpler and more flexible if I had such a generic sound generator/processor. I figured that granular synthesis would be a good candidate for a sound processing method that would allow for this degree of flexibility. Inspired by Curtis Roads' 'Microsound', I set out to design an "all-in-one" granular sound generator, because all existing implementations in Csound and elsewhere did miss one bit or another to make my puzzle complete. The design method was to go through all types of GS mentioned in Roads' book, making sure that my ideal generator would be able to produce that variant of GS. If I found that one variant required an additional parameter, I added it, making sure that the added functionality did not present conceptual problems for any of the other supported GS types.

My first prototype was written with basic Csound opcodes, implementing each grain as an enveloped instrument event. I knew this would not be computationally effective but it was a good way to test the desired feature set. At the same time I was contacted by Sigurd Saue, then supervising two diploma students (Thom Johansen and Torgeir Strand Henriksen), at the department of acoustics. They were in need of an interesting task/theme for their diploma and they were also interested in music and sound processing. This was perfect timing for me, so I asked if they would be interested in implementing the new granular synthesis opcode. I am very pleased with the result these two students produced, optimising the implementation, discussing features, and generally following up everything in the best possible manner. We named this new opcode "partikkel" (Norwegian for particle, the twist to the name a suggestion from Sigurd Saue). The reason for using the term particle synthesis is that we saw this as a kind of "granular plus", an all in one approach that needed to be termed appropriately. Roads had also used the term particle synthesis in a chapter heading, while he did not follow up using the term further on in the chapter.

During my artistic research project I build a software instrument called ImproSculpt4, where the partikkel opcode was used as a core sound generator. ImproSculpt contains numerous functions for algorithmic composition and improvisation. After the project was finished in 2008, I wanted to develop some parts of ImproSculpt further. I realized it might be a good idea to strip down and modularise the functionality. This led me to start with the particle synthesis generator, as I saw that there was unrealised potential. I was also fresh out of a job, as my research project was finished, and I wanted to see if perhaps I could make an attempt at commercialising the parts of the software. I received good support and help from the NTNU Technology Transfer, a bureau at the university specially targeted towards commercialisation of research products. I also tried my luck with "Innovasjon Norge" (Innovation Norway) a state agency for support of commercial start-ups. After a long process, of which I will spare you the details, it did not work out so well with Innovation Norway. They just did not see the value of open source software, neither were they able to imagine that open source software could be used as the basis for a commercial enterprise. For me it was a key issue that I kept the software open, as I feel strongly about the idea. Most of what I know about software I have learned from open source communities, with the Csound community being the most important. For me it is not so much about "giving something back" as it is about believing that this is a good way to organise society, benefits and further development for all on account of shared knowledge and resources.

Early 2008, I got in touch with Yukio King at Ableton and I suggested that my particle generator could be developed into a plugin for Live. I did not yet know how to take care of the open source aspect in that relation, but figured it would be good to start talking and see what we could find out. Yukio immediately responded positively towards the idea of doing something but wanted to direct my attention to a new product they had plans for, namely Max for Live. I was invigorated over the prospect of combining a fully-fledged tool like Live with the flexibility of Max, especially since Max can be used to interface to almost anything else you might want to throw into the mix. We decided to go forward with the collaboration and I changed my design to accommodate Max as an interface between Csound and Live. I started collaborating with my master student Bernt Isak Wærstad, as he is a much better Max programmer than I am. I tend to lose my temper with all the cables… At the same time I also initiated collaboration with product design student Arne Sigmund Skeie for the design of the user interface. Arne has brought a lot of fresh ideas to the table, and the combination of an XY pad with four expression controllers has been conceived in collaboration with him.

We tried to develop a VST plugin simultaneous to the Max for Live version, with (previous master student) Erik Blekesaunet handling the initial work on VST interfacing via JUCE. Due to lack of resources, we had to make some priorities, and decided to go for the MFL version first.

We saw the opportunity of getting some marketing and visibility support from Ableton as it was in their interest to show inventive and practical applications of their product. There were a few technical issues to be solved in this relation, as Ableton prefers (requires) all necessary code to reside inside the Live library on the end user computer. We wanted to use open source libraries (Csound), and needed to enable these to be installed elsewhere. A certain amount of fudging was needed to figure out how to handle this. Currently we install the core Hadron files in a separate folder, while the Live devices are installed into the Live library, linking to the external components. The MFL version of Hadron was released in July 2010, and it seems we did indeed get some extra attention due to the Ableton affiliation.

IM: *How long did it take to develop Hadron? What was the developmental process?*

ØB: From the very first prototyping of the partikkel opcode to the Hadron release it took about 5 years. The more specific design and implementation of Hadron was about 2 years. The development process was first to create a basic building block that gave a lot of potential (partikkel), and then gradually find a form where this potential could be applied and developed into something practically usable. A lot of effort went into the design of an interface that should be simple enough to be playable in real-time whilst retaining a great degree of flexibility. The partikkel opcode by itself has some 40 control parameters, where some of them are multidimensional "per grain" controls containing many sub-parameters. Building further on top of this to create a practically useful instrument we of course need things like envelope generators, LFOs and the like, each of them bringing a few more parameters that need to be specified and controlled. The current Hadron implementation uses more than 200 parameters. This gave rise to the idea of utilising some kind of preset interpolation routine and a 2-dimensional surface to control it. Inspired by the work of Ali Momeini et al, we implemented this in Csound using the hvs (hyper vectorial synthesis) opcodes. Now, preset interpolation in itself reduces flexibility significantly, as the 200-dimensional parameter space is collapsed onto a 2-dimensional control space. I wanted something to enable direct modification and control over some aspects of the parameter space.

As a generalization to reduce complexity, I figured we could look at all envelopes and LFOs etc. as modulators, affecting the control parameters. This led to the design of the dynamic modulation matrix, where all modulators could affect any parameter including its own control parameters. I also included the "expression faders" of the Hadron GUI as modulators, together with pitch/amp/centroid analysis tracks (analyses of the source waveforms used for partikkel). The modulation matrix was initially implemented with basic Csound opcodes, and later optimised when implemented as a Csound opcode (modmatrix). Again, Thom Johansen came to the rescue providing an excellent optimisation of my clunky initial attempt. I see the preset interpolation system as a means to enable the user to move around to specified locations in the 200-dimensional parameter space, while the modulation matrix allows local modification of position and orientation. Seen together, the term "preset" did not seem to completely fit the bill so we opted for the term "state" to describe the items that we interpolate between.

After the MFL release in 2010, we picked up the work on a VST version again. At this time I had the great fortune of getting a regular position at NTNU music technology, and even greater fortune of Sigurd Saue getting a position at the same department simultaneously. As Sigurd had taken part in the early stages of partikkel development, it was natural to bring the collaboration up to speed now. Sigurd took up the source from Erik Blekesaunet (he left to work with "Verdensteatret" building robotical performances and travelling worldwide) and made the current VST implementation. Bernt helped accommodate this implementation for OSX and we brought Arne back in to redesign the GUI for the new platform. The VST version was released late 2012.

IM: *Can you describe to me the relationship between Hadron and Csound?*

ØB: I very much consider Csound, partikkel and modmatrix to be the enabling technologies for Hadron. Csound is used as the audio processing engine, and we install a separate version of Csound with Hadron on the end user computer. The purpose of using a separate Csound version is that we do not rely on the end user having Csound installed, and if they have Csound installed we also avoid any possible version conflicts etc. in this manner. We also install a Csound standalone version of the Hadron orchestra and score, so that Hadron can be run conventionally in Csound without the MFL or VST bindings. I suspect this is mostly practical as a demo case for those who want to pull Hadron apart and use the components to build their own version.

IM: *Can you explain for me a little bit about the commercial aspect of the Hadron project and how this fits in with Csound's LGPL license?*

ØB: Yes, I think the basic promise of open source to enable sharing of knowledge is very important. I've tried to find a model that allows open source software to be the basis of a commercial product, hopefully allowing resources to be generated to enable further development of both Hadron and Csound. Formally, we comply with the LGPL license in terms of a dynamic link, using Csound as a library, and we also install the core Hadron DSP code as text files for every end user. The Max for Live interface (Max patch) files are also open and editable. The VST interface source code for JUCE has not been distributed yet, but we have no secrets there, and will find an appropriate way of distributing it soon. The one thing we keep as a commercial and closed product is the state files for Hadron. These contain parameter settings and modulation matrix routings that expands the applications for Hadron, for example new effect processor modes, new synthesiser modes etc. The design of new states files is quite time consuming and requires careful handling of the modulation matrix coefficients. As there is full flexibility in the modulation matrix, it is also quite possible to make things go haywire, especially when interpolating from one state to another. Still, I do see this model as an experiment, being open to change if formal or practical issues arise that make that necessary. Also if there is any opinion that this model is trying to look pretty but is, in fact, reaping benefits in a non-moral manner, I am more than happy to participate in a discussion about it and change it if it needs to be changed.

IM: *What sort of users are using Hadron now?*

ØB: We've had a large amount of users downloading Hadron, especially after the release of the VST version. I would not dare to make generalisations as of yet. The few support emails we've had suggests that we have users working on sound design, musicians, composers, sound artists etc, so quite a wide range of users. It is very inspiring to see how other users employ the tool in different ways and with different aesthetics than what I would do myself.

IM: *Do you use Hadron yourself?*

ØB: I use Hadron extensively, and in many cases almost exclusively. I perform regularly with an ensemble called Trondheim Electroacoustic

Music Performance (T-EMP), which is an ensemble based on free improvisation within the electroacoustic domain. Here I work with the audio signals I get from the other musicians, sampling or processing live for example the signal I get from the drummer Carl Haakon Waadeland. I find that there is a new kind of musical interaction found in the combined effort, two performers collaborating on making a single musical output. There is indeed one sound coming out from two instrumentalists, and the actions of each performer directly influence what the other one can do or how he will sound. Similarly I work with inputs from our singers, any guest performers we might bring in, and I also use my own voice as an input to the process if needs be. My set-up for this kind of musicking is four instances of Hadron with a free routing of any input to any Hadron instance, and with each Hadron instance free to feed its output back into other Hadron instances.

I find that performing with Hadron is quite different from any other instrument I've used, in that the complexity of the underlying engine and parameter mapping provides a wide range of potential, while the controls are still relatively simple, even with four instances of Hadron. I would say that the instrument, more than any other I've used, requires me to play by ear, as the interaction between different states is complex. Some performers and composers like to have a random element in the mix, I like more to have a completely deterministic but very complex instrument.

***IM:** What's next for Partikkel Audio?*

ØB: We really should try to make some more states packs, exploring further the possibilities of Hadron. I clearly see that there is much unreleased potential in the instrument. On the side, we have also started researching some other kinds of effects, most of them quite a bit simpler than Hadron. Csound will reside at the heart of what we do in any and all cases in the foreseeable future.

DEVELOPING CSOUND PLUGINS WITH CABBAGE

RORY WALSH

Introduction

In an industry dominated by commercial and closed-source software, audio plugins represent a rare opportunity for developers to extend the functionality of their favourite digital audio workstations, regardless of licensing restrictions. The beauty of plugin development is that developers can focus entirely on signal processing tasks rather than getting distracted by low-level audio and MIDI communication protocols.

Cabbage is an audio framework that provides users with a truly cross-platform, multi-format Csound-based plugin solution. Cabbage allows users to generate plugins under three major frameworks: the Linux Native VST, Virtual Studio Technology (VST), and Apple's Audio Units. Plugins for the three systems can be created using the same code, interchangeably. Cabbage also provides a useful array of graphical widgets so that developers can create their own unique plugin interfaces.

In using Csound as the language for development users have at their disposal a vast array of audio and MIDI processing options, with new features being added all the time. Csound is one of the oldest and most extensive audio processing language around. Coupling it with a framework like Cabbage means that users can now integrate it, and thousands of existing instruments, into any number of high-end audio workstations.

I. Overview of Cabbage

The ability to run existing audio software in tandem with commercial DAWs is not something new to computer musicians. Systems such as Pluggo, PdVST, CsoundVST, Max4Live and Csound4Live all provide users with a way to develop audio plugins using existing audio languages. CsoundVST is still available for download but can be tricky to build. It does not provide native GUI widgets, but Python interfaces can be built for it with relative ease using Csound's Python opcodes. Much to the dismay of many Max/MSP users, Pluggo has been discontinued and is no longer available. PdVst is still available, but has not been updated in quite some time. Max4Live is a commercial product that provides a way of integrating Max/MSP into Live. Csound4Live provides Csound users with a way of accessing Csound within Live. Because Csound4Live is built on top of a Max4Live patch, it means users must already have Max4Live installed. The software presented in this paper may well have been inspired by the systems mentioned above but is in fact an amalgamation of several projects that have been rewritten and redesigned in order to take full advantage of today's emerging plugin technologies, not to mention the outstanding developments made to Csound itself in the past decade. Before looking at the system in its present state it is worth taking a look at the different projects that have made Cabbage what it is today.

The Csound Library

The main component of the framework presented here is the Csound 5 library. Since the release of the host library Csound users have been harnessing the power of Csound in a variety of different applications. The library is accessed through its application programming interface, or API. APIs can be described as libraries that allow users to access internal functions of a particular software. A Csound host application can for example start any number of Csound instances through a series of different calling functions. The API also provides several mechanisms for two-way communication with an instance of Csound, through the use of 'named software' buses. These 'buses' operate like the auxiliary sends and receives you see on mixing desks, data gets sent to and from Csound. Cabbage accesses the named software bus on the host side through a set of channel functions provided by the API. Csound instruments can then read and write data on a named bus using the *chnset/chnget* opcodes.

All this allows Cabbage to control Csound in a very flexible way, and in turn provides Csound with a means of controlling Cabbage interfaces during run-time. Examples of type of two-way communication are providing in the sections below.

csLADSPA/csVST (2007)

csLADSPA and csVST are two lightweight audio plugin systems that make use of the above mentioned Csound API. Both toolkits were developed so that musicians and composers could harness the power of Csound within a host of commercial and open source audio software. The concept behind these toolkits is very simple and although each makes use of a different plugin technology, they were both implemented in the very same way. A basic model of how the plugins work is shown below in figure1.

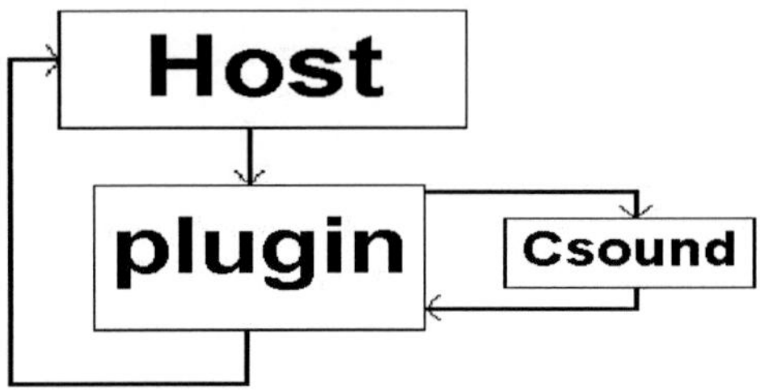

Figure 1. Architecture of a Csound plugin

The host application loads the csLADSPA or csVST plugin. When the user processes audio the plugin routes the selected audio to an instance of Csound. Csound will then process this audio and return it to the plugin, which will then route that audio to the host application.

The main drawback to these systems is that they do not provide any tools for developing user interfaces. Both csLADSPA and csVST use whatever native interface is provided by the host to display plugin parameters. csLADSPA is no longer under development, while csVST continues to be distributed with major releases of Csound.

Cabbage, First Release (2008)

Cabbage was first presented to the audio community at the Linux Audio Conference in 2008. The framework provided Csound programmers with a simple, albeit powerful toolkit for the development of standalone cross-platform audio software. The main goal of Cabbage at that time was to provide composers and musicians with a means of easily building and distributing high-end audio applications, without having to well versed in various low-level programming languages. Users could design their own graphical interfaces using an easy to read syntax that slotted into a unified Csound text file(.csd). This version of Cabbage had no support for plugin development, and although certain aspects have changed dramatically in the intervening years, the basic modus operandi remains the same.

II. Cabbage Today

The latest version of Cabbage consolidates the aforementioned projects into one user-friendly cross-platform interface for developing audio plugins. Combining the GUI capabilities of earlier versions of Cabbage with the lightweight approach of csLADSPA and csVST, users can now develop customised high-end audio plugins armed with nothing more than a rudimentary knowledge of Csound and basic programming. Early versions of Cabbage were written using the wxWidgets C++ GUI library. Whilst wxWidgets provides a more than adequate array of GUI controls and other useful classes, it quickly became clear that creating plugins with wxWidgets was going to be more trouble than it was worth due to a series of threading issues.

Cabbage now uses the JUCE Class library. Not only does JUCE provide an extensive set of classes for developing GUIs, it also provides a relatively foolproof framework for developing audio plugins for a host of plugin formats. On top of that it provides a robust set of audio and MIDI input/output classes. By using these audio and MIDI IO classes Cabbage can bypass Csound's native IO devices completely. Therefore users no longer need to hack Csound command line flags each time they want to change audio or MIDI devices.

The architecture of Cabbage has also undergone some dramatic changes since 2008. Originally Cabbage produced standalone applications which embedded the instrument's .csd into a binary executable that could then be distributed as a single application. Today Cabbage is structured differently and instead of creating a new standalone application for each instrument Cabbage is now a dedicated plugin system in itself.

Cabbage Syntax

Each Cabbage instrument is defined in a simple Csound text file. The syntax used to create GUI controls is quite straightforward and should be provided within special xml-style tags <Cabbage> and </Cabbage> which can appear either above or below Csound's own <CsoundSynthesizer> tags. Each line of Cabbage specific code relates to one GUI control only. The attributes of each control are set using different identifiers such as colour(), channel(), size() etc. Where identifiers are not used, Cabbage will use the default values.

Cabbage Controls

Each and every Cabbage widget has 4 common parameters: position on screen(x, y) and size(width, height). Apart from position and size all other parameters are optional and if left out default values will be assigned. To set control parameters you will need to use an appropriate identifier after the control name. In the following example, *form* is the Cabbage specific control, while *size()* and *caption()* are two identifiers used to control it how it appears.

```
control size(400, 400), caption("Hello World")
```

The different identifiers and their roles will be discussed shortly, but first is a full list of the different GUI controls currently available in Cabbage, and a short description of what they do.

Available GUI Controls	**Description**
Form	Main window.
groupbox	A container for placing control on.
Image	Used to display an image from file.
keyboard	MIDI keyboard.
Label	Used to display text.
csoundoutput	Will show a window with the output from Csound in it.
snapshot	Can be used to record presets.
infobutton	When pressed will display a web browser with a user defined file. Can be useful for displaying plugin help in HTML. (Only available on OSX and Windows)
Line	Used to display a line. Useful when designing GUIs.
Table	For displaying Csound function tables. Tables are notified to update from Csound.
rslider, hslider, vslider	Rotary, Horizontal and Vertical sliders. Range can be set, along with an increment value. A skew factor can be set in order for it to behave non-linearly.
button	Button. Toggles between 1 and 0 when clicked.
combobox	Pressing a combo box causes an indexed drop-down list to appear. The item index is sent to Csound.
checkbox	A toggle/check box. Will show when it's on and off. Sends a 0 or 1 to Csound.
xypad	A xyPad which can be used to controls two parameters at the same time. Animation can also be enabled to throw the ball around. It's also possible to draw a path for the ball.

Cabbage Identifiers

As mentioned above, not all controls support the same identifiers. For example, a groupbox will never need to have a channel assigned to it because it's a static control. Likewise buttons don't need to use the range() identifier. Below is a table showing all the available identifiers in Cabbage. Parameters within quotation marks represent string values, while those without represent floating point decimals, or integer values. A list of available identifiers is given in the table below.

GUI Control – Supported identifiers	Description
pos(x, y)	Sets the position of the control within it's parent.
size(width, height)	Sets the size of the control.
bounds(x, y, width, height)	Sets a controls position on screen and size.
channel("channel")	Sets up a software channel for Csound and Cabbage to communicate over. Channels should only contain valid ascii characters.
caption("caption")	Used to set the name of the instrument and also used to automatically place a control within a group box.
min(min)	Set minimum value for a slider.
max(max)	Set maximum value for a slider.
value(val)	Set initial value for sliders, combo boxes, check boxes and buttons. When used with a keyboard controls it can be used to set the lowest note seen on screen.
range(min, max, val, skew, incr)	Sets range of slider with and initialises it to val. Users can get the slider to a have in a non-linear fashion by selecting a skew value less than 1, while incr can be used to control how big each step is when the slider is moved.
rangex(min, max, val) rangey(min, max, val)	Set the ranges of the xyPad's X and Y axis.
colour("colour") colour(red, green, blue) colour(red, green, blue, alpha)	Sets the colour of the control. Any CSS or HTML colour string can be passed to this identifier. The colour identifier can also be passed an RBG, or RGBA value. All channel values must be between 0 and 255. For instance colour(0, 0, 255) will create blue, while colour(0, 255, 0, 255) will create green with an alpha channel set to full.

fontcolour("colour") fontcolour(red, green, blue) fontcolour(red, green, blue, alpha)	Sets the colour of the font. Please see the *colour* identifier for details on the parameters.
tracker("colour")	Set the colour of a sliders tracker. See the *colour* identifier for details on the parameters.
outline("colour")	Set the outline colour of an image. See the *colour* identifier for details on the parameters.
textbox(val)	Used with slider to turn on or off the default textbox that appears beside them. By default this is set to 1 for on, if you pass a 0 to it, the textbox will no longer be displayed.
text("string")	Used to set the text on any components that displays text.
file("filename")	Used to select the file that is to be displayed with the image control.
populate("file type", "dir")	Used to add all files of a set type, located in specific directory to a combo boxes list of items.
author("author's name")	Used to add the author's name, or any other message to the bottom of the instrument.
items("one", "two", "three", …) items("on", "off")	Used to populate buttons, combo boxes and snapshots. When used with a button the first two parameters represent the captions the button will display when clicked. When used with a snapshot each item represents a saved preset.
preset("preset")	Used to tie a snapshot control to a particular control
plant("name")	Used to turn an image or group box into a container for controls. Each plant must be given a unique name and must be followed by a pair of curly brackets. Any widget declared within these bracket swill belong to the plant. Coordinates for children are relative to the top left position of its parent control. Resizing the parent will automatically cause all children to resize accordingly.
shape("shape")	Used to set the shape of an image, can be set to *rounded, ellipse* or *sharp* for rectangles and squares.

pluginID("plug")	Used to set the plugin identifier. Each plugin should have a unique identifier, otherwise hosts may not be able to load them correctly.
tablenumbers(1, 2, 3, 4, ...)	Tells table controls which function tables to load. If more than one table is passed function table will be stocked on top of each other with an layer of transparency.
midictrl(channel, controller)	Can be used with sliders and button to enable the use of a MIDI hardware controller. Channel and controller set the channel and controller numbers.
line(val)	This identifier will stop the group box line from appearing if passed a 0.

II. Modes of Operation

Users will run their Cabbage instruments in two distinct ways. One is through the standalone host, where each instrument functions as a single piece of audio software. The other mode of operation is through instruments that are loaded as plugins within a larger host software. Both modes of operation offer certain pros and cons. For example, when running in standalone mode there are less of the computer's resources being used so it is possible to run some pretty CPU intensive processes, but you lose the extra functionality offered by a fully featured host. On the other hand, because many hosts demand a lot of resources themselves, you'll find that computationally expensive instruments don't always run so smooth when loaded as plugins and in many cases run much better in standalone mode.

The Cabbage Native Host

The Cabbage native host loads and performs Cabbage instruments, as plugins. The only difference between the Cabbage host and a regular plugin host is that Cabbage loads .csd files directly as plugins. To use Cabbage plugins in other hosts users must first export their instrument through Cabbage, in the form of a shared library. The type of shared library created is determined the operating system in use. The Cabbage host provides access to all the audio/MIDI devices available to the user and also allows changes to be made to the sampling rate and buffer sizes.

The function of the Cabbage host is twofold. First it provides a standalone player for running GUI based Csound instruments (in this context it functions similarly to the Max/MSP runtime player). Secondly it provides a platform for developing and testing audio plugins. Any instrument that runs in the Cabbage native host can be exported as a plugin and used in any plugin host. The host also provides a way of triggering MIDI instruments through the virtual keyboard widget, and comes with an integrated text editor which can be launched at any time during the playback and performance of your instrument.

Cabbage Plugins

When users export their instruments as plugins they can be accessed in plugin hosts such as Live, Cubase, AudioMulch, Sibelius, Renoise, etc.. Any host that loads VST plugins will load Cabbage plugins too. At the time of writing Cabbage only supports VST plugins, but future versions will also feature the option to create Audio Unit plugins on OSX.

When you load a Cabbage plugin in your host, it is most likely that a native interface of sliders will be used to display the plugin parameters, if you chose not to open the plugin's editor window. The number of parameters shown in your host will always match the number of software channels used in communicating between Csound and Cabbage. What's more is each parameter in your host will be named with whatever was passed to the channel() identifier when the control was created. With this in mind, it is important to remember to use clear and meaningful names for your channel strings, otherwise users of your plugins will not know what each parameter does!

While sliders can easily be mapped to the plugin host GUI, other controls must be mapped differently. Toggling buttons for example will cause a native slider to jump between maximum and minimum position. In the case of controls such as combo boxes, native slider ranges will be split into several segments to reflect the number of choices available to users. If for example a user creates a combo box with 5 elements, the corresponding native slider will jump a fifth each time the user increments the current selection.

The upshot of this is that each native slider can quickly and easily be linked with MIDI hardware using the now ubiquitous 'MIDI-learn' function that comes with almost all of today's best audio software. Because care has being taken to map each Cabbage control with the corresponding native slider, users can quickly set up Cabbage plugins to be controlled with MIDI hardware, or alternatively, through automation provided by the host.

Cabbage Plants

Cabbage plants are GUI abstractions that contain one or more controls. These abstractions are used as anchors to the child widgets contained within. All widgets contained within a plant have top and left positions which are relative the the top left position of the parent. The screen shot below shows a Cabbage instrument that contains several plants, all of which can be used across a whole range of instruments.

Figure 2. Simple bass synthesiser which uses plants to organise panels on screen

While all widgets can be children of a plant, only `group boxes` and `images` can be used as plants themselves. Adding a plant identifier to an image or group box definition will cause them to act as containers. The plant() identifier takes a string that denotes the name of the plant. Plant names must be unique within an instrument or plants will end up being placed on top of each other. When using an image or a group box as a plant, you must enclose the code from the controls that follow in curly brackets, to indicate which controls belong to the plant. In the code below a groupb box control is set up as a plant.

```
groupbox bounds(10, 10, 400, 300), text("I'm a plant!"),
plant("plant"){
;all plant controls should be placed here
}
```

The big advantage to using plant abstractions is that you can easily move and resize them without needing to modify the dimensions of the child components contained within. You can also save your plants and recall them later from a plant repository. Plants are intended to be reused across instruments so users don't have to keep rebuilding GUIs from scratch. They can also be used to give your plugins a unique look and feel.

Figure 3. Plants can be used to give applications their own unique look and feel.

Examples

When writing Cabbage plugin users need to add -n and -d to the CsOptions section of their .csd file. -n causes Csound to bypass writing of sound to disk. Writing to disk is solely the responsibility of the host application(including the Cabbage native host). If the user wishes to create an instrument plugin in the form of a MIDI synthesiser they can use the MIDI-interop command line flags to pipe MIDI data from the host to the Csound instrument. Note that all Cabbage plugins are stereo. Therefore one must be sure to set "nchnls" to 2 in the header section of the csd file. Failure to do so will result in extraneous noise being added to the output signal. Below are 3 simple examples of Cabbage instruments. The examples were written to be simple, clear and concise Please do not judge the entire project on the examples you see below!

Example 1

The first plugin is a simple effect plugin. It makes use of the PVS family of opcodes. These opcodes provide users with a means of manipulating spectral components of a signal in realtime. In the following example the opcodes *pvsanal*, *pvsblur* and *pvsynth* are used to manipulate the spectrum of an incoming audio stream. Users can use the first hslider to average the amp/freq time functions of each analysis channel for a specified time. The output is then spatialised using a jitter-spline generator. The speed of the spatial movement is determined by the second hslider.

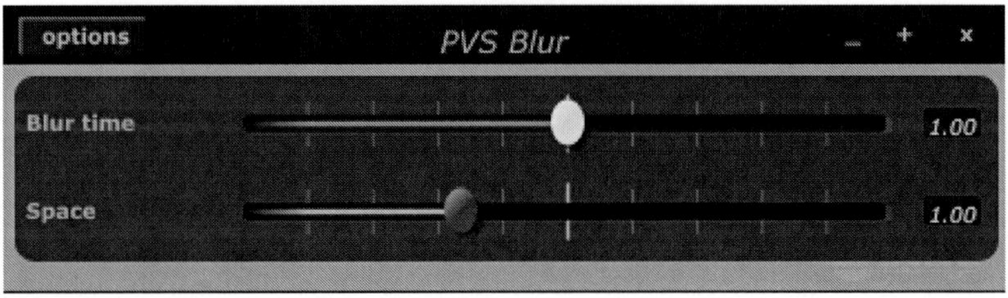

Figure 4. A simple PVS processing effect

```
<Cabbage>
form caption("PVS Blur") size(450, 110), colour(70, 70,
70)
hslider bounds(10, 1, 430, 50), channel("blur"),
range(0, 2, 1), textbox(1),\  text("Blur time")
hslider bounds(10, 40, 430, 50), channel("space"),
range(0, 3, 1), textbox(1),\  text("Space")
</Cabbage>
<CsoundSynthesizer>
<CsOptions>
-d -n -+rtmidi=null -M0 -b1024
</CsOptions>
<CsInstruments>
sr = 44100
ksmps = 32
nchnls = 2

instr 1
kblurtime chnget "blur"
kpanfreq chnget "space"
asig inch 1
fsig  pvsanal   asig, 1024, 256, 1024, 1
ftps  pvsblur   fsig, kblurtime, 2
atps  pvsynth   ftps
apan jspline 1, 1, kpanfreq
outs atps*apan, atps*(1-apan)
endin

</CsInstruments>
<CsScore>
f1 0 1024 10 1
i1 0 3600
</CsScore>
</CsoundSynthesizer>
```

Example 2

The second plugin is a MIDI-driven plugin instrument. This instrument uses the MIDI-interop command line parameters in the CsOptions section to pipe MIDI data from the host into Csound. This plugin also makes use of the virtual MIDI keyboard widget which can be used to play the instrument when a real keyboard is not available.

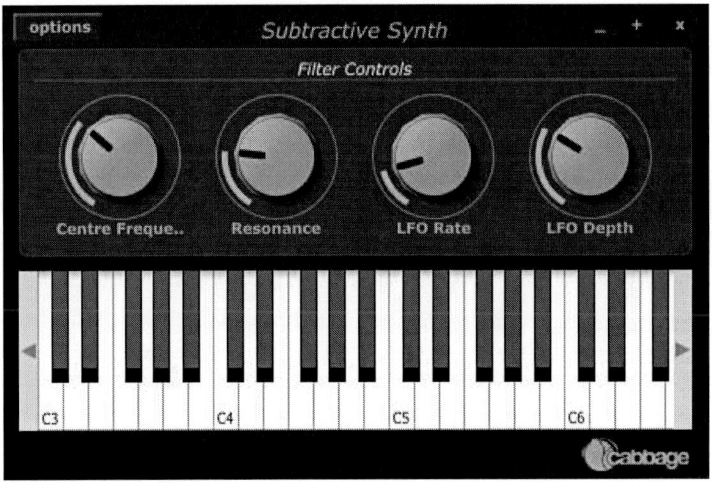

Figure 5. A simple MIDI driven snythesiser

```
<Cabbage>
form caption("Subtractive Synth") size(450, 270),
colour("black")
groupbox text("Filter Controls"), bounds(10, 1, 430,
130)
rslider bounds(30, 30, 90, 90), channel("cf"), \
range(1, 10000, 2000), text("Centre Frequency"),
colour("white")
rslider bounds(130, 30, 90, 90) channel("res"), range(0,
1, .1),\ text("Resonance"), colour("white")
rslider bounds(230, 30, 90, 90) channel("lfo_rate"),\
range(0, 10, 0), text("LFO Rate"), colour("white")
rslider bounds(330, 30, 90, 90) channel("lfo_depth"),\
    range(0, 1000, 0), text("LFO Depth"),
colour("white")
keyboard bounds(10, 140, 430, 100)
</Cabbage>
<CsoundSynthesizer>
<CsOptions>
-d -n -+rtmidi=null -M0 -b1024 --midi-key-cps=4
--midi-velocity-amp=5
</CsOptions>
<CsInstruments>
sr = 44100
ksmps = 32
nchnls = 2
0dbfs = 1

instr 1
;access data from named channels
kcf chnget "cf"
```

```
kres chnget "res"
klforate chnget "lfo_rate"
klfodepth chnget "lfo_depth"
aenv madsr .1, 0.4, .6, 1
asig vco2 p5, p4
klfo lfo klfodepth, klforate, 5
aflt moogladder asig, kcf+klfo, kres
outs aflt*aenv, aflt*aenv
endin

</CsInstruments>
<CsScore>
f1 0 1024 10 1
f0 3600
</CsScore>
</CsoundSynthesizer>
```

Example 3

The last example shows how Cabbage can be used to create MIDI effects plugins. This instrument takes an incoming MIDI note and arpeggiates it according to a variety of parameters which the user can control in real time. It is worth noting that Cabbage can also be used to create generative MIDI plugins that don't just modify notes, but create an entirely new stream of MIDI notes from scratch.

Figure 6. A simple MIDI arpeggiator

```
<Cabbage>
form size(300, 150), caption("MIDI Arpeggiator"),
colour(30, 30, 30)
groupbox bounds(9, 5, 281, 113), text("Controls"),
colour("black")
rslider bounds(20, 33, 67, 71), text("Transpose"),
range(0, 11, 0, 1, 1),\       channel("range")
```

```
rslider bounds(91, 33, 67, 71), text("Tempo"), range(1,
10, 1, 1, 1),\   channel("tempo")
combobox bounds(161, 33, 122, 72), caption("Chord"),
channel("combobox"),\   items("Major", "Minor", "7th")
</Cabbage>
<CsoundSynthesizer>
<CsOptions>
-n -d -+rtmidi=NULL -M0 -Q0 --midi-key=4
--midi-velocity-amp=5
</CsOptions>
<CsInstruments>
sr = 44100
ksmps = 64
nchnls = 2
0dbfs=1

;trigger instrument 1000 with incoming midi
massign 0, 1000

instr 1000
;retrieve channel data from Cabbage
kTransp chnget "transpose"
iChord chnget "chord"
kTempo chnget "tempo"
kTrigger metro kTempo;
kIndex init 0

;if a type of chord is selected, proceed
if(iChord>0) then
    if(kTrigger==1) then
    ;read through table of notes
    kNote tab kIndex, iChord
    ;start instrument one each time we enter this test
    event "i", 1, 0, 1/kTempo, p4+kNote+kTransp
    ;increment out table index
    kIndex = (kIndex>3 ? 0 : kIndex+1);
    endif
endif

endin

instr 1
;output MIDI notes
noteondur 1, p4, 120, p3
endin
</CsInstruments>
<CsScore>
;tables containing chord types, maj, min, 7th
f1 0 4 -2 0 4 7 4
f1 0 4 -2 0 3 7 3
f1 0 4 -2 0 4 7 11
f0 3600
</CsScore>
</CsoundSynthesizer>
```

3. Future Development

Cabbage development is moving along relatively quickly despite the small number of developers. Duties such as work, sleep, and eating all draw resources away from development, but there are still a lot of interesting new features in the pipeline. First is the continued development of the table editor. As it stands users can view and superimpose function tables on top of each other, and also position a playback scrubber that will move along the table in time with the current index. Direct manipulation of the table data through the mouse is not yet supported but work is already under way. 8-channel plugins are now working and will be supported soon. A new GUI drag and drop system is almost complete and should be available in the next release. This feature allows users to easily design GUIs by manipulating controls and plants using the mouse when in 'edit' mode. The text editor is also undergoing some updates and integration between the editor and the standalone host will only get better over time.

Apart from the above, work is also under way on a new Cabbage patcher. The Cabbage Patcher is a fully functional plugin host that allows direct editing of Cabbage plugins. Plugins, both VST and Csound derived Cabbage ones are patched together is a modular fashion, similar to Pure Data, AudioMulch and Max/MSP. When users design a patch, the possibility is there to group all the Cabbage instruments together into one larger plugin. This opens up a whole new way of developing effects and instruments in Csound and has already proved to be very powerful in early experiments. Unfortunately development on the patcher is slow due to various time constraints and it would be unreasonable to expect its release any time before the end of 2013, if not later.

4. Conclusion

From reading the above article one could be excused for thinking that Cabbage began life in 2008. In reality it is quite different. In 2003 I worked on an audio software not unlike Cabbage, called AIDE, which made use of Victor Lazzarini's SndObj C++ library. AIDE let users design standalone audio software through a GUI drag and drop system. Users could also edit C++ code directly, and have it compiled on the fly. Unfortunately for me, the research institute in which I was working at the time ran out of funding so the project stopped. Not long after this Csound 5 was released, and with it the possibility to embed Csound into other software. It wasn't long before I was replacing the C++ processing code in my applications with Csound code, much to the auditory relief of my friends it must be said!

Cabbage as it stands today is more than the sum of it's parts. It is the product of every discussion I've had with musicians about what draws them to Csound, and it is the product of every thread I've engaged in on the Csound mailing list. Cabbage is an open source project that belongs to the entire Csound community.

Giving users access to Csound within their preferred audio software opens up a plethora of new possibilities. Who knows, it might also encourage those computer music professionals who have rarely, if ever used Csound, to take another look. It really has grown into something quite extraordinary!

For downloads, news and samples instruments please visit: http://www.TheCabbageFoundation.org

Acknowledgements

I'd like to express my sincere thanks to everyone on the Csound, Renoise and Juce mailing lists. Without their help and assistance this project would not have been possible. I'd also like to thank Stefano Bonetti for help in debugging various issues over the past few months. Finally I'd like to thank the other developer on this project, Damien Rennick. His attention to detail in the look and feel development means Cabbage users have at their disposal, free and professional quality GUI controls that could compete with any commercial software on the market.

References

ffitch, John, “On The Design of Csound5,” *Proceedings of Linux Audio Developers Conference. ZKM, Karlsruhe, Germany*, 2004.

Lazzarini, Victor and Walsh, Rory, “Developing LADSPA plugins with Csound,” *Proceedings of the Linux Audio Developers Conference TU Berlin, Germany*, 2007.

Walsh, Rory; Lazzarni, Victor and Brogan, Martin. "Csound-based cross-platform plugin toolkits," *Proceedings of the Internation Computer Music Conference, Belfast, NI*, 2008.

Walsh, Rory, “Cabbage, a new GUI framework for Csound,” *Proceedings of the Linux Audio Conference KHM Cologne, Germany*, 2008.

"Linux VST Homepage," website accessed April 12, 2013 http://www.linux-vst.com/.

"Steinberg Hompage," website accessed April 12, 2013 http://ygrabit.steinberg.de/~ygrabit/public_html/index.html.

"Apple Audio units Developer Homepage," website accessed April 12, 2013 http://developer.apple.com/audio/audiounits.html.

"WinXound Homepage," website accessed April 12, 2013 http://winxound.codeplex.com/.
"Cycling 74," website accessed April 12, 2013 Homepage http://cycling74.com/.
"PdVst," website accessed April 12, 2013 http://crca.ucsd.edu/~jsarlo/pdvst/.
"CsoundVST," website accessed April 12, 2013 http://michael-gogins.com.
"WxWidgets," website accessed April 12, 2013 www.wxwidgets.org.
"Juce," website accessed April 12, 2013 http://www.rawmaterialsoftware.com/juce.php.

Wavelets in Csound

Gleb G. Rogozinsky

This chapter describes the application of wavelets for sound synthesis and signal processing. It provides some theoretical background as a basis for further research and also introduces Csound's new *GENwave* utility, designed specifically for the generation of compactly supported wavelets, the most notable and popular type of wavelet.

It has been more than 30 years since wavelets first appeared in the fields of signal processing theory and applied mathematics. We can find the origins of wavelet theory in the works of Dennis Gabor, Alfred Haar, Paul Levy and others. The term "wavelet" was first introduced through the work of Alex Grossman and Jean Morlet; they were interested in the analysis of seismic signals, using techniques related to windowed Fourier atoms, but with the possibility to change the length of the window function. In the late 1980s Ingrid Daubechies and Stephane Mallat proved the existence of finite impulse response filters, capable of producing wavelets with finite length (or compact support) and building compact bases (Daubechies, 1992; Mallat, 1998). Since that time, the number of wavelet applications has grown (Chui, 1992). Some years ago wavelets began to emerge within the field of music and sound processing (Batista, 2000). Further aspects of their implementation and application within Csound are given in this chapter.

Theory

A wavelet $\psi(t)$ is defined as a function of finite energy and zero average value. The equation (1) is called the admissibility condition and it means that the spectrum of the wavelet must have zero at the zero frequency:

$$\int \frac{|\Psi(\omega)|^2}{|\omega|} d\omega < +\infty$$

Equation 1.

Zero at the zero frequency means that the average value of the wavelet in the time domain must be zero.

$$\int \psi(t)dt = 0$$

Equation 2.

The entire wavelet basis ψa,b(t) is derived from the so-called mother wavelet through scaling and translation. The parameter a, is responsible for changing the scale of the wavelet (also referred to as dilation), whilst b defines a translation (or shift) of the wavelet along the time axis.

$$\psi_{a,b}(t) = \frac{1}{\sqrt{a}} \psi\left(\frac{t-b}{a}\right)$$

Equation 3.

Factor 1/√a, normalizes the energy of the wavelet, ensuring that all wavelets possess the same energy. Figure 1 shows dilation and translation of the wavelet referred to as the "Mexican hat", which is actually a second derivative of a Gaussian function.

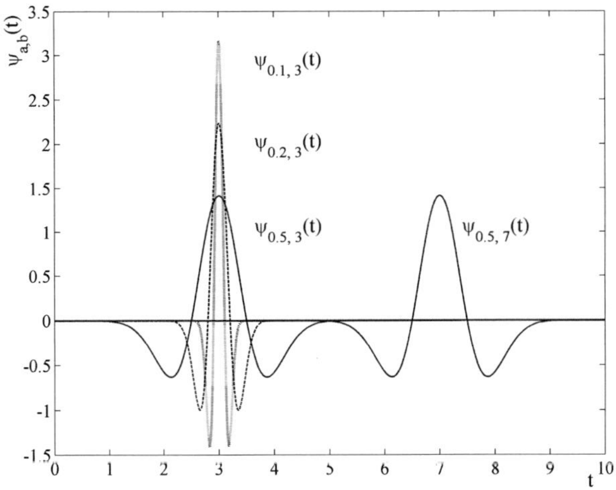

Figure 1. Scaling and dilation of a wavelet

All of these given definitions and formulae simply mean that the wavelet should oscillate, or in other words it must be a wave that exists for some finite duration. The fact that the wavelet possesses finite energy means that the wavelet cannot persist indefinitely, unlike *sin* or *exp* functions. When this is compared to the classic Fourier transform, which uses sinusoid as its only base function, the wavelet transform works with a huge number of basis functions. It is possible to build a unique wavelet to suit each new application. If the reader is interested further in the construction of wavelets, it is recommended to investigate *Building Your Own Wavelets at Home* (Sweldens and Schroeder, 1996).

There are several different variants of wavelet transform. In most cases, Discrete Wavelet Transform (DWT) is the preferred variant, whilst Continuous Wavelet Transform (CWT) is used mostly for the detailed analysis of non-stationery time series. DWT supports a fast algorithm for the calculation of coefficients called the *algorithm of Mallat*. On each step of the procedure, the input signal is convolved with two filters: a high-pass filter *h[n]* and a low-pass filter *g[n]*. The high-pass filter relates to the wavelet function and the low-pass filter relates to the so-called *scaling function*. Both of these filters create a quadrature mirror (QMF) pair. Their magnitude responses are symmetrical about 0.25 of the sampling frequency. If we already know the impulse response of one filter, its mirror can be calculated using the equation:

$$g[n] = (-1)^n h[n]$$

Equation 4.

When using the fast algorithm of DWT, the input signal *x[n]* is convolved with each of those filters. The output of the high-pass filter is referred to as the "details" and the output of the low-pass filter is referred to as the "approximation". Because we feed the signal through the QMF pair, we can downsample their outputs. This procedure can be repeated several times to obtain coefficients for different levels (or scales) of wavelet transformation.

$$y_a[n] = \sum_k x[k] \cdot g[2n - k]$$

Equation 5.

$$y_d[n] = \sum_k x[k] \cdot h[2n - k]$$

Equation 6.

In classical DWT only approximation is divided further. Another type of wavelet transform called Discrete Wavelet Packet Transform (DWPT) divides both of the filter outputs to obtain better resolution.

Why Wavelets?

Classical Fourier analysis deconstructs the input signal into a set of harmonics and, as already mentioned, the sole basis function used in Fourier is the sinusoid. But imagine now that you have a set of differently shaped Lego building blocks from which you can reconstruct the sonic world. This can be compared to the Fourier hegemony of only one basic building block type. Classical Fourier analysis does not provide any time resolution. The only way to solve this problem is to use a window function that slides along the signal (Short-Time Fourier Transform). In this procedure the window's length is fixed, so that only the number of oscillations within the window varies.

In the case of wavelets the number of oscillations is constant, while the window length varies. This feature of wavelet transformation provides some remarkable peculiarities of which the most important one is the *variable time-frequency resolution*. This means that we can retain good localisation in the time domain at high frequencies and vice versa, therefore short bursts are detected well in time domain while low tones are estimated better in the frequency domain (or the "scale" domain, in terms of wavelet theory).

There are a number of areas in which wavelets are commonly used. In most cases, they should provide better results compared to Fourier when we are dealing with an input signal of a non-periodic or chaotic nature. The list of wavelet applications includes machine vision, data processing, de-noising and encoding. For example, the JPEG2000 encoding algorithm (http://en.wikipedia.org/wiki/JPEG_2000) uses wavelets for encoding images. Paul Addison's book (Addison, 2002) provides multiple examples of wavelet usage.

Many aspects of the connection between wavelets and the sound they produce remain undisclosed however. From a traditional point of view, most sound signals are fundamentally related to the Fourier domain on account of their periodic characteristics. Conversely, many sounds that display more aperiodicity are much closer to the wavelet domain. For example, speech contains of a lot of non-stationary elements. It is also worth mentioning that the techniques of granular synthesis have a lot in similar with wavelets in how they employ grains of sound for sound synthesis. Curtis Roads' book (Roads, 2001) about granular synthesis includes a chapter about the application of wavelets for producing grain-like sounds. There are a number of papers about wavelets and sound (Kronland-Martinet, 1988; Darlington and Sendler, 2003), most of them describe the application of wavelets in the field of sound processing, compression etc. although some of them offer interesting examples of the use of wavelets in music (Poblete, 2006).

Wavelets in Csound

The Csound Book CD1 contains a chapter written by Pedro Batista about the application of wavelets in Csound (Batista, 2000). Batista's procedure (based on loops, tables and several instruments) is rather complicated for everyday use in sound programming.

The aim of this project is to provide an easy method of wavelet application for Csound, based on a new GEN utility. The code is based on the algorithm proposed by M.V. Wickerhauser, originally written for the Mathematica system (Batista, 2000).

The Csound manual page gives the following description of the new *GENwave* utility for the construction of compactly supported wavelets and wavelet packets.

f # time size "wave" fnsf seq rescale

Initialization

size -- number of points in the table. Must be a power of 2 or power-of-2 plus 1.
fnsf -- pre-existing table with scaling function coefficients.
seq -- non-negative integer number which corresponds to sequence of low-pass and high-pass mirror filters during deconvolution procedure.
rescale -- if not zero the table is not rescaled

The function table *fnsf* should contain the coefficients of the wavelet filter impulse response. It does not actually matter which one of two QMFs you use here since it is sufficient to fix one impulse response to obtain another. If, however, you want to follow the typical formalities, then you should put the coefficients of the scaling function in that table.

Seq defines the sequence of filters used in the convolution. In the binary form of this number, *zero* means a low-pass filter and *one* means a high-pass filter (see example below).

Rescale normalises the function table. It is recommended to leave the table without normalisation, if uniformity of the wavelet's energy is required.

The usage of the *GENwave* utility is quite simple. One could easily construct wavelets without delving deep into wavelet theory. The only thing required is a suitable filter impulse response.

The most popular wavelets are compactly supported ones. Their popularity can be explained by their capability for perfect reconstruction and finite length of impulse responses. Most wavelets of this type do not have a formal description. The whole wavelet is obtained through the iterative deconvolution of the delta-function and the wavelet filter coefficients. If we have a vector in which only the first element is one, whilst the others are zeroes, it means that the last level of the wavelet transform had a wavelet function as the input signal. If we perform the reverse procedure we will obtain the wavelet function. Following this procedure step by step, we can re-construct a wavelet of any length.

It is worth mentioning here that the world of wavelets goes much further than just compactly supported families. The success of Daubechies wavelets, Symlets and Coiflets (see figure 2) can be explained by their remarkable uses in signal processing of which the greatest are multi-resolution analysis and alias-free synthesis. Other wavelets possess features of a more analogue nature, for example, the 'Mexican hat' wavelet which belongs to a small group of wavelets that can be described mathematically. Wavelets of this type are not applicable for DWT and are used mostly in CWT.

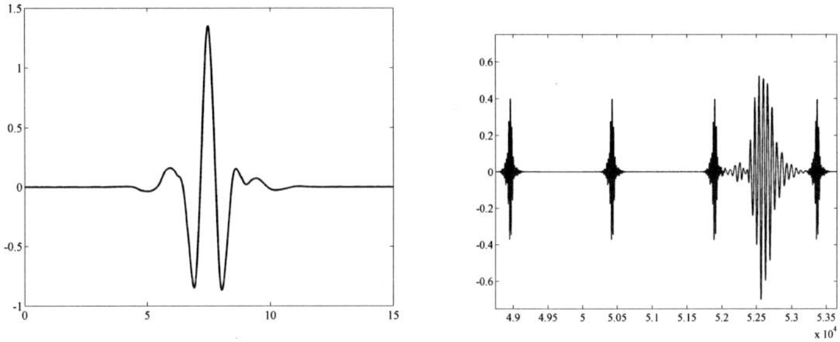

Figure 2. Symlet of 8th order (left), Biorthogonal wavelet 2.4 (right)

Examples

One of the most obvious applications of wavelets is to simply employ them as sound objects. Since wavelets have much in common with grains it is not unusual to use them in this way. Curtis Roads describes in his book the so-called *grainlet* method, which is wavelet re-synthesis based on operating with wavelet transform coefficients in the wavelet domain and with further synthesis of audio.

The Csound code shown below implements the generation of several wavelets available for further manipulation. It should be mentioned here that aliasing always appears with wavelets. The smaller order wavelets, such as *Haar*, or any other wavelets with relatively short IRs due to their short length in the time domain, have quite a substantial length in the frequency domain. This basically means that a 20 Hz wavelet generator will produce sound containing strong high harmonics. To make matters worse, these harmonics will be mirrored at the Nyquist frequency, therefore one should be aware of the frequencies produced when working with wavelets in this way.

First we will generate some wavelets using *GENwave*. For this we will define several FIR filters which are capable of producing wavelet families. One could input filter coefficients manually using GEN02 or read them directly from a text file. We define Daubechies filter of the 2nd order manually using GEN02 and we also define a Symlet of the 10th order using GEN23. PyWavelets can obtain most of the known compactly supported wavelets from the Wavelet Browser on *wavelets.pybytes.com*. You can select the family and the order of the filter and then copy the desired coefficients into a text file to be used with Csound. Note that for a correct interpretation of the results you should use the coefficients of the decomposition low-pass filter.

Table 1 below provides the coefficients of the low-pass filter IR for Daubechies wavelets of the 2nd to 5th orders. The values for these coefficients were copied from PyWavelets Wavelet Browser.

n	db2[n]	db3[n]	db4[n]	db5[n]
1	.48296	.33267	.230378	.16010
2	.83652	.806892	.714847	.60383
3	.22414	.45987	.630880	.72430
4	.129410	.135011	.0279838	.13842
5		.085441	.1870348	.24229
6		.035226	.0308413	.03224
7			.0328830	.07757
8			.0105974	.00624
9				.01258
10				.00334

Table 1. Rounded Daubechies filters coefficients for db2 – db5

This is not formally applicable to wavelets but it is nice to have the ability to use a wavelet prototype for the creation of wavelet-style grains. This instrument provides control of the wavelets' amplitudes and frequencies. The *osciln* opcode is used to access the table values at the user-defined rate.

```
sr = 44100
kr = 4410
ksmps = 10
nchnls = 1


instr 1             ; wavelet synth instrument
iamp  =     p4      ; wavelet gain
ifreq =     p5      ; wavelet frequency
itab  =     p6      ; selected wavelet function
inum  =     p7      ; number of wavelets to be created
a1    osciln iamp, ifreq, itab, inum
out a1
endin
```

Next we produce several wavelet granules. They can be used in wavelet synthesis. Tables of large sizes should produce smoother copies of wavelets. We should take the array of filter coefficients from *ftable 1* and iteratively deconvolve it until the output length is 16384.

The order of filters used throughout the deconvolution process is given as 14 which is 1110 in binary, therefore the first filter is LP ("0") and the others are HP ("1"). The text file *sym10.txt,* which contains the Symlet of the 10th order coefficients, is included in the Csound Manual directory.

```
; Daubechies 2 filter coefficients
f  1  0  4  -2  -0.1294095226  0.2241438680  0.8365163037
0.4829629131
; Symlet 10 filter coefficients
f 2 0 0 -23 "sym10.txt"

f 3 0 16384 "wave" 1 14 0
f 4 0 16384 "wave" 2 1  0
f 5 0 16384 "wave" 2 7  0
f 6 0 16384 "wave" 2 6  0

; Let's hear how some wavelets could sound
; instr start dur amp  frq wave      times
i 1     0     1   0.6  15  3      8
i 1     0.5   .   0.9  20  4      5
i 1     0.9   .   0.7  8   5      .
i 1     1.1   .   0.4  30  6      9
```

Next we can estimate how the wavelets might sound. The score given produces several portions of granular-style wavelets with different amplitudes and frequencies. A fragment of the rendered file is shown in figure 3.

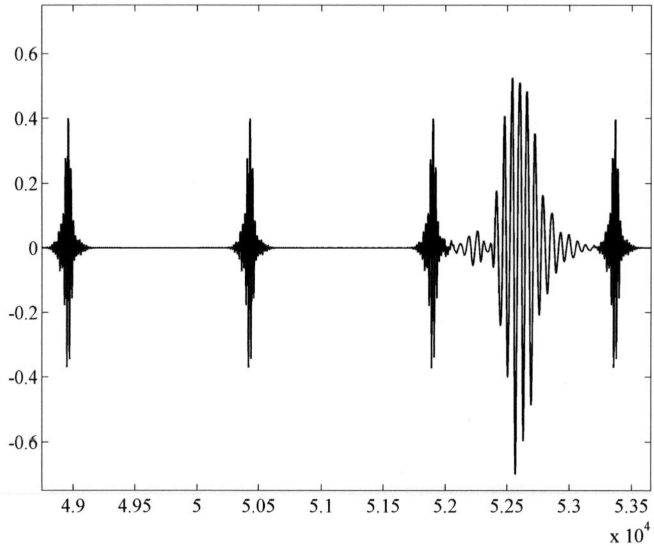

Figure 3. Fragment of wavelet granular signal

The main purpose of using wavelets is the wavelet transform. It is not that easy to perform a classic DWT in Csound on account of the fact that down-sampling of the audio signal is needed at each step of the wavelet decomposition. Through using *GENwave* it is possible to create a number of up-sampled wavelets and perform a so-called 'undecimated wavelet transform' (also known as a 'stationary wavelet transform'). This form of wavelet transform suffers greater redundancy but stays shift-invariant and uses the same lengths of wavelet coefficients for each level of decomposition, therefore we need to create some up-sampled children of the mother wavelet. The direct convolution opcode *dconv* is used to perform convolution in the time domain.

Note that some coefficients of the wavelet transform can reach rather large values so sometimes judicious attenuation is advisable.

We establish *zak* space in order to be able to connect different levels of wavelet transform with each other.

```
zakinit 3,1

instr 2    ; wavelet analysis instrument
a1 soundin "fox.wav"
; Decomposition Structure:
;      1 LEVEL   2 LEVEL
```

```
;       HP->ah1
; a1->|      HP(up2)->ah2
;       LP->al1->|
;              LP(up2)->al2
;
ain = a1*.5         ; attenuate input signal
                    ; since wavelet coefficients
                    ; could reach big values
ah1 dconv ain,ftlen(8),8
al1 dconv ain,ftlen(7),7
ah2 dconv al1,ftlen(10),10
al2 dconv al1,ftlen(9),9

zaw ah1,0
zaw al1,1
zaw ah2,2
zaw al2,3

aout zar p4
out aout
zacl 0,3
endin
```

Next we need to fill tables with wavelets and the scaling functions required for undecimated wavelet transform.

```
f7  0 16 "wave" 1 0 -1 ;db2 scaling func. for 1st
iteration
f8  0 16 "wave" 1 1 -1 ;db2 wavelet func. for 1st
iteration
f9  0 32 "wave" 1 0 -1 ;db2 scaling func. for 2nd
iteration
f10 0 32 "wave" 1 1 -1 ;db2 wavelet func. for 2nd
iteration

; Now we can try to decompose input file using
wavelets
i2 2 4  1; approximation 1st level
i2 5 .  2; details 2nd level
```

The details and approximation coefficients are the result of filtering. One can pick out a band with noise and zero it and then re-synthesize the signal in order to obtain the de-noised version. It is also interesting to analyse a signal using one pair of filters and re-synthesize it with another.

Conclusion

During recent years, Csound has become one of the most popular music programming languages. It is important to extend Csound's possibilities to make it suitable for many interesting purposes including experimental applications. The implementation of wavelets provides an easy interface for wavelet-specific applications like wavelet de-noising or wavelet synthesis in Csound. I have demonstrated only two of the possible applications for wavelets. For future work, applications based on the *multi-fractal* properties of wavelets will be applied to algorithmic composition and chaotic dynamics.

References

Addison, Paul, *The Illustrated Wavelet Transform Handbook,* Introductory Theory and Applications in Science, Engineering, Medicine and Finance. Bristol and Philadelphia: Institute of Physics Publishing, 2002.

Batista, Pedro A.G., "An Introduction to Sound Synthesis with Wavelet Packets," *The Csound Book*, edited by R. Boulanger. Cambridge: The MIT Press, 2000.

Chui, Charles, *An Introduction to Wavelets*, San Diego, CA: Academic Press. 1992.

Darlington, David and Sendler, Mark, "Audio Processing in Wavelet Domain," AES. Convention paper 5849. 2003.

Daubechies, Ingrid, *Ten lectures on wavelets*, 2nd ed. Philadelphia: SIAM 1992.

Kronland-Martinet, Richard. "The Wavelet Transform for Analysis, Synthesis and Processing of Speech and Music Sounds," *The Computer Music Journal,* 12(4), 1988.

Mallat, Stephane, *A wavelet tour of signal processing: the sparse way,* 3rd edn., San Diego, CA: Academic Press, 2009.

Poblete, Raul Diaz, "Manipulation of the Audio in the Wavelet Domain Processing A Wavelet Stream Using PD," IEM, Graz 2006.

Polikar, Robi, "The Wavelet Tutorial," accessed: January 30, 2013, http://users.rowan.edu/~polikar/WAVELETS/WTpart1.html.

Roads, Curtis, *Microsound*, Cambridge: The MIT Press, 2001.

Sweldens, Wim and Schroeder, Peter, "Building Your Own Wavelets at Home," In *Wavelets in Computer Graphics*. ACM SIGGRAPH Course notes, 1996.

Valens, Clemens "A Really Friendly Guide to Wavelets," accessed: January 30, 2013, http://www.polyvalens.com/blog/.

MUSIC

PERFORMING WITH CSOUND: LIVE AND WITH CSOUNDFORLIVE

AN INTERVIEW WITH DR. RICHARD BOULANGER (A.K.A. DR. B.)

Richard Boulanger (aka Dr.B., born 1956) holds a Ph.D. in Computer Music from the University of California at San Diego (awarded 1985). For the past 25 years, Boulanger has been teaching computer music composition, sound design, performance and programming at The Berklee College of Music. He has collaborated, performed, lectured, and published extensively with the father of computer music, Max Mathews, the father of Csound, Barry Vercoe, Csound5 Developer, John ffitch, and electronic musician BT (Brian Transeau). For MIT Press, Boulanger has authored and edited the foundational books in Computer Music, "The Csound Book", released in February 2000, and "The Audio Programming Book", release in November 2010.

Alex Hofmann: *We were really happy that you arranged and played that wonderful opening concert at the First Csound Conference on 30th September 2011 in Hannover, Germany. The concert was dedicated to live-electronic music viewed from different perspectives.*

Dr.B. - I was very happy too! After all these years of teaching Csound, of writing about Csound, of designing Csounds, and composing with Csound, it was so wonderful to share my music with a concert hall filled with equally passionate Csounders at the first ever conference dedicated entirely to Csound. It is quite incredible to think of how far that Csound has come, how much it has evolved from the early days, and how the community of Csounders has grown. The future looks incredibly bright for

Csound thanks to the dedication of many of those talented and selfless developers and the inspiring work of the researchers, sound designers and composers who were in the audience; and especially to Joachim Heintz and to you Alex Hofmann for organizing this truly historic event.

Alex Hofmann: *Csound is often associated with traditional "pre-rendered" computer music (tape-music), which is played back to the audience during the concert. You gave an impressive overview of Csound's live-performance features. Was this a specific intention?*

Dr.B. - From the outset, I wanted to show that in 2011 we could "play" Csound. Csound is arguably the worlds' most powerful and versatile software synthesis and signal processing language. It has been for years. But I wanted to show that it had evolved to being a powerful and versatile performance system as well. In fact, I re-orchestrated a number of my earlier works using Csound specifically for this concert. In 2011 there is not a single composition that I have composed over the past 40 years that I could not today play "live" and in real-time using Csound. This is not to say that I don't appreciate and love "tape-music". Sound systems are better today — quieter, cleaner, more powerful, more speakers, and with a much better frequency response. Performance spaces are better today — better suited for the presentation of sound through speakers and through multiple speakers. Audiences today are, in fact, raised on loudspeaker music and immersed in virtual sound environments via the virtually constant use of headphones. Given that Csound is an amazing tool for sound exploration and sound composition. And the audience today is hungry for new sound experiences, I think that it is equally wise to focus our attention on sound painting — CsoundScaping. I was inspired by what I heard at the second concert, which featured more traditional audio art works that were beautifully composed and diffused in a church. Sacred Csound. I like that too very much. For me, for this concert, I wanted to show that "all" of my work could be "played" live—expressively played using wireless controllers - such as the Nintendo WiiMote, the iPad, the Mathews Radio Baton, and the P5-MIDIglove.

Alex Hofmann: *There is a lot of software specially designed for live computer music performance such as Max/MSP, SuperCollider, Chuck, Ableton Live. What role do you see for Csound in that domain?*

Dr.B. - I use Max/MSP and Ableton Live all the time—in my teaching, in my design work, in my software development, in my systems development

—and in concert. At Berklee, I have been teaching Max for more than 20 years and using it on stage to interface and expand the Mathews Radio Baton. In fact, I knew it and used it back when Miller Puckette called it "Patcher". Then it was being used to control RTCsound from MIDI keyboards at MIT—and by (Jean-Claude) Risset to control MIDI pianos. I am a good friend of both of its creators—David Zicarelli and Miller Puckette. I was there, in fact, with Miller and David, on the evening that they presented the first copy to Max Mathews: "Max, this is Max." It was always an important performance tool for me—mapping, thinning, massaging data from the Radio Baton, but I especially fell in love with Max/MSP/Jitter when David Zicarelli hired and revealed the inner secrets to Matt Ingalls that allowed him to write the "csound~" external. Incredible! This "single" object brought "all" of Csound into Max and allowed one to take, integrate and use all the MIDI, spatial, GUI, plugin, preset, visualization, and multimedia capabilities of Max/MSP/Jitter and still synthesize and process the audio with the high-end and high-level audio opcodes in Csound. Bringing these two worlds together was a dream of mine for many, many years. Max wasn't only the interface, but with Max I could now render any Csound Piece and build custom performance systems in which Csound was an integral part. Today, because of MaxForLive and the integration of Max into Ableton Live, via csound~, Csound becomes a part of this incredibly powerful performance and production tool—part of the premier 21st century DAW and performance tool. Max is for media artists, installation artists, visual artists, performance artists, algorithmic composers, experimenters, prototypers, and developers. Live is for producers, improvisors, players, remixers, DJs. Csound is under the hood in both of these programs, and it is being used by artists now from all of these communities. That is incredibly exciting to me. Csound for everyone.
Alex Hofmann: *Ableton Live is a commercial software sequencer, which has a big community especially in electronic dance music. You decided to develop CsoundForLive and thereby make Csound's synthesis power available for music producers from a non-programming background. How can Csound benefit from Ableton and Ableton-users from Csound?*

Dr.B. - CsoundForLive has changed the way my students compose and produce and work with Csound. More of them are using it, and more of them are using it more often. CsoundForLive is fast becoming their go-to "instrument" or their very special "effect". I love when people make music with Csound - all types and genres of music. I really like when I hear the academic avant-garde infiltrating and infecting "pop" and "dance" and film and advertising. I especially like when I hear Csound in these mainstream venues. And I am proud of the work that these talented and gifted composers, performers, and remix artists are doing with Csound today. They might not (yet) fully understand the mechanics of the streaming phase vocoder or the mathematics of Chowning FM, or the algorithm that underlies Csound's beautiful waveguide reverberator, but they sure know how, and when, and where to use them! Commercial musicians are hungry for new sounds and new ways to transform sound. Csound is a treasure chest filled with exotic and rare jewels. I want to make Csound easier to use and make it more useful to all. I don't want anyone to be tuned off or turned away. Whatever ways that musicians are working, and whatever tools that they are using, I want to make sure that Csound is right there too—at their disposal. Ableton Live is fluid, dynamic, intuitive, spontaneous, powerful. CsoundForLive is all that… and then some. Live is all about remixing and composed improvisation. With it, one can develop incredible flow. And CsoundForLive is now a part of that process - in the creative flow, dynamic, improvisatory, spontaneous! Csound? Spontaneous? Intuitive? Dynamic? CsoundForLive makes things that were "impossibly difficult" to do with the Csound language, a piece of cake; one can remix multiple .csds simultaneously, one can "hot-swap" Csound instruments and effects without restarting Csound! It is simple now to synchronize LFOs, lock controllers and oscillators to a common clock, relate tempo to BPM, automate any and all parameters, drive all .csds from a simple and clean graphical interface but still be able to open the underlying .csd and edit it. Most importantly, CsoundForLive supports the seamless integration of Csound opcodes and instruments with an infinite assortment of Audio Units, VST plugins, and Ableton Live instruments and effects. Ableton Live is huge and it makes Csound even bigger.

Alex Hofmann: *Max Mathews developed the Radio Baton as an interface to conduct parameters and interpret the playback of traditional scores in computer music performance. 'Three Shadows' is a duet, especially composed for the Radio Baton and Violin. Can you describe how you started working on that piece?*

Dr.B. - Max Mathews was the father of computer music. He was a visionary thinker, a brilliant researcher, a pioneering programmer, a great engineer, and a good friend. Computer music started with him and Csound is a direct decendent of his pioneering MUSIC1-MUSICV languages. (I like to think of my "Csound Book" as the sequel to his "Technology of Computer Music" book—both published by MIT Press. He would comment on how far computer music had come by the fact that his book, written in 1969, was a couple hundred pages, and mine, written in 2000 was a couple thousand pages!) In addition to inventing the systems and the languages that would allow computers to make and process sound, he also wanted to be able to "play" the computer like an instrument. To do so, he invented the Sequential Drum, the Radio Drum, and finally the Radio Baton. I am fortunate to have been one of the first composers to work with his Radio Drum at Bell Labs back in 1986, and as this system evolved into the wired and wireless Radio Baton, I continued to work with him at Stanford University and Interval Research at MIT and here at Berklee. We traveled together, wrote together, performed together and collaborated on the software and hardware. (What that meant was, I had many ideas and requests as each composition brought new challenges and inspiration, and Max Mathews was generous enough and supportive enough to implement them for me. Here in my studio, I have many generations of Radio Batons, computers, interfaces, and programs that support them. His final "wireless" system was by far the most portable and most versatile.) For more than 25 years now, I have been performing on this incredibly expressive controller that Max built for me and it has allowed me to take to the stage around the US and the world with some of the greatest virtuoso players, and the finest orchestras. A large antenna surface measures and reports the location and strength of two wands as they move continuously above. These X,Y, and Z control signals (each are sampled 1000 times a second), can be mapped or assigned to any MIDI controller or just captured as raw data. In addition two "planes" are established above the surface - one several inches, and the other about 1 foot - the (re)Set and Hit threshold. When either baton crosses the hit threshold a trigger is registered. This is used to trigger sounds, tap tempo, and register "beats" (Max devised a very interesting tempo tracking algorithm that was at the heart of his *Conductor* program.). Also, there was a measure of the time it took to cross from the Set to the Hit plane and this was known as the Whack parameter and could be associated with MIDI velocity or any other variable in Csound. One could use Max Mathews conducting program and code "traditional scores" in his ASCII-based expressive sequencer language. Or one could use Max/MSP to map all the data and write one's own performance system - a superConductor. Or, one could write C programs that would interpret the buttons, knobs, footswitches, and XYZ, triggers and whacks. I did all of the above, but in *Shadows* I was using Max's *Conductor* program to play a traditional score that had been transcribed.

To think of the computer as a unique and expressive new form of performance "instrument", one must find a way to "play" it "expressively" —and the Mathews Radio Baton is just one such "expressive" and dynamic interface—a particularly good one! How do you "play and explore" a complex, multi-faceted, multi-layered, sound object? How can you connect real-time controls to the sound to articulate it, trigger it, apply an envelope to it, spatialize it, twist it, trim it, stutter it, process it and mix it—all while it is growing, evolving, and percolating of it's own internal design? Max Mathews wanted an interface that would let him both "conduct" and "follow" and "remix" a traditional score while at the same time allowing him to "touch" the sounds themselves and his Radio Baton, with it's Conductor and Improve programs allowed one the means to do just that. In *Shadows*, there are times when I am conducting a synthetic orchestra and times where I am playing a duet on my physically modeled violin with a live acoustic violinist, and times where I am transforming and spatializing textures and tones that have no physical correlate. Csound particularly lends itself to sound design and sound design-based composition. (I like to think of this style of composition as SoundPainting, SoundSculpting, or SoundScaping). Systems and controllers like Max Mathews' Radio Baton and Conductor program make it possible to play in this new world and associate this new world with traditional instruments and traditional scores. When I compose for the Radio Baton and Csound, I am working on the chamber music of the future. Today, there are many controllers and sensors that are affordable, adaptable, and readily available for this purpose - for sound exploration. Using existing game controllers, using built-in accelerometers, using video cameras, using the keyboard, the trackPad, MIDI pads/sliders/keys and then using the Arduino or Max/MSP to map, adapt, filter, assign, and re-assign the sensor/controller data and apply it to parameters of the sound is relatively easy (and fun). This is, the age of *controllerism* and customization in which each composer (each Jedi knight) can and should build their own interface (a personal "audio light saber"). I have several classes at Berklee that focus on developing these skills and building custom expressive controllers and learning to play them.

Shadows was composed in Max Mathews' Lab in Murray Hill New Jersey in 1986/1987. I would make the four hour drive down from Boston every weekend for months to study, practice, compose. Bell Labs was a high security facility, and so Max had to be present with me when I worked. To "support" my research and timetable, he would sleep on the floor in his Wenger sound-proof booth while I composed through the night. At the time, we were controlling MIDI synthesizers with the Baton and running a program that he called RTlet (for real-time letter carrier). This design and architecture of this program was what inspired Miller Puckette to develop the "Max" program - and thus the name. At the time, the only way to "perform" computerized sounds in real-time was to use MIDI and MIDI synthesizers We were controlling the Yamaha DX7 and TX816 and I programmed all sorts of expressive timbres for them, but certainly none sounded like an "acoustic" orchestra or violin. Now, the work has been fully re-orchestrated for CsoundForLive instruments and is much closer to my original conception and realization. This is the version that we premiered in Hanover.

Alex Hofmann: *You also performed 'Toccata From Sonata #1 For Piano' with the Radio Baton. How did the idea to interpret a piano piece with a computer come about?*

Dr.B. - I have been opening every one of my concerts with some version of this piece since 1990. It was composed the summer I went to The Aspen Music Festival to study with Aaron Copeland and premiered there by an amazing pianist from Juilliard - Robert Woyshner. It has always been a dream of mine to be able to play the piano that well, but I never reached that technical level. In 1990, while I was a Fulbright Professor in Computer Music at the Krakow Academy of Music in Poland, I was teaching Csound there and the US Consulate was setting up solo concerts for me all over the country. I did over 12 concerts in less than 3 months and set a goal for myself that I would premiere a new work on each program. Somewhere along the line I got the idea to re-orchestrate some of my earlier works and the Piano Sonata—then labeled the Radio Sonata—became a great way to start the show as it demonstrated clearly that I was in total control of the performance and that this instrument required and rewarded practice and a level of virtuosity. It was a great showpiece for the technology as in some cases I am beating time and in others I am soloing and in others I am playing quite lyrically and expressively. It was only a matter of time when I was able to re-orchestrate and revisit this "score" with Csound and that has opened up a new world of possibilities and a new palate of incredibly rich colors and textures. My Piano Sonata from 1975 was one of the first "classical" works that had "my voice" and showcased "my musical soul". Recasting the work in Csound retains the underlying structure, but adds a whole new message and enthralls a whole new audience. The work is still played by Pianists around the world - most recently in Seefeld Austria by Slawomir Zubrzycki—amazing—from memory (most players don't "memorize" contemporary music!), and with such passion and power. I was blown out of my seat. But… I love being at the helm and interpreting the work myself—and tossing the notes all around the audience—turning a tiny droplet into a thunderous torrent. When I was first getting into computer music, I remember dreaming that I would one day move my fingers and control the articulation and evolution of all aspects of a sound—revealing and expressing with very subtle and nuanced gestures. With the invention of his Radio Baton, my dear friend Max Mathews made this dream of mine come true.

Alex Hofmann: *The Radio Baton lets the performer manipulate 6 sound-parameters through the movements of two batons. Physical modelling sound-synthesis often lacks the right interface to control multiple-parameters during performance. Do you see an application of the Radio Baton as a control-device of live performances with physical models in the future?*

Dr.B. - You are right to think that the Radio Baton would be an ideal controller for the expressive performance of physically modeled instruments. In fact, at Interval Research in Palo Alto California, some years ago, I was brought in to join a team there led by Bill Verplank and Max Mathews and including Paris Smaragdis and Perry Cook to use the Radio Baton to control a unique Physical/Mechanical Model that they had pioneered there—Scanned Synthesis. This was Max Mathews using his instrument to help him realize his dream of sound design and performance—of controlling the evolution of a sound at "haptic rates" and use the baton to "warp" the 3D surface of this model—effecting a set of masses and springs and tensions, damping, and reconfigurable interconnection matrices. I was brought in as a composer and sound designer. Paris Smaragdis was brought in to convert the code into Csound opcodes so that I could design more complex synthesizers and systems with these building blocks. It was an incredibly exciting time. There was incredible innovation at Interval and I was so lucky to be there in the middle of it all and to bring Csound into the work there too! Recently, I have enjoyed using the MultiTouch capabilities of the Lemur, the iPad3, and the Nexus7 to control Csound opcodes (using TouchOSC or custom Boulanger Labs code in the csGrain or csSpectral iPad Apps), and it has been so stimulating and fulfilling to play with 10 parameters of a granular opcode simultaneously or to control many parameters of a complex instrument all at once. To explore new sonic vistas that can so rapidly transform at the sweep of a finger - literally at your fingertips. In a concert situation, it is much more visual and engaging to be doing all this control with 2 batons or 2 wiiMotes or 2 PowerGloves, (bigger venues require broader gestures), but there is a lot more control when you involve all 10 fingers. With video projection, we can focus on and grow to appreciate the auditory correlation of more delicate movements and I do foresee a lot more audio art spaces (concert halls specifically designed for computer music, and mixed media performance and remixing) being designed to support and showcase these modalities—venues for fully immersive visual music—that is "performed, triggered, and remixed live"—and that is being produced by Csound of course!

Alex Hofmann: *With traditional instruments the performer has to provide energy to the musical instrument to excite its mechanism of sound generation. The manner in which this energy is provided shapes the sound produced and defines expressivity. How can we overcome the limitation of only shaping electronic sounds to excite the electronic sounds?*

Dr.B. - With flashing, blinking, pulsating, indicating, articulating light. With immersive video. With well composed music. Music in which the relationship between the sound and the gesture is clear. Not necessarily always, but often enough. I can imagine a new audioVisual counterpoint that will engage the listener at many levels. You are right to point out that there is a wonderfully complex relationship between the excitation/articulation of a sound, the resonating body of the instrument and the resulting timbre. Add to this the next level of complexity that comes from the transition between notes and sounds produced by physical performers and instruments. We need to build more complex multidimensionally-interconnected Csound instruments that manifest this richness and controllers that map our motions into these complex systems in equally complex ways. For my own audio art, I am dedicated to creating fewer notes and focusing on the design of a smaller set of more noteworthy instruments - that breath, and scream, and cry, and whisper, and sing.

Alex Hofmann: *For the concert, you were exploring different ways to get in touch with computer-synthesized sound during improvisation. You designed environments where players were using data gloves ('In the palm of your hands'), touch-devices ('Trapped Remixed') and game-controllers ('WII_C_Sound'). How was your experience with these interfaces?*

Dr.B. - I wanted to show others that they can touch and explore sound, that they can play and paint with sound using game controllers, sensors, and multiTouch Tablet interfaces that are readily available and quite affordable. The Radio Baton is quite a special and rare piece of hardware. In fact the one that I play now was built for my by Tom Oberheim and Max Mathews. It is model 0001 of Max's final line of batons. I was so honored and touched when it arrived and they had signed the back and named it - "The Boulanger". With a couple of wiiMotes or some sensors and an Arduino, every audio artist can create their own interface—the Hofmann? In addition to showing that there are many "types" of Radio Baton out there, I was also trying to show, through the compositions and the sounds that we were controlling in them how perfectly adapted these sounds were to the interfaces that I was using to control them. The Glove piece required more training and practice, and for this I had my dear friend and Csound Guru, John ffitch play along with myself and one of my students. The piece is scored. There are sections, and gestures, and button combinations that move from section to section, from sound to sound. I designed all the sounds and mapped all the fingers and XYZ parameters to them. I made sure that the sounds work with each other that they compliment each other and our progression through them, projects and evokes an interesting and compelling Cinema for the Ear. John ffitch has performed this work with me in Bath, England and in Maynooth, Ireland. Trapped Remixed used the iPad2 to bring to life the first Csound piece, Trapped in Convert. It was originally composed in 1979 in Music11 and then revised as a test-piece for Barry Vercoe's new version of Music11 that he had written in the C programming language in 1986. Back then, even on some of the fastest computers at MIT, it took a month of 20 hour days to compose the piece and it took days to render the audio for the final analog tape performance at Boston's famed Kresge Auditorium. For 15 years the work was revised on other mainframe computers and workstations, on desktops and laptops, on the ADI shark DSP, on the $100 laptop by OLPC and now, on the iPad, the iPhone, and the Google Nexus7 (Android). I wanted to play this "sonic mobile" and set the frozen timbres free (they were locked in time via the classic note-list score of the Csound, Music11, MusicV language). What would it be like to dust off these old friends and thaw them out after years of hibernation. Everyone in this audience knows this piece and these sounds almost as well as I do. I thought it would be especially satisfying for all of these "insiders" to get inside these sounds and hear them blossom into something radically new. Finally, Wii-C-Sound was composed as a piece for the audience to play and to pass the controllers around. I thought that it would be a fitting way to end my "solo" concert, by turning the stage over to the audience. That is the spirit of Csound. All that we have learned in computer music is embodied in this program and it is freely given so that we can use it, add to it, share it, and pass it on. There is a score to this piece, and I have performed it with multiple performers in the Opera House in Seoul Korea with speakers surrounding the audience on each of the four floors and balconies. Sounds were flying all around and that version was pretty powerful, symbolic, ritualistic and ultimately liberating. Here in Hanover, there was some structure in that we advanced from one "room" or "scene" to another, but how we explored the sounds, and how we combined the sounds, and how we played with each other and played off each other was left to the quartet of Csounders who had the controllers in their hands at the time. What is especially nice about the Nintendo WiiMote and NunChuck as a controller pair is that they are wireless and reach the Csound host computer from every seat in the concert hall. Not only were the sounds flying around, but the performers were all over the place too. It was so much fun. At a time in my life when I was very, very "serious" about my music, I wanted it to be perfectly composed and dreamed of the day when it would be perfectly realized and performed, one of my great teachers - Pauline Oliveros reminded me, that we "play" music, that we might wish to keep the joy and playfulness in the mix. This piece surely realized that goal.

Alex Hofmann: *Players of conventional instruments must practice for many years in order to reach a level at which they can perform in front of an audience. Should performance of live-computer music also be taught from a much earlier age or should the education of music performance begin with traditional instruments such as violin, recorder or piano?*

Dr.B. - My first instrument was the guitar, then trumpet, then voice, the synthesizer, and then the computer and Radio Baton. Lately it's been the iPad and EuroRack and Laptop. I still play them all a little bit, but mostly focus on composition, writing, and teaching. When I was young, I was fortunate to have played in wedding bands, and jazz bands, and concert bands, and marching bands. I was fortunate to have played in chamber groups, in pit orchestras, in college orchestras, and community orchestras including the Richmond Symphony and the La Jolla Symphony. I was fortunate to have sung in bars, night clubs, coffee houses, church halls, and church choirs, and concert choirs, in barber shop quartets, and in a capella chamber groups. On synthesizer I played with the Newton, the New Haven, the Krakow and Moscow Philharmonic and now perform with my Berklee students. On voice, I recorded with The Boston Symphony, and sang at Carnegie Hall in New York, in Notre Dame, and

Westminster Abbey and in the Vatican where I sang for the Pope. For the past few years I have been touring and performing with my son Philip, who is a virtuoso classical cellist and is currently the "teaching artist" for The Chicago Symphony. I am not sure I could ever write music that is better than he is a cellist, but I am so blessed to be able to play with him at his level using my Radio Baton. I cherish each of these memories and miss them. Playing music with others, playing music together is one of the greatest joys in life. Playing your music. Playing the great and challenging music of others - old music, new music, art music, pop music, it's so life affirming and truly life changing. I have been teaching music since I was very young and I have made my living as a Professor of Music at The Berklee College of Music ever since I finished my PhD work at the University of California in San Diego. I remind my students every day that they need to keep playing acoustic instruments, that they need to keep singing. That complex physical connection with source and sound resonates with the very core of us and informs the synthetic, algorithmic, simulations and designs that are a manifestation of this experience. I don't think that we need to worry too much about young children needing to learn how to play their computer instruments with alternate controllers. Long before they reach their teens, they have spent thousands of hours "gaming" and texting, and gesturing with iPads, with Game Controllers, with wiiMotes and full-body control via the Kinect 3D camera interfaces. They are learning to manipulate these complex systems in very expert ways through years of practice. The challenge seems to be how to translate these skills into higher-level artistic or shared community experiences; how to make ensemble "games" that are soulful and artistic. I am not sure that Guitar Hero is the "ultimate" model here, but it is certainly one that bears some consideration as people do play music together in the home and online, and there is some skill required to actually "play" through the songs, and some "training" involved when you sing along and it shows the accuracy of your pitch. To answer your question, I think that it takes new music and new interfaces to turn the laptop or iPad/Surface/Tablet into a new and expressive musical instrument. I have dedicated my life to composing and performing such music - with Csound. And, I think that it is such a wonderful thing to make music with instruments that do not require electricity to produce sound, or speakers or headphones to hear the sound that they produce. To learn to listen closely, carefully and deeply is mind expanding.

***Alex Hofmann:** Computers in the form of smartphones are very common today, nearly everybody has one. If children were better trained in creating live-computer music, do you think that this could result in a big "self made music" revival?*

Dr.B. - I am not sure that the "smart" phone will become the popular folk instrument of the 21st Century. It may just be too smart for that. And since we go through software and hardware so fast, before we get to bond with our smart phone we are upgrading it. Musicians carry their instruments around for years and they clearly develop quite a "relationship" with it. They are drummers, singers, guitarists and cellists. The instrument becomes an extension of the physical self. We do carry our smart phones everywhere we go and it does say a lot about us musically; as we can be identified by all the music that we carry in it. Sadly, however, rather than make us more musical, we seem to use the tunes to "tune out" the sound world around us. Our "smart" phones use music to isolate us. Music, this most powerful "instrument" of self awareness, of self expression, of communion, community and deep communication is, via the "smart" phone, having just the opposite effect - it is helping us to become completely alone in a crowd, insulated from reality. Worse, by giving us access to all knowledge, there is no need for us to develop an acquire any of our own. The answer is in the phone. I can Ask Jeeves or Ask Siri or do a Google search. I don't ever need to speak with a person. I don't need to make a sound. It's all in my head and all at my fingertips. Smart? Maybe not. I do not place my hope in technology. I place my hope in humanity. I have faith that teachers and parents will use technology in smart ways. That they will use these new audio apps and games, these intuitive new controllers and sensors, these new recording, sampling, synthesis, and processing technologies to creatively and artistically capture, assemble, transform, study, and grow; and that they will use them to play together, to sing together and to make music together, using the newest tools to perform one of the oldest socially and personally enriching activities.

Fingers in the Waves

An Interview with John Clements

John Clements is a student of Electronic Production and Design at the Berklee College of Music and is currently also co-webmaster of www.Csounds.com along with Dr. Richard Boulanger.

Alex Hofmann: *Can you describe how you started working on your piece 'Fingers in the Waves'?*

John Clements: I wanted to create interfaces for sound generation that respond intuitively to drawing and touch, employing real-time wavetable creation and additive inharmonic synthesis over a dense chordal landscape. Timbre, motion, spatial placement, and other dimensions of synthetic sound are also explored through assignment of multi-touch gestures like pinch, rotate, drag, and swipe; the instruments provide graphical feedback on the screen of the iPad, which are projected for the audience as a visual index of the performance.

It began as an effort to create touchable graphic synthesis instruments inspired by drawing systems like Iannis Xenakis' UPIC, or the recent HighC. The piece highlights our physical relationship with technology and the possibilities (and limits) of controlling machines by touch. This new technology offers a question: "How do we represent gesture—and the subtlety of human touch—with computers?"

Alex Hofmann: *You decided to use the iPad, a commercial multi-touch tablet computer, to control your sounds. What do you think about the pros and cons of that technology for live computer music usage?*

John Clements: I think that the proliferation of tablet computers, with wireless capability and fast graphics processors, allows for the design of interfaces for computer music controllers that can be performed separately from the computer that is generating the audio, or networked with multiple computers at once to provide interactive ensembles of controllers. Multi-touch input is a good step toward making interfaces that respond more closely to direct hand gesture, as physical controllers. The use of video output from the screen of the tablet can provide a graphical connection for audiences to more closely connect with the performance, and other controllers and interfaces can be connected directly to a tablet to make hybrid wireless digital instrument interfaces.

Using an open-source iPad application called Fantastick (www.pinktwins.com/fantastick/), along with Max/MSP or Pure Data, I have been able to quickly prototype many interfaces that control Csound using multi-touch, and use the application's OpenGL graphics capabilities to make creative and expressive visual feedback.

The cons of using this device to perform are the lack of haptic feedback, the design limitations of what can be connected simultaneously to the device, and the fact that the iPad operates within a closed publishing ecosystem of software, tightly controlled by Apple. Purchasing an Apple Developer License will allow access to writing one's own software for the device, but there is also the limitation of the closed hardware design that prohibits the user from making modifications to the device. Wireless control also has latency and interference issues. In fact, during my performance at the 2011 Csound Conference, the laptop lost its connection to the two iPads immediately prior to my taking the stage, and this was quite frustrating. Apple has improved the iOS operating system since to provide more robust and dependable WiFi connections, yet the issue of dependence on a closed design ecosystem still remains.

Alex Hofmann: *What do you like about working with Csound?*

John Clements: I like Csound because of its sound quality, the ability to tightly define the relationships of control to audio rate per instrument/instance, and the real-time control via OSC or MIDI, which has become my primary way of performing with Csound. I am primarily a designer of systems for improvisation, education, and music therapy/accessibility and the dependability and efficiency of Csound's runtime makes it a great choice for these applications. The fact that Csound can be objectified within Max/MSP/ Ableton Live, Pure Data, Processing, and used as a sound engine on iOS and Android is also a reason that I use it more than any other synthesis environment.

I also like the Csound community, for its diversity, warmth, and human resources. As well, Csound's direct lineage in the history of sound synthesis (Music-N systems) makes it a great tool to explore the cookbooks and patches of pioneers like Risset and Chowning.

SPINNING PENDULUM CLOCK

AN INTERVIEW WITH TAKAHIKO TSUCHIYA

Takahiko Tsuchiya is a student at Berklee College of Music, who studies programming, sound synthesis and alternate controller design with Dr. Richard Boulanger. As a violinist, he played in several professional orchestras. Currently his focus is on making CsoundForLive instrument packs, developing sensors and programs for Music Therapy, as well as creating a 3D interactive music system for his senior thesis.

Alex Hofmann: *You have a classical music background as a violin player. What was your first contact with live-electronic music?*

Takahiko Tsuchiya: My first contact with (live) electronic music was with the FM-synth chip playable in MML (Music Macro Language) on an MS-DOS computer. I was about 12 years old. I could sequence notes (or "beeps"), experiment with basic sound parameters, and interact with the sound outcomes line by line.

Alex Hofmann: *In your piece 'Spinning Pendulum Clock', you, as a violinist, play with an interactive performance system built in Csound. How far does your playing influence the computer's output?*

Takahiko Tsuchiya: The piece was actually played with a 3D-mouse and computer keyboard (and not with the violin). I sequenced the basic structure of harmonies and rhythms, and left certain melodic and textural parts playable in real-time, either by playing notes or by changing timbre.

Alex Hofmann: *Why did you start to use Csound?*

Takahiko Tsuchiya: I was first introduced to Csound in Dr. Boulanger's Csound class at Berklee College. I was amazed by its diverse opcodes, and how you could realize any kind of synthesis you can imagine. Also the syntax was fairly easy to learn.

Alex Hofmann: *Would you recommend Csound to other young performers to build their interactive music systems? Why or why not?*

Takahiko Tsuchiya: I mainly use Max/MSP for interfacing and Csound for the 'audio engine' of performance system. I do recommend using Csound for audio part because it makes it easy to change/experiment/ expand the code as you go. Also it is stable and fast enough when run in the csound~ API.

Alex Hofmann: *Interactive music systems require low level signal-analysis of the input, higher-level processing of musical information and sound synthesis to generate the output. In which domain would you like to have more tools/opcodes/language features in Csound?*

Takahiko Tsuchiya: I think all of them have room to expand. I would love to see more waveshaping/phase distortion-type DSP opcodes, or a greater variety of table-based tools/opcodes with which you can quickly record gestures, manipulate them and morph them easily.

RAZOR CHOPPER

AN INTERVIEW WITH ØYVIND BRANDTSEGG

Øyvind Brandtsegg is a composer, musician and professor of music technology at the Norwegian University of Science and Technology (NTNU). His field of interest lies in Compositionally Enabled Instruments and Particle Synthesis. Sound installations have a natural place in his work, and he sees an installation as an autonomous musical instrument. Øyvind has performed with the groups *Krøyt* and *Motorpsycho* throughout Europe. He has written music for interactive dance, theatre and TV, and he has programmed instruments for other performers. His main programming tools are Python and Csound. At the Csound Conference Concert he performed a live improvisation together with guitarrist Bernt Isak Waerstad.

***Alex Hofmann:** You are working at a technical university, how would you describe your background - is it more musical or technical?*

Øyvind Brandtsegg: I think that my approach has always been music first, then to find the tools and technologies to enable me to make music the way I imagined. I have no technical education but have learnt what I needed as I went along. I started out as a drummer but also had a fascination for technology. I used to read up on old synthesizers, and I acquired a simple 4-track cassette tape machine to experiment with in the late 1980s. I also used a xylophone and a simple delay machine with a guitar amp, playing "space rock odysseys" with my teenager band mates Bent Saether and Hans M. Ryan (later to become Motorpsycho). I also wanted to add electronic sounds to the drums, and started using a simple Simmons pad, just a single pad with a single sample that you could change by replacing a chip, accessible from the control panel on the pad. I quickly found that it was not so flexible, and I wanted to record my own samples. To do that you would need a special EEPROM burner to transfer the sounds to the chip, and that was beyond my budget at the time. Around 1989 or 1990 I got my first digital sampler, it was a Roland S-330 with 14.4 seconds of internal memory (split on two banks of 7.2 seconds each). This sampler had an internal sequencer, video out and mouse input so it was a kind of compact music production and composing environment. I used that a lot, also for live triggering with an Octapad.

I changed my main instrument to vibraphone when I started studying jazz in the early 90's. Then after a while I realized, although the vibes were sounding nice, perhaps too nice… I needed some more varied timbral expression, so I started using effects pedals on the vibraphone sound via contact microphones. These contact mikes came with a midi triggering system, so natural expansion was to use midi triggering in tandem with the processed miked vibe sound This led me to the need for gesture sensors, since I had two mallets in each hand and no limb free (on the vibes you stand on one foot and use the other on the sustain pedal) to push buttons for selecting patches on the synthesizer etc. The gesture sensors needed interfacing and programming for mapping, so I learnt Max in order to do this. There was no MSP at the time, only Max.

Alex Hofmann: *What was your first contact with Csound?*

Øyvind Brandtsegg: I began by reading the Csound manual, as I realized this was a tool that could let me overcome the limitations of commercial hardware synthesizers. I used to be proud to twist and turn the hardware synths and samplers to do stuff they were not intended to do, but it was also quite cumbersome. I realized that I was always hungry for the latest developments, and wanted to buy a new synth or effects machine once a year because they had put some new and interesting feature in it. Then I saw Csound as a tool to enable me to create my own implementations of these new and interesting features without having to buy new hardware every year. I also realized that all features I wanted seldom came in the same hardware box, and this limited the manner in which the different tools and features could be combined. With software synths I could combine whatever I wanted, as long as I could figure out how to implement it. … and I spent quite some time in trying to figure out how Csound worked. At that time, the Csound manual was more or less the only resource, so I started reading it trying to figure out how to make Csound make any sound at all. I must admit I read the whole manual straight through, and still did not get it. When I turned it over and started reading it for the second time, it slowly clicked into place and I was able to make some simple sine beeps… You could say it was an insane thing to do, but the features that I read about in the manual kept my interest up, as I realized more and more that all the tools I could imagine needing were in there, I just had to unlock the box.

Alex Hofmann: *There was no real-time Csound back then?*

Øyvind Brandtsegg: There were some attempts, I used Gabriel Maldonado's DirectCsound, as it could do simple instruments in real-time on my computer (still with a lot of latency). I figured that by the time I had learnt to use it, computers would have become fast enough to do something interesting in real-time too. For some time then I used Max as a control and mapping module running on a laptop, combined with hardware samplers and synths, and doing selected custom processing with Csound on a 40 kg rackmount computer.

I was getting less and less satisfied with Max due to some instability problems, for example that the loadbang object did not always bang at load time, so I was starting to look for alternatives. Then my mac laptop died during a tour, and I had to reprogram my Max patches in Csound. That was quite a hassle as it involved translating between two quite different ways of thinking in programming. After that exercise I found it hard to go back to the intense mouse-labour of programming by drawing patch cables in Max. After this I used Csound as my only live synth/sampler for many years, for example in the band Kroyt. I still use Csound for composition and performance, and I rarely use anything else. The occasional VST if it is convenient, and I've also started using Csound inside other host software (Ableton Live, AudioMulch, Cubase…even in Max if I have to), relying on the host software for routing and patching things together.

Alex Hofmann: *'Razor Chopper' is a duo improvisation, performed by Bernt Isak Waerstad and you. You are using a touch interface to control the 'Hadron Particle Synthesizer', an instrument you have been developing in Csound. Can you describe its' functionality?*

Øyvind Brandtsegg: Yes, I actually think that the general idea for Hadron is rooted in my old desire to have all features in the same box, so that combinations of different methods can be done flexibly. Hadron can be an effects processor, and synthesizer or a sampler, and it can morph between these different modes of operation. The mode of operation is defined completely by parameter values, so the set of parameters is necessarily quite large (> 200 parameters for a single monophonic event). We call such a setting of all the parameters a "state" in hadron, as the term "preset" did not quite cover the concept of changing between different working modes. Hadron can morph seamlessly between different states and this is how it can gradually change from being a synthesizer to being an effect processor. To be able to use it intuitively as a live instrument, I wanted a simple set of controls, so Hadron actually just has a few user controls. It has a joystick type control for morphing between 4 states, and it has 4 expression controls for fine-tuning selected parameter values.

The audio processing core of Hadron uses particle synthesis, implemented with the partikkel opcode in Csound. There is one single instance of partikkel doing all of the significant processing, I would consider the rest of the code mainly "support" for partikkel. There are modulators (LFOs, envelopes, random generators, pitch trackers and other audio input analysis methods, and there are some simple effects on the outputs (delays and filters). The audio for partikkel processing is read from Csound tables, these can be filled from sound files, by live sampling, or by streaming live audio input into a circular buffer.

Alex Hofmann: *Electronic music setups can be adapted to meet new needs very quickly by adding functionality, but this also changes the usability and demands retraining on the instrument. How often do you change your live-setup?*

Øyvind Brandtsegg: That is an interesting question, I have been thinking about this quite a bit lately. I realize that we have (at least) two kinds of latency when performing. One *technical latency*, that we know from soundcard audio buffer sizes and such, then we have the *mental latency* that stems from our reaction time to an unexpected musical situation. I realize that my mental latency on the instrument may increase significantly when I have changed something substantial on my instrument. Sometimes I just rearrange the controls to make for a more intuitive control situation, then again it will take some time to *retrain* before the instrument can be used optimally. I have wondered if there are techniques we could use to train ourselves for quicker adjustment to a new instrument. I guess it becomes better over time, just by doing it. For me, the usual way of preparing for a performance is to program, bug check, re-think and configure the control interface, and just make sure that I know where every function is and reassure myself that everything actually works. I'd say that it is almost never an issue of instrumental-technical challenges that I need to practice, like a violin player, singer or wind player who need to condition their muscles and embouchure and so on… it is more the mental picture of the instrument, knowing what all controls do and checking that they actually do what I expect them to. Now, to your question… how often do I change the live setup: I do change it a little bit almost for every performance. This is mostly because I want to adapt the instrument to musical ideas that arose during or after the previous performance, things I wanted to do but was not able to. Sometimes it is just a matter of adding one or two new functions or controls, or moving things around to make it easier to access. I generally use the same "instrument model" for many months, perhaps even some years. What I mean by the instrument model is the general selection and combination of tools. For example during the Csound conference concert, I used 4 instances of Hadron all connected via Ableton Live and used the mixer, routing and a simple delay and reverb in Live to knit it all together. In this setup, two of the Hadron instances were used for effects processing, one for live sampling and one as a synthesizer. So you see, even if Hadron *can* change its mode of operation while performing, perhaps my instrumental mind still organises the available resources in a traditional way. … but I also keep changing the selection of Hadron states in the setup, throwing in an occasional joker here and there, for example putting a synth state in one corner of the effects processing Hadron instance, I sometimes do this if I feel I get too secure and want something to throw me off a little bit. I have used this instrumental model now for over a year, changing the number of Hadron instances, the configuration of the signal routing between them, and the Hadron states. It seems that I have been able to keep it longer than usual, probably because Hadron in itself is quite deep, and I've used the model to explore what Hadron can do. It probably makes sense to keep some parts of the instrument or setup constant while experimenting with selected parts of it.

..*ED IO STO AL CENTRO*

AN INTERVIEW WITH ENRICO FRANCIONI

Enrico Francioni graduated in Electronic Music and Double-Bass at the "Rossini" Pesaro (Italy). At the Csound Conference Concert he presented his 4 channel tape composition named .. *ed io sto al centro*.

Alex Hofmann: *You have a classical music background as a double-bass player. What was your first contact with Csound?*

Enrico Francioni: Maybe it was during my journey of bass playing (as a soloist and in orchestras) especially while composing (self-taught). My interest in contemporary music is the main reason for my constant curiosity for Csound. It supports me with electroacoustic composition, or with live electronics. I also like to investigate old patches of historical repertoire with Csound.

My first contact with Csound was in the ordinary course of Electronic Music at the Rossini Conservatory in Pesaro (Italy) - Maestro Eugenio Giordani. That was in 2003 and all the students of the course were asked to use Csound as it is free software. We were working in a Windows environment, with WinXound by Stefano Bonetti. Later I switched to Mac and used MacCsound by Matt Ingalls, which is what I'm still using.

Alex Hofmann: *Was it a barrier to express musical ideas in a programming language?*

Enrico Francioni: Probably the programming syntax, which in Csound, tends to accentuate the distance between the cold linguistic code and a musical idea. Especially at the beginning of the musical idea this is strongly influenced by the characteristics of the language, in any case, this obstacle can also occur using other languages (Max/MSP, Supercollider, or other ...). In general, unlike the others, Csound deals with the logic of my thinking at the root, forcing me to think in a strictly mathematical way. When I open my .csd file to create something and to overcome this obstacle, now I force myself to think about this: "Using Csound my FIRST question must always be: 'what' I want to do musically, and not what I can make with the software." Csound perhaps requires more time than other programs, at least in the learning phase, it maybe takes more time to understand, design and test.

Alex Hofmann: *Csound contains thousands of opcodes, and sometimes it's hard to find the right one for the sound you have in mind. How do you organize sounds and opcodes?*

Enrico Francioni: I think that the choice of certain opcodes, rather than others, is the consequence of the work and the experience that have accrued up to that moment. The auto-update on the latest operational codes and user's guide is extremely important, and this requires a lot of sacrifice and desire to understand, to do better, to save time, to develop a personal syntax that takes into account all (rationalisation of resources, pleasantness of sound synthesis, functionality, portability, ...).

However over the years I've created my own personal archive "libraries" with valuable examples (with .csd files) that have become models for me to be able to achieve in a short time what I have in mind.

Alex Hofmann: *Do sounds inspire the composition?*

Enrico Francioni: Yes, I think that new ideas often begin by experimenting with an instrument carefully in Csound. Often small things (a sound, an attack, a subtle element) have an opportunity to give birth to ideas, even complex ones that are sometimes very musical and sometimes fascinating. Reflect a little on what is happening within your musical instrument before you radically modify it, then connect multiple elements and develop the musical ideas, which I can call 'gestures' which in turn build to larger structures I call 'textures' or even more complex musical images.

Alex Hofmann: *You also work with live-electronics and Csound, what were your experiences with it?*

Enrico Francioni: My experiences with live electronics with the aid of Csound were: the aforementioned algorithm *Solo* by Karlheinz Stockhausen but also other works of mine for female voice, live electronics and sound support, *Cluster_I* for double-bass, live electronics and sound support; *Alchemy of Fear* for violin, cello, piano and recorded sounds.

After doing a search through the forums and social networks of Csound, I must say that this software has been used relatively little for live electronics. However, I recall with pleasure the work and patches for live electronics by Iain McCurdy, John ffitch, Matt Ingalls, Bruce McKinney, Rory Walsh ... and with them I also had direct comparisons which I could use for troubleshooting technical language and syntax problems of my own. However I'm sure there is still a long way to go in this direction because it is much easier and faster to work with other software these days.

Alex Hofmann: *Would you recommend Csound to young electronic composers? Why, why not?*

Enrico Francioni: In all honesty, if I were a teacher of electronic music, I do not know whether I would recommend the use of Csound to young composers: in fact I see that more and more young composers have very little time to lose, to realise their ideas. In short, today there is no time to lose! Unfortunately, the facts are that I have seen, that after their Csound introduction, many students move on to other software such as Max/Msp.

GEOGRAPHIES

AN INTERVIEW WITH GIACOMO GRASSI

Giacomo Grassi (*1984) has a BA and an MA in Music in Interpretative and Compositional studies from the Musical Institute *Giovanni Paisiello* in Taranto. He is currently studying Electronic Music at the *Niccolò Piccinni* Conservatoire in Bari.

Alex Hofmann: *Your piece 'Geographies' has the intention to translate vastness into music; how did you go about writing this piece?*

Giacomo Grassi: The piece evolved very slowly. It all started with intense research into all topics: research about sound first, together with a search for the meaning of everything.

At the beginning there was just one need and a strong desire about communicating something. This something had no defined boundaries, and the more I searched, the more I was discovering vast spaces. I like to imagine in the piece to be flying over the earth. I see all the things one does not see when on the surface. From this derives the title "Geographies". I have tried to represent the lines of the earth with sound. In this I am trying to reflect nature more than the world itself but also the lines of myself and humans generally. Who knows which is bigger, which contains which? Besides the easy distinction, one draws the lines of the other in only one way. There is a lot of French existentialism in it, I reference Merleau-Ponty in this for instance.

***Alex Hofmann:** How would you describe the form and development of the piece?*

Giacomo Grassi: The piece begins with shaped trails that converge into a dome of sound. Out of this climax, there is a sudden depression, an empty floating space where one can start to listen what I like to call interferences. These increase quickly and build to another climax, where most of the pathos is, for the impetus of the sound and the use of the voice. It all ends with the same overview of the intro, this time in a lighter way, like flying where it is no longer visible.

***Alex Hofmann:** Technically, it sounds to me, that the piece evolves from FM-sounds to granular-based-sample processing, which thus explores two different worlds of sound synthesis. Was this a decision you made right at the beginning or did it evolve during the development process of the piece?*

Giacomo Grassi: Yes, there is a radical change of sound synthesis technique along the different sections. What you perceive as FM are just a lot of linsegs in the Csound code; linsegs of many sounds with slight differences of pitch. There are few proper granular sounds; the granular effect has come about as a consequence of the multiplication of different signals: so-called *ring modulation*, which gives a sort of aggressiveness to the climax of the piece. Usually I don't have a lot of ideas *a priori*, except a general idea, even if it is not particularly defined. The various techniques chosen arise during the process of composition. I reflect on how to create a specific quality of sound that could give the right meaning and expressiveness at a particular part of the piece and this then suggests an appropriate technique.

***Alex Hofmann:** You decided to use voice-samples from Jean-Luc Godard's movie "Masculine Feminine" (1966). Has this movie a special meaning to you? Why did you decide on these parts?*

Giacomo Grassi: Well, in that period I was watching many movies of the *Nouvelle Vague*, and I felt very close to the main character of "Masculine Feminine", concerning the way he feels about life. In the centre is his relationship to the world, to others, the other key character being the woman, with her beauty but also the frequent misunderstandings. The nuance of the first scene sets the mood for the entire movie. The parts I've taken for my piece are some lines read by the young man in the café, where shortly after, the girl will appear. In those lines he expresses the impossibility of a total communion among different human beings. Now, coming back to the piece, it is not just about this. These lines and the music sketch a terrain where the man had never been before, and where he is alone. He is adjunctive to the nature, and yet he could stand there as the moon shines above.

ZEITFORMATION

AN INTERVIEW WITH JAN JACOB HOFMANN

Jan Jacob Hofmann (*1966) holds a Diploma in architecture and conceptual design. Since 2000 his work has concentrated on research into sound spatialisation using ambisonics and other techniques.

Alex Hofmann: *When I hear about your background, it makes me wonder whether this influences the way you think about sounds and acoustics?*

Jan J. Hofmann: I am trained as an architect. I do assume it makes me think a bit differently about sounds and music compared to people who were trained as musicians or composers. My former education is probably influential on both scales: The small scale of a single sound but also on the large scale of the whole composition.

Especially during my postgraduate training in conceptual design at the Staedelschule — a school of art that counts architecture, filmmaking and even cooking among the arts — I was taught a way of thinking that might be unusual even for most architects. Architecture there was regarded as an art form which has a strong relationship and interaction with its context. It was not merely about taking the context into account when making a design. It was also about using the context as a source of inspiration, but deriving from it parameters and information that fed a process of design. We were trained with an entirely different approach to design. It became a rather structured process while the unconscious and the inspiration were in exchange with all the context of the project and the project itself. I like the approach of evolving development and process in design. It may lead to projects full of vividness and movement. I got the idea that this approach was valid for all arts generally, not only architecture. I do believe there is a certain essence, which all arts share in common. Still, at a certain point I felt it would be easier to apply these ideas to the realm of music. That does not mean that it is not possible in architecture, but in architecture there are certain economic conditions, which make it extremely difficult to work in such a way there. So shifting to sound, I retained my preference for 3-dimensionality, texture and material but now enhanced it with movement of sounds and development within the composition, which I do like a lot. I now think of sound as a material with certain characteristics that may be adjusted as desired or by the demands of the composition. I then place these sound objects into specific locations, equip them with their appropriate behaviour and let them interact within the composition. One could name the result a “sculpture of sound”, or "choreography of sounds", or "sonic architecture". While working, the piece gets more and more refined by reworking its components over and over, just as would be done in architecture. The character of the sound also helps me in finding an appropriate structure for the composition, and vice versa.

Alex Hofmann: *How do you make notes or sketches during the composition process?*

Jan J. Hofmann: I like to work very precisely. I elaborately plan every single sound and each group of sounds in their relation to each other by listening and reworking them until I feel there is a certain logic or vividness that convinces me. It usually takes some time until I reach that point, which suggests that things have to be that way “naturally”. Sometimes I make a quick sketch to capture an idea for a new piece until I find time and circumstances to work on it. However, during the process of creation, I find it more useful to interact with the sounds and the demands of the composition. I even find it useful to make no notes at all, firstly so that I am not distracted and secondly to prevent any permanence. It is open-ended and if things turn out differently than I first intended, I am quite glad about it.

Alex Hofmann: *What was your first contact with Csound?*

Jan J. Hofmann: Perhaps my first contact with Csound—or its predecessor MusicV—was through listening to electronic music at the age of 18 or 19. I especially liked a CD of music by John Chowning, which I listened to repeatedly through headphones without realising consciously that it had been binaurally processed. I liked the strange and avant-garde sounds and the propagation of the composition. Especially in the piece "Stria", I felt a sense of material and space, which must have influenced me. Before this, I had already started to make 4-track tape studies just for myself with a Korg MS20 analog synthesizer. After my second degree in architecture I had the idea of making a performance of "spatial music". I thought I might just buy a small and cheap electronic device, which would place the sounds at a certain position and then play back the tape through four speakers. Pretty soon, I realised that there was no such device and that it would not work that way anyway, but I got into contact with the Italian composer Michelangelo Lupone after listening to a radio-programme about him. I felt that he dealt with similar questions and he invited me to visit his master class about "sound and space" in Rome. I learned a lot about acoustics and perception there. He invited me to his and Laura Bianchini's studio and they showed me their work and their DSP-system "fly 30", which I hoped could do the job. Instead he recommended using Csound and a computer for what I intended. I had an image of the MIT computer of the seventies in mind and said that I didn't think I could afford such an advanced system. He said that the software was free and would run on any computer. I could hardly believe that I could have a whole electroacoustic studio in my hands so I bought my first computer, downloaded and learnt Csound.

Alex Hofmann: *You worked with 3rd order ambisonics for spatialisation in 'Zeitformation'. Why did you choose this?*

Jan J. Hofmann: Well, I chose Ambisonic right from the start in 1999 when I wanted to start producing pieces of spatial music. I had certain technical requirements. First of all the technique had to be suitable for many listeners at the same time and also be capable of reproducing the height of a sound. It also had to be as precise as possible regarding spatial definition. On the surround-list it was discussed, that a certain method called "Ambisonics" might be more convincing and efficient than amplitude-based panning, which was the other main possibility. By the time, I had realized that my project would not be accomplished within a few weeks, so I wanted to choose the most appropriate platform from which to begin. I had the chance to visit Richard Furse in London and meet people from the University of Derby to find out more about Ambisonics. When I had listened to examples of, mostly recorded, sound, I knew that I was on the right track. I decided to use 2nd order right away, because the computer was capable of doing it and I preferred the best spatial resolution possible. Then followed several months of programming and conceiving Csound instruments for spatialisation – without knowing if it would finally work in the end. Now the 3rd order equations are out, and as I prefer to work with the higher resolution for my new pieces, I am glad that I can re-render my older pieces with the new algorithms.

Alex Hofmann: *You were using Blue and Cmask in addition to Csound. How far did these tools help you to compose and realize your music?*

Jan J. Hofmann: I composed my first pieces without Blue, it did not exist then. For some pieces I used Cmask to generate stochastic textures within the composition. I found Cmask very useful for that but it had always been a complicated and long-winded workflow to generate a composition and spatialize it. I could listen to the exact results only several steps later in that workflow and often I had to go back to adjust, for example, volume and pitch because they would both change in respect to the distance and velocity of the sound and may sound different when the sound is at a certain location and speed. I also appreciate a minimal graphical representation of the composition in time to be able to move a sound back and forth in time when I am working on it.

I encountered the program Blue when I met Steven Yi by chance at a Festival in Ireland. He presented his latest version of Blue there and I had the impression that it could be fruitful for me to integrate my environment for spatialisation into Blue. To be really sure, I visited Steven again some months later to find out if it would be possible to transfer my rather complicated environment to Blue. We achieved promising results and I totally reconfigured my code within several months (or let's say years) after that visit to take full advantage of Blue. Now it indeed is very useful for me as I can, for example, change the volume or the pitch instantly using lines and graphs. The main reason I reconfigured my code was that I wanted to be able to do a kind of spatial granulisation of sound. I wanted to be able to place an unlimited number of sound-grains in different locations in space. By now Cmask was no longer available, as it did not run on OSX anymore. I contacted Andre Bartetzki and he decided to make Cmask open source. Consequently Anthony Kozar was able port it to OSX and Steven was so kind to make it addressable via Blue. He even created a Java-based graphical representation of Cmask called Jmask, which I find very useful to work with too.

Now I have all possibilities of manipulation just one click away; I can alter the sound or its timbre, change the spatial distribution of its grains, alter the volume or the pitch and change its distribution in space or the whole composition very easily. It is now possible to arrange the grains on a plane or a spherical surface and to distribute them according to frequency or amplitude.

I am very grateful to have this environment for spatialisation, which is now much more powerful than I ever thought possible. To collaborate with developers in this was is something that is very precious to me and is something that I have never experienced before.

Still, I want to move forward in my modular approach to make the sound and some chains of effects more interchangeable: like plug-ins. I also want to make the whole system more robust and intuitive to use so that others may take advantage of my code, too.

...UND LÄCHELND IHR ÜBEL UMARMEN...

AN INTERVIEW WITH WOLFGANG MOTZ

Wolfgang Motz (*1952) studied in Venice with Luigi Nono and Alvise Vidolin. He wrote several larger compositons like „Krypsantes" and „non svanisce", which are played worldwide. He also works as a professor for aural training at the University of Music Freiburg.

Alex Hofmann: *You decided to play music you composed about 20 years ago. What makes it still relevant today?*

Wolfgang Motz: It is definitely not an up-to-date piece, especially not concerning today's technology. But as a musical piece it is still innovative, this is what I also experienced from the positive reactions of the audience.

Alex Hofmann: *During production, you worked in the 'Elektronisches Studio der TU Berlin' with Folkmar Hein. Can you describe the process of realizing the piece and the way you both communicated about sound and synthesis?*

Wolfgang Motz: 1989 the electronic studio of technical university Berlin was not as today. It was a very small chamber in which you were not able to work for longer than two hours. That time I worked with "cmusic" and "CHANT" together with a "Vax" Workstation. Computers were quite slow and working with my complex scores, controlling several parameters, took hours to process a minute of sound. During processing-time I went for dinner or worked on something else. In the beginning, Folkmar Hein mainly gave technical support. But during the working process we began to collaborate more and he gave useful advise to sound-parameters. For that I am very thankful and this is why the piece is also dedicated to him.

Alex Hofmann: *How did you make notes or sketches?*

Wolfgang Motz: There is a real paper score in DIN A2 format. I scored every sound-parameter, all the envelopes and data. Each event is defined by several (up to 30) parameters and all of them had to be entered into the computer, a time consuming procedure. The computer was only used for sound-synthesis, not to generate the structure of the piece. For sound-synthesis I mainly used frequency modulation. I used that technique in previous compositions so I knew a lot about the sounding results of the parameters. Nevertheless it was necessary to do several sketches to optimize the sounding result, develop a kind of sound family, and to finalize the structure of the parts.

Alex Hofmann: *All sounds were synthetically produced, how do you design synthetic sounds?*

Wolfgang Motz: This electronic composition is an introduction to a larger orchestral work, which also includes parts for a choir. The concept of the electronic sounds was to have a familiarity to the orchestral instruments and the singing voice, but with an artificial approach, so they can disappear and reappear like chimeric.

Alex Hofmann: *You hold a professorship in 'aural training' at the University of Music Freiburg/Germany. When I remember my aural training, we mainly practiced transcriptions of melodies, chords and rhythms in western music tonal system. Today synthetic or computer processed sounds play an important role in various music styles, from new music to pop music. Do you think aural training should include identification of basic sound waves, synthesis methods and sound processing?*

Wolfgang Motz: This is probably an interesting aspect to enhance musical training especially for composition students.

Alex Hofmann: *Have you been working with Csound in the last couple of years?*

Wolfgang Motz: Unfortunately not, because I mainly wrote instrumental pieces and taught a lot. But the Csound Conference gave me a lot of new impulses, I'd like to include in new compositions. I'm especially interested in working with algorithmic processes to control masses of sound and I see Csound as a great tool to continue my working process based on Music V and cmusic.

Alex Hofmann: *Would you recommend Csound to young electronic composers?*

Wolfgang Motz: I definitely would recommend it, although it takes some effort to start with Csound compared to existing programs where you can tweak knobs and immediately hear the sounding result. But Csound forces you to first think about your sounds more physically and thereby you perfectly learn to master the sound world you create. This requires self-discipline and some time but you get an enormous freedom and a deep insight to structures of sound. A young composer should definitely know about these possibilities.

THE ECHO

AN INTERVIEW WITH REZA PAYAMI

Reza Payami is an Iranian software engineer and musician. He received his B.Sc. and M.Sc. in software engineering from Sharif Polytechnic and his M.A. in composition from the University of Art in Tehran. He is currently studying for his Master's in Music, Science and Technology at Stanford University and its Centre for Computer Research in Music and Acoustics (CCRMA). Some of his recently composed pieces include "Immortality" for symphony orchestra, "Irreversible" for ensemble, "Seven", "Serial Seconds" and "Twisted" for electronics. In addition to composing, he has also been involved in computer music through the implementation of music software and frameworks for sound synthesis, signal processing and algorithmic composition.

Alex Hofmann: *How would you describe your background – is it more musical or technical?*

Reza Payami: I have been trying to improve my experience and knowledge in both areas and it is hard to choose one of these two aspects. I got involved in playing musical instruments in early childhood and I started programming using home computers around that time. On account of my dual interests, I studied both software engineering and composition at university. Practically, I have been interested in developing software as well as performance and composition, in parallel, or in combination in the computer music field.

Alex Hofmann: *What was your first contact with Csound?*

Reza Payami: My first practical contact with Csound was when I took part in the composition and audio software classes held by Mr. Joachim

Heintz which were so inspiring, not only on account of using Csound but also on account of the electronic music composition component. At that time I was using environments and languages such as Max/MSP and C++ and I liked Csound particularly on account of its programmatic approach— which is similar to C or Java — and its easy-to-use opcodes which remind me of Max/MSP objects. I am also a fan of having an object-oriented version of Csound through extending its current syntax.

Alex Hofmann: *I'd like to talk about the writing process of "The Echo". What was your initial idea? When did you start to work together with the flute player Mehrdad Gholami? And at which step in the process did you incorporate the live-electronics?*

Reza Payami: The initial idea was to write a piece for flute and live electronics in which the flute part becomes extended though electronic modifications. These modifications include buffering and transformed playback in order to create a polyphonic texture, as well as real time audio manipulation using different effects. I started to work with Mehrdad after finishing the piece to review some points especially about extended techniques on the flute. He is an excellent player and was a motivation for me to write this piece, ensuring a nice performance. I made the initial design of the electronic part while writing the flute part, but the final implementation was done after writing the part for solo flute.

Alex Hofmann: *You decided to use Csound for live-processing of the flute part. How much freedom has the flute-player on stage to interpret the piece through his performance?*

Reza Payami: In this piece there is a set score for the flute player with different pedal markings. Whenever the player pushes the MIDI foot pedal, a command is sent to the underlying Csound program as a simple type of human computer interaction. It can be regarded as a standard type of flute score with the addition of using the performers foot to control the electronic part as the accompaniment. The flute player may perform expressively in interpreting the part, especially in regard to rubato.

***Alex Hofmann:** Do you see Csound as an instrument — like a limitless modular synthesizer — or as more, because of the programming language it provides?*

Reza Payami: Like other computer music languages and environments, Csound may enable you to do almost everything. That may include building an instrument or synthesizer, writing an audio effect, composing a piece, developing a software application, etc. It only depends on the user's imagination and the underlying design, which may result in some strange imaginings coming into existence.

TRÊS QUADROS SOBRE PEDRA

AN INTERVIEW WITH LUÍS ANTUNES PENA

Luís Antunes Pena (*1973) is a composer of electroacoustic and instrumental music. He studied composition in Portugal with Evgueni Zoudilkine and António Pinho Vargas. In Germany, he was a student of Nicolaus A. Huber, Dirk Reith and Günter Steinke. He currently lives in Germany working as a composer.

Alex Hofmann: *For your composition 'Três Quadros Sobre Pedra' you worked together with the percussionist Nuno Aroso. Have you worked together before?*

Luís A. Pena: I met Nuno Aroso for the first time during an ensemble project in Germany in 2006 where he played a piece of mine about two years before *Três Quadros Sobre Pedra*. This piece was called *Musik in Granit* and it was the first time I used granite stones in a music composition. Nuno liked the sound and the idea and challenged me to write a new composition using mainly granite stones. So actually *Três Quadros Sobre Pedra* was the first creative collaboration with Nuno Aroso.

Alex Hofmann: *You decided to generate sound material with stones. Can you describe the research process for the sounds a little?*

Luís A. Pena: When Nuno Aroso came to Karlsruhe so that we could work together at ZKM, I didn't know exactly what kind of stones he would bring. I heard these stones for the first time on our first working day. The process of creation was a discovery of the possibilities with these granite stones. We had some ideas and some tools, such as brushes of different sizes and materials, and so we started experimenting. We had about a week in the studio to create the piece, so the processes of discovering and creating ran simultaneously. It was a very naïve process but we were completely fascinated by the sounds we were creating.

***Alex Hofmann:** In your introduction to the piece you said you decided to work with stones because they are not a common part of the percussion family. After finishing the piece, do you think that stones should now be included?*

Luís A. Pena: I am interested in starting the composition process by choosing the setup to work with. Of course, to choose to work with stones involves already a certain notion of sound, timbre, and texture. It is already a compositional decision. So for me they definitely became part of the percussion setup. I have used them again in other pieces such as "Im Rauschen Rot" for double bass, percussion quartet and electronics and Nuno Aroso uses them also when he is playing in our trio *ruído vermelho*.

***Alex Hofmann:** What was the technical process during the composition?*

Luís A. Pena: One of the three pieces was written during the working phase at ZKM. Nuno got the score, we discussed some parts, he studied it and then played it. The other pieces involved more improvisation. We worked more on the sound. Nuno played something and we discussed and changed it until we got something that would satisfy both of us. For the first piece, the only technical condition I had, was to work with different kinds of brushes. I was interested in these kinds of iterative sound-rhythms.

***Alex Hofmann:** At which point of the process did you incorporate Csound?*

Luís A. Pena: Csound was used to produce sounds involving sound synthesis. Re-synthesis using the phase vocoder opcodes interested me particularly. I also used Csound to execute simple tasks with samples.

Alex Hofmann: *What do you like about working with Csound?*

Luís A. Pena: I use Csound because I prefer text based programming and because of the quality of the synthesis. I also enjoy connecting Csound with other programs like PWGL or simply executing Csound in the Shell with some simple script. It is a very flexible program. I also find the aspect of being free of superfluous graphics and working at quite a low level of programming very appealing.

VINETA

AN INTERVIEW WITH ELKE SWOBODA

Elke Swoboda studied music pedagogics and recorder until 2007 at Folkwang University in Essen. At present, she studies electronic music composition, composition and visualisation with Prof. Thomas Neuhaus and Prof. Dietrich Hahne. Her interests lie in the interdisciplinary fields of dance, physical theatre, photography, and video.

Alex Hofmann: *What was your first contact with Csound?*

Elke Swoboda: My first contact with Csound was in sound synthesis classes during my studies at the Folkwang UdK.

Alex Hofmann: *Can you describe how you started working on your piece 'Vineta'?*

Elke Swoboda: I started experimenting with some samples and just found some interesting sounds. Then I started to work closer on these samples, the result let me think of the story of Vineta.

Alex Hofmann: *You have a strong musical background, was it a barrier to express musical ideas in a programming language?*

Elke Swoboda: No, once I knew how to work in a programming language, I just had to translate my musical ideas into code.

Alex Hofmann: *Electronic music can deal with both composing and sound design. How do you combine both fields?*

Elke Swoboda: I feel that I am working in the field of composition but I think composing electronic music includes many aspects of sound design.

Alex Hofmann: *What do you like about working with Csound?*

Elke Swoboda: What I like about Csound is that you can determine every parameter of your composition, as you want.

CHEBYCHEV

AN INTERVIEW WITH TARMO JOHANNES

Tarmo Johannes (*1976) is a flutist, his work is mostly dedicated to performing contemporary music. He has graduated from the Estonian Academy of Music in the major of flute in 2000, supplemented by the post-graduate course of Conservatory of Amsterdam with Harrie Starreveld in 1999-2001 and in 2004 with Annamaria Morini in the Conservatory of Bologna. In 2005 Tarmo Johannes completed his doctoral studies with a thesis on "The influence of musical analysis to performance on the examples of Bruno Maderna, Franco Donatoni and Salvatore Scirrino". At the Csound Conference he presented an interactive sound-game for four conductors, four groups of performers on tumbler-switches and a Csound synthesizer.

Alex Hofmann: *Your piece 'Chebychev' is highly interactive. The sound is controlled by joystick actions from the audience. Can you describe which parts are determined and what is improvised during performance?*

Tarmo Johannes: In fact the main "instruments" in the hands of public are simple on-off switches, joysticks (or mice) are played by just two players. The final sound is formed from three levels of processing in the Csound score:

1) sound generation – six predefined synthesis types (additive, subtractive, wave terrain, FM, granular, noise through resonant filters)
2) envelopes and wave shaping of the generated signal
3) occasional additional filters.

When the notes are triggered, what kind of sound is generated and almost every single parameter in the sound generation of any of the operations depends on the state or actions of the controllers (sometimes it means a choice from predefined pool of waveforms or envelopes). Also a general score was prepared for the four conductors – where to conduct, which tempo, where to give solos, interruptions etc. The score is responsible for granting some sort of overall form.

Alex Hofmann: *You implemented a probability function based on Chebychev's theory to process the incoming data from the players. Can you explain the algorithm behind it?*

Tarmo Johannes: It's not that complicated. I used different Chebychev polynomials defined via GEN 13 routines. There were two groups of f-tables, one resulting less, the other more modification to the spectrum of the sound. Which function and from which group to choose (and many other parameters) depend on the density of on-off actions by the players – the more enthusiastic the players get (more actions in one time interval), the more the sound gets "shaped".

Alex Hofmann: *Can you explain a bit more about the hardware you used or built?*

Tarmo Johannes: The state of switches (on or off) was read by a digital input-output controller RedLab 1024LS. It has 24 digital input/output ports and has USB connection to the computer. It took a long time for me to find out how to program it, but knowing the right commands that the device expects, it turned out not to be so difficult. Now I would have used probably an Arduino Mega instead. The movements with joysticks (in Hannover I changed them to mice – smaller to carry) controlled some filtering to add some linear changes to the sound. The interface reading their state was written in C++. From the joystick/mice movements the average value was calculated and it was sent to Csound only when both players had pressed down a certain button. So the two players had to work as a team but could not know what the other was doing - I liked it as it added some randomness to the actual result and supported the idea that in fact nobody is in total control of the situation.

Alex Hofmann: *You decided to use the CsoundAPI in C++ to realize your piece. How was it involved in the setup?*

Tarmo Johannes: In the first performance I used Csound python API that is basically a wrapper to C++ API. I like it a lot since I find the C++ (or python or other similar languages) classes and methods much more convenient to use than C, less lines in the code and more close to human thinking. At first, I had to use the python API since the RedLab device came with its software only in Windows and I did not know any other way how to bind it with Csound then. I loaded the library via python ctypes module, ran my csd in Csound performance thread and fed the values to it with sendChannel function. Actually, in the second version, played in Hannover, I separated the program communicating with the hardware and Csound - the hardware info was sent as OSC messages, the csd ran in CsoundQt where I had all the time a checkbox “Emulate” ready – just for any case, if something had gone wrong. But it did not, huhh.

Alex Hofmann: *Would you recommend the CsoundAPI to young electronic composers and performers for interactive artworks?*

Tarmo Johannes: Absolutely. Of course, it is quite a bit of learning. When I first had the idea of the piece in the beginning of 2011 – starting just from a picture of audience turning switches according to conducting and actually not understanding what they actually do – I knew very little about Csound, nothing about C++ and had done some C programming years ago in secondary school. It was a huge process of learning, extremely interesting and I think, very fruitful. An interface using CsoundAPI written and compiled in C or C++ is fast and effective. For example, I wrote another similar interactive project “Csound in kindergarden” in C++ using Qt framework and Csound C++ API. The program used remarkably less CPU than similar test application in CsoundQt and thus allowed to have more users behind it. It is wonderful that Csound has wrappers to most widely used programming languages. If someone has learnt the language of Csound, he would be definitely able to learn another programming language of his choice. It opens up so many new possibilities, especially for algorithmic composition, interfacing with hardware and using system libraries. There is much to gain.

THE RITE OF JUDGMENT

AN INTERVIEW WITH NICOLA MONOPOLI

Nicola Monopoli (*1991) graduated from 'N. Piccinni' Conservatory with a Bachelor's degree in Music and New Technologies. His compositions have been selected and performed at several festivals such as De Montfort University SSSP, SICMF, Stanford LAC, ACL Conference and Festival, Emufest, Fullerton Annual New Music Festival, Musiche Nuove, FIMU, Festival Internacional de Música Electroacústica 'Punto de Encuentro', Shanghai Conservatory of Music International Electronic Music Week and UCM New Music Festival.

***Alex Hofmann:** Your piece 'The Rite of Judgment' is very much about sound. Did sounds inspire the form of the composition?*

Nicola Monopoli: I think that form and materials are closely linked in the musical discourse: it is not possible to "design" a credible form without knowing the materials with which you are working; materials without form are like sentences in a random order, which will hardly make sense.
So, Yes! The materials have influenced the form, but, at some point of the compositional process, the logic of the form has led me to a more thorough selection of the materials.

***Alex Hofmann:** Csound contains thousands of opcodes so sometimes it can be hard to find the right one for the sound you have in mind. How do you organize your sounds and opcodes?*

Nicola Monopoli: Deep knowledge of a number of opcodes is essential. This knowledge comes only with practice. With sufficient expertise it is a very natural thing to achieve the sound you have in mind. Personally, I first identify the musical result I want to obtain, and then move to the second step of 'transcription' so that the computer generates the required sound. I think every composer who wants to work with Csound must create a series of .csds related to his/her compositional technique.

Alex Hofmann: *What do you like about working with Csound?*

Nicola Monopoli: I find Csound extremely comfortable and pleasant to work with, primarily for the following reasons: At first Csound potentially allows the user to create any sound. The .csd files, divided into orchestra and score, make it extremely easy to create external applications that can automate the writing. Also, Csound scores, if written in a valid manner, can turn a gesture, a structure, a composition project in reality. They allow the composer to accurately assess his or her own choices leaving nothing to chance. Furthermore Csound is cross-platform and I use it on Windows, Mac and Linux.

CSOUND HAIKU: A SOUND INSTALLATION

IAIN MCCURDY

I. Introduction

Csound Haiku is a sound installation that comprises a suite of nine generative Csound pieces and a book with nine pages of designs with each page relating to a different piece. When the piece is installed, the book is placed in the middle of a public space with a pair of loudspeakers nearby.

Visitors to the installation are invited to select a page in the book, which will then start the piece corresponding to that page (sensors within the book sense what page is selected and send that data wirelessly to an offstage laptop that generates the music). If a page is turned, any currently playing piece stops before the new one begins. Figure 1 shows the page for Haiku IV (the sensor holes are evident in the spine of the book). Pieces are "performed" in real time by a computer. Random number generators employed within the piece's mechanisms are seeded by a time and date reading from the computer's system clock so that each performance will be unique. All sounds are synthesised so no sound samples are used.

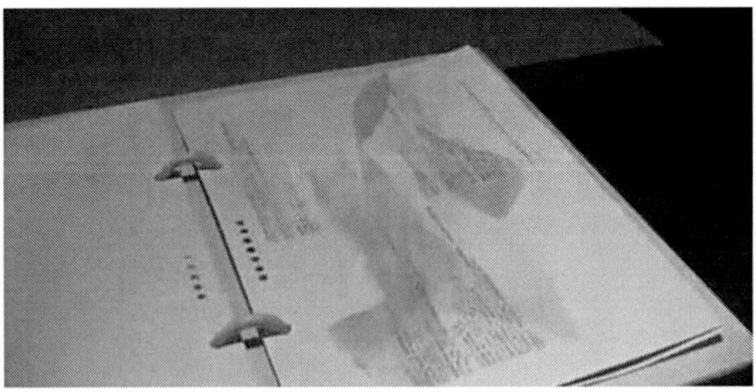

Figure 1. Csound Haiku IV

The remit imposed was to compose in as concise and pared down a fashion as possible, both in terms of musical structures employed and in terms of the amount of Csound code used to achieve this. The longest piece is constructed from 96 lines of code but the average length is closer to 70 lines. Most of the code used in each piece is included in the design on that page—typed on transparencies using an antique typewriter—to allow the visitor to examine to inner workings of the piece. An understanding of the code is not required but it is so brief that visitors completely ignorant of Csound should still be able to derive some connection between the code shown and the resulting music. The aim of the artwork—with its inherent imperfections—is also an attempt to step back further from digital representation and storage of information; to remind ourselves of less perfect and precise materials. In a way, the interface for this piece represents a kind of "play-list" in which tracks are accessed through a very raw and physical means. The idea of offering the visitor some choice and influence in how the piece will turn out has been important in much of my recent work. The physical component of this piece is also intended to encourage visitors to linger a while and contemplate the pieces. The inclusion of a degree of indeterminacy also figures prominently in my recent work. Despite being the creator of the systems my pieces employ, I want to occasionally be surprised by their results.

I feel that composing in this reduced manner imbues the pieces with a levity and directness often lacking in larger, more complex pieces.

Csound Haikus installation at the Csound Conference at the Hannover HMTM was the piece's premiere (figure 2) where it ran for three days. The pieces can be downloaded as individual csd file from the composer's website (http://www.iainmccurdy.org/compositions.html). It is recommended that the pieces be listened in their unfixed state from the Csound csd files rather than from the fixed mp3 versions.

Figure 2. Visitors to the installation

II. Composer's Biography

Iain McCurdy is a composer of electroacoustic music and sound art originally from Belfast and currently based in Berlin. Having come from a background of writing for fixed medium, more recent work has focussed on sound installation, exploring physical metaphors of compositional structures through the creative use of electronic sensors and innovative human interface design. Physical designs are minimalistic, using primary shapes and colours and utilising instinctive user inputs.

References

http://www.iainmccurdy.org/compositions.html mp3 renderings of the pieces.
http://www.iainmccurdy.org/csoundhaiku.html programme note and csd files.

CONTINUOUS FLOW MACHINES

CLEMENS VON REUSNER

Abstract

This article concerns the concept and realization of the composition CONTINUOUS FLOW MACHINES. The circular movement of turbomachinery and the varied noisy and tonal sounds which result lead to a multichannel spatialization concept, which was realized with Csound and 3rd-order ambisonics

Introduction

Besides working with purely electronically generated sounds, my interest as a composer also focusses on specific sound locations which tend to be outside most people's everyday experience. The Pfleiderer-Institute for Fluid Machinery (PFI) at the Technical University of Braunschweig (Germany) with its numerous test rigs, pumps, compressors and turbines is an example of this type of special sound location. When the Pfleiderer Institute took a new direction in 2011/12, the institute moved to the regional airport in the north of Braunschweig. My composition (2010-2011) can therefore also be seen as an historical documentation of the soundscape of the institute's original location.

Beyond the theoretical foundation and technical realization which will be discussed below, listening to this environment means listening to the unremarkable stasis of steady flow, moving aimlessly forward in always new sound layers by gradual compression and uncompression, speaking for nothing other than itself. Even the cavitations (which will be discussed below) do not detract from this – they simply demonstrate the living nature of the processes.

For me, the diversity of the noise in this particular soundscape, and the possibilities of working with it compositionally in a manner which can extend to acoustic modeling, were a strong, durable motivation for aesthetic exploration and shaping the sound-world of the continuous flow machines.

Figure 1. Main plant floor of the Pfleiderer-Institute for Fluid Machinery (PFI) at the Technical University of Braunschweig (Germany)

Material

Definition 1: "A flow machine is a fluid energy machine, in which the energy transfer between fluid and machine is carried out in an open space by means of a flow which follows the laws of fluid dynamics via the re-routing of kinetic energy." – translated from http://de.wikipedia.org/wiki/Strömungsmaschine, accessed November 26th, 2012

Definition 2: "Cavitation is the formation and then immediate implosion of cavities in a liquid – i.e. small liquid-free zones ("bubbles") – that are the consequence of forces acting upon the liquid." – http://en.wikipedia.org/wiki/Cavitation, accessed November 26th, 2012

The acoustic material upon which this composition is based was digitally recorded in numerous sessions at the PFI in Braunschweig. Contact microphones were mounted directly on the machines, both in order to avoid cross talk from test rigs which were operating in parallel and to simultaneously record usually inaudible processes inside the machines and tubes. In the studio, the material was then modified with filters and other methods of digital sound analysis and processing. At times they were changed extensively. One of the criteria for the combination of different sounds was their spectral complementarity.

Finally the material was spatialized in a virtual acoustic space (3rd order ambisonic).

Turbomachines work with rotating solid cages (blades, vanes) in gases and liquids, and often acoustically produce a uniform noise in a wide frequency range. They usually manifest a tonal component (expressing the number of blades multiplied by the speed), which is audible in a manner akin to a root or fundamental. By cavitations in fast flowing liquids, acoustically significant deviations from the uniform noise are induced. These deviations mostly have a percussive character.

The circle and the circular motion are important (indeed, essential) for the operation of turbomachines. Both the shape and the structure of this work are derived from this overarching idea of a circle, the constant flow and rotation as a key aspect of turbomachinery movement and the increase and decrease in vertical density.

This contrasts with cavitation as a quasi-chaotic element. It will be audible to the point of distortion in both the recorded material and in its acoustic processing.

Next to the numbers "pi" and "60" and its multiples, the sine function – both as an elementary trigonometric function to define the unit circle on the one hand, and as a means of describing acoustic and other waves on the other – is the organizing principle of the structure and form of the composition, which even in a graphical representation appears as a waveform.

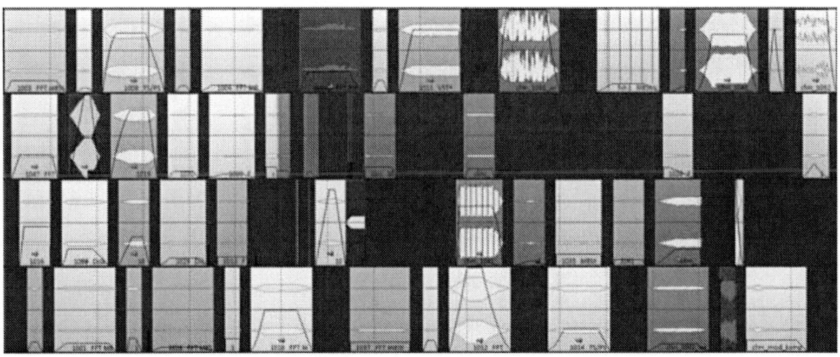

Figure 2. Grafic score of the soundobjects

Placed on four stereo tracks (A-D) the individual parts are limited in their duration, and arranged in their start times in such a way that the space (offset) between all sections describe a sine curve. Acoustically this layering of sounds means a constant increase and decrease in vertical density, which corresponds to changing pressure phases. The idea of cavitation, i.e. the "hollowing out", is also formally expressed in the omissions in the second third of the composition. Dimensions of the four parts as follows:

A – 266.5 sec.
B – 199.9 sec.
C – 133.2 sec.
D – 66.6 sec.
Offset – 47.1 sec.

Total duration of the composition: 60 minutes

Scientists working in the field of continuous flow machines not only work with real test rigs and real machines, but also and increasingly with computer simulations. This is reflected in the composition in that as the piece progresses the edited recordings of turbomachinery are replaced by "acoustic models". These models were obtained from spectral analysis of the recorded sounds and then resynthesized by means of additive sound synthesis.

Spatialization

The spatial concept of the piece reflects the principle of rotation of turbomachinery. The 3rd order ambisonic method, realized here with the sound synthesis language Csound, makes it possible to individually place sounds in a two-or three-dimensional acoustic space and move them along discrete trajectories. In the virtual acoustic space of this composition the individual sounds are moved in circular orbits with different radii at different speeds and in different directions.

Ideally the audience is placed (whether standing or walking) in a darkened room within a circle of 8 speakers; the diameter of the circle might exceed ten meters. The speakers are numbered counterclockwise.

I want to thank Jan Jacob Hofmann for his support in customizing his 3rd-order ambisonic Csound-codes of spatialization in the context of this composition.

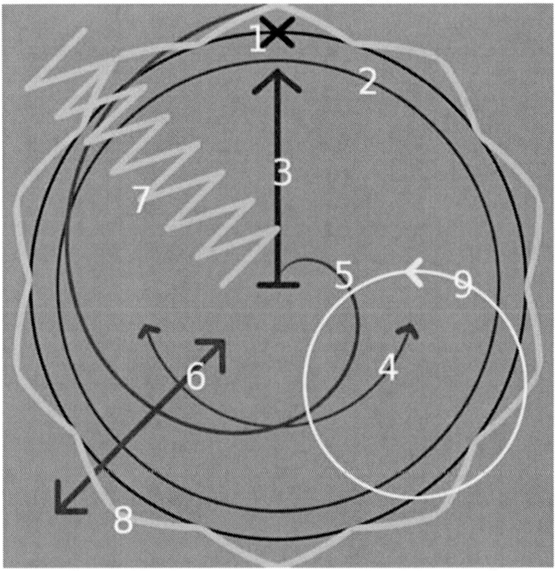

Figure 3. Synopsis of the spatial movements

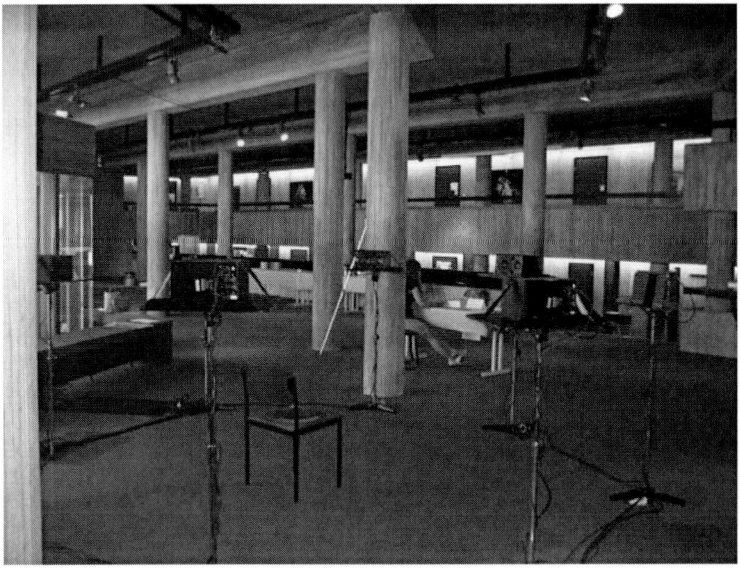

Figure 4. Installation at the HMTMH Hannover

USAGE

THE CSOUND JOURNAL

INTERVIEW WITH STEVEN YI AND JAMES HEARON

The Csound Journal is an online journal hosted at www.csounds.com. It is released roughly three times a year and contains articles on a wide range of subjects related to Csound and its use. It can be considered as the main forum for discussions in the Csound community besides the Csound Mailing List.

Pictures: Steven Yi (left), James Hearon (right)

Steven, Jim, you have been editing the Csound Journal together since it began. When, why and how did you start this project?

James Hearon: This was shortly after Hans Mikelson had ceased work on *Csound Magazine* due to a more demanding day job. Steven and I were both living in San Francisco at the time and had formed a Csound Users Group, primarily along with Matt Ingalls.

Steven Yi: Yes, at the time the three of us were regularly meeting for the Bay Area Csound Users Group. It was at one of these meetings that Jim and I had discussed what a great resource the *Csound Magazine* was for learning and sharing things related to Csound. After some discussion, we decided to create a new journal and the community response was very positive. We have been working on it since.

Can you give a short overview of the main subjects?

JH: I think *Csound Journal*, following on the heels of *Csound Magazine*, provides a look into the author's views of research with Csound. Each author has his/her own way of continuing to expand their use and application of Csound, and it is always interesting how the authors utilize and write about those experiences.

SY: For the Journal, I think we're really looking at it as a place for people to share their experiences with working with Csound. I've really enjoyed the diversity of articles people have contributed. Some of the subjects that have been covered are: Csound coding practices, exploring opcodes, composing with Csound, using Csound for audio research, synthesis and signal processing, and tools built for use with Csound. I always learn a lot from the articles people contribute, most especially, people use Csound in many different ways!

How do you work together? What tasks are required for a new issue of the journal?

JH: Currently we are using a Bitbucket account setup by Steven which works with GIT for versioning over the internet. Although we publish a template for authors, we usually have to do quite a lot of editing on the articles. We try to stick to IEEE standards.

The editing can sometimes become tedious, but in the end it helps to give the issue a uniform appearance, and hopefully also makes it easier to read and comprehend. I like to think that the effort put into the editing is helpful to the Csound community in some small way, especially to those who read the articles and who may want to try out some of the approaches, techniques, and workflows listed in the articles.

SY: The general process for a new issue is that we first put out a call for articles. Interested authors then contact us to see if a topic for an article would be appropriate for the Journal. When the deadline for submissions approaches, we start to contact the authors again to see their status. After we receive the articles, our real work begins.

Once we receive the articles, we take the articles and convert them to HTML. Next, we spend time going over the HTML formatting to make sure it matches the standard that we use. Afterwards, Jim and I both do editorial passes over the articles. It is during this time we look at the content of the article as well as the writing style. When we have questions regarding the content, we will email the authors for clarification. Through this process, we will also make edits to the document or request them from the authors. Once we have each finished reviewing the articles, we will do a final check with the authors. At this time we may get some additional corrections, then a final sign off. When all of the authors have given their sign off, we publish the issue.

Jim has mentioned that we use GIT for collaboratively editing the issues. That repository is private to Jim and myself. What we publish to our staging site (where authors have access to the articles in progress) and the published site on csounds.com is an exported version of the articles from the GIT repository.

Is there anything you would like to change in the future? Any wishes?

JH: *Csound Journal* seems to work well for those who know and typically use Csound. For several issues we followed the *Csound Magazine* tradition of having a bit of computer generated artwork on the cover, but changed that a few issues back, opting for a more refined look which would concentrate just on the articles, not the artwork. But I think pictures or images help in someway, and I would like to possibly add images of the various authors, say alongside their contact email address usually listed at the top of each article.

SY: I have had the thought that the Journal might benefit from moving away from hand-edited HTML to using something like LaTeX or Docbook. It would then give us options to publish not only HTML, but PDF and EPUB as well. The only reservations I have had regarding this is that the current published URL's are referenced by other articles, and it would be quite some work to redo the existing articles. However, I think we might gain a lot in making the change to either LaTeX or Docbook.
Other than that, I'm largely happy with how things have been going with the Journal. If others have suggestions on how the Journal might be improved, I'd love to hear them!

Interview: Joachim Heintz

DEVELOPING CSOUNDQT

INTERVIEW WITH ANDRÉS CABRERA

CsoundQt, formerly known as QuteCsound, is at the time of publishing this book the way most users come into contact with Csound. They use CsoundQt as code editor, they run their .csd files, they work with the in-built tutorial or check its vast collection of examples.

Andrés, along with many other people, you have done a lot of work for the Csound community in the past decade. An example of this would be your maintanance of the Csound manual. How did you first come into contact with Csound, and how did you get hooked?

I was introduced to Csound by my teacher Juan Reyes around the middle of the 1990s. I was immediately amazed that you could generate sound artificially (it doesn't sound like a big thing nowadays, but it was pretty surprising then...). Although I didn't use it for a couple of years, I eventually had some ideas that required it. I wanted to use a VST plugin I was using within Csound itself, and I realised that I would have to write a VST hosting opcode myself. So I decided to do this and learn C++ at the same time. I managed to hack something together that miraculously worked, and with the help of Michael Gogins finally produced something usable for VST hosting. I then started porting some opcodes over from CsoundAV to the "canonical" Csound version, because I realised that I could improve the tool I was using to make it better. During this process, and from my own usage, I saw the manual could be improved, so I got very involved into making it more complete and easier to consult. The process of becoming involved with Csound development and the Csound community came very naturally, as it was the tool I was using, and I needed to make improvements to it. It is wonderful when you understand that it's fairly easy to contribute to open source projects, and that you can shape programs to be what you want them to be and learn a lot in the process as well.

CsoundQt is now the most widely used front-end for Csound. How did you decide to develop it?

I had been teaching sound synthesis at Universidad Javeriana and Universidad de los Andes in Bogotá, exploring different tools for the job. I started using Pure Data, which I thought, because it is a graphical language, would be simpler for the music students facing programming for the first time. This did not work as I had hoped, and it seemed to me that students got easily confused by the ways algorithms are expressed in PD. I was a Csound user, and I felt that it was a good learning environment because of its simple and straightforward syntax, and its musical terminology (instrument, score, note, etc.). However, I found that beginners who were not used to the command line struggled with running Csound, because at the time the front-ends for Windows (most of my students only had Windows systems available) were not beginner-friendly. Mac users had a great front-end called MacCsound written by Matt Ingalls which allowed the creation of widgets to control Csound in real-time. I didn't have a Mac either and MacCsound is not open source, so I decided to write a cross-platform version of MacCsound because I saw nobody else would do it for me. But although the main use I envisioned for CsoundQt (then called QuteCsound), was pedagogical, I also wanted the system to have no roof and accommodate advanced users as well.

What were the main decisions in the development process, concerning programming language, design and license?

The only thing I had clear from the start was that I wanted to use a free license like the GPL. I knew this could encourage other people to contribute to the project and it would help spread the usage of the program. The way this has worked out has far exceeded my expectations as many different users have contributed ideas, code, examples and documentation which have made the program much better than what I could have made it by myself.

The choice of a programming language and GUI toolkit was more fortuitous as I went with C++ and the Qt toolkit (recently acquired by

Digia from Nokia). I went with this toolkit as it was in widespread use in the Linux community and I liked how cross-platform applications looked with it. I think this has turned out to be a great choice as the Qt toolkit has made a lot of the work simple and quick and it now presents an interesting future with Digia committing to support for Android and OS X.

How would you describe the current (summer 2012) state of the application?

The 0.7 version has been in development for more than a year and a half, and has seen many significant additions such as the Python interactive API for real-time scripting of both the CsoundQt application and GUIs as well as running the Csound engine, work towards enabling the generation of standalone applications and split view editors with spreadsheet-like functionality for scores. This has proved to be major work, which is why there hasn't been a "stable" release for a long while. When released (although it is currently available as alpha versions on OS X), this version should provide greater stability and performance and open up new possibilities for the usage of Csound.

What are your future plans for CsoundQt?

The short-term plan is to get the 0.7 release out the door. This still requires work, particularly in the standalone application generation, as making sure it works properly on all supported platforms is time consuming.

In the longer term, as Csound 6 takes shape, I think CsoundQt is in a great position to take advantage of the new features that will be available, such as real-time modification of the running engine through the Python interface as well as better debugging and development environments.

As you described, such a development is both an individual and a collective work. What would you, as a main developer, like to see more of, in terms of support, from the Csound community?

I haven't really asked myself this question before, but it's actually a good time to do so as I'm finding I have a lot less time to spend on CsoundQt these days. Ideally, I would like more eyes looking over and improving the application code, as much of it was written several years ago, when I was less experienced in Qt and C++, but I think that might be difficult as it requires significant programming knowledge and a serious time commitment. However, something the community could provide, which up to this point I haven't asked for, is help with the maintenance of things like the web page, which is a bit outdated, and with the testing and updating of examples, in order to catch errors and regressions in the CsoundQt application.

Interview: Joachim Heintz

PYTHON SCRIPTING IN CSOUNDQT

ANDRÉS CABRERA

Abstract

This article presents the Python scripting facilities within CsoundQt. The interactive Python API exposes both portions of the CsoundQt application and the running Csound engines within it.

Introduction

Adding Python scripting to CsoundQt comes from the motivation of integrating a powerful interactive language like Python with CsoundQt to provide new possibilities for real-time control and scripting which can open the door to more interactive methodologies for algorithmic composition and to a broader range of applications and interfaces for arts and research through Python's extensive support of a broad range of technologies and infrastructures.

Using Python in CSoundQT

There are three ways of running Python code in CsoundQt:

1. As a whole Python file which is run in the interpreter or a separate shell using the Run and Run in Term actions from the menus or the icon bar.
2. Directly on the interactive Python Console, which reports from the main interpreter, and shows the results of any Python code executed in the internal interpreter.
3. By evaluating code from editors or the Python scratch pad (using the Evaluate selection or Evaluate Section actions). The Python scratch pad is a disposable buffer to prepare constructs like function definitions or loops which are not practical or possible to type into the console directly. Section separators are marked using two

number signs ##. These section separations are shown in the Inspector.

It is important to note that there is only one internal Python interpreter, so any variables, functions and objects will be available from any places where code can be evaluated by the interpreter.

Additionally, there is a menu on the interface called "Scripts" which lists the Python files found in the Scripts folder, which can be configured in Preferences. This simplifies the execution of common Python tasks, and results in a sort of "plug-in" system, since it is possible for the script to act on the active content, for things like modifying indentation of a certain content, to performing text transformations of the score, or interacting with external applications such as Lilypond or a browser.

Architecture

The Python scripting capabilities in CsoundQt are implemented through PythonQt[1], a C++ library that automatically wraps C++ and Qt classes for exposure in Python. This greatly simplifies the work, reducing the amount of manual code wrapping that is normally required. PythonQt simplifies the creation of Python interpreter instances and provides console widgets with code completion based on the active objects and variables of the interpreter instance.

An additional benefit of PythonQt is that it wraps most of Qt, giving the possibility of building GUIs in Qt directly from Python, without the need for PyQt[2] or PySide[3].

Elements of CsoundQt and Csound are exposed through a custom object called "q", which is available by default in the interpreter. This object wraps a lot of diverse functionality from the CsoundQt interface, Live Event Sheets, code editors and running instances of Csound, in an integrated and hopefully succinct way.

The CsoundQT Python Object

The CsoundQt class (called PyQcsObject in the sources) is the interface for scripting CsoundQt and it exposes a set of functions for various elements of the CsoundQt application and any instances of Csound

---

1 http://pythonqt.sourceforge.net/

2 http://www.riverbankcomputing.co.uk/pyqt/

3 http://www.pyside.org/

associated with currently open documents. The various functions available are presented below, grouped according to the elements they affect.

As mentioned, by default a PyQcsObject is already available in the interpreter called "q", so all the methods described below should be called as member functions of this object.

CsoundQt Interface

The CsoundQt object offers control of execution of any of the open documents by index. Giving an index of -1 or omitting it, executes the order on the currently active document.

```
play(int index = -1, realtime = true)
pause(int index = -1)
stop(int index = -1)
stopAll()
```

There are also functions to find the index of a document by its name, and to set a particular index as active. Setting a document like this will make it visible, as if the tab for it had been clicked.

```
setDocument(index)
getDocument(name = "") # Returns document index. -1
if not current open
```

Csound files can also be loaded from the disk, or new files created:

```
newDocument(name)
loadDocument(name, runNow = false)
```

Editors

Operations on text for open files can be done through the API, for example:

```
insertText(text, index = -1, section = -1)
```

will insert the text at the current cursor position, for document *index*. Text for individual sections of the file can also be inserted using the functions:

```
setCsd(text, index = -1);
setFullText(text, index = -1)
```

```
setOrc(text, index = -1)
setSco(text, index = -1)
setWidgetsText(text, index = -1)
setPresetsText(text, index = -1)
setOptionsText(text, index = -1)
```

And text can also be queried with the functions:

```
getSelectedText(index = -1, int section = -1)
getCsd(index = -1)
getFullText(index = -1)
getOrc(index = -1)
getSco(index = -1)
getSelectedWidgetsText(index = -1);
getWidgetsText(index = -1)
getPresetsText(index = -1)
getOptionsText(index = -1)
```

Additionally information about the file being edited can be queried with:

```
getFileName(index = -1)
getFilePath(index = -1)
```

Widgets

Widget values and properties can be changed and queried through the API for any of the open documents with the functions:

```
setChannelValue(channel, value, index = -1)
getChannelValue(channel, index = -1)
setChannelString(channel, stringvalue, int
index = -1)
getChannelString(channel, index = -1)
setWidgetProperty(channel, property, value,
index= -1)
getWidgetProperty(channel, property, index= -1)
```

And widgets can be created and destroyed through the API. The functions to create widgets return a string with the UUID (unique id) of the widget, which can then be used in the destructor function. The channel can be set directly in the Python line, but if it is not, the properties dialog for the widget will be shown.

```
createNewLabel(x, y, channel, index = -1)
createNewDisplay(x, y, channel, index = -1)
createNewScrollNumber(x, y, channel, index = -1)
createNewLineEdit(x, y, channel, index = -1)
createNewSpinBox(x, y, channel, index = -1)
createNewSlider(x, y, channel, index = -1)
createNewButton(x, y, channel, index = -1)
createNewKnob(x, y, channel, index = -1)
createNewCheckBox(x, y, channel, index = -1)
createNewMenu(x, y, channel, index = -1)
createNewMeter(x, y, channel, nt index = -1)
createNewConsole(x, y, channel, index = -1)
createNewGraph(x, y, channel, index = -1)
createNewScope(x, y, channel, index = -1)
destroyWidget(QString uuid)
```

Presets can also be loaded from the python API:

```
loadPreset(presetIndex, index = -1)
```

And information about existing widgets can be obtained:

```
getWidgetUuids(index = -1);
listWidgetProperties(widgetid, index = -1)
```

Csound Functions

Several functions can interact with the Csound engine, for example to query information about it:

```
getVersion() # CsoundQt API version
getSampleRate(int index)
getKsmps(int index)
getNumChannels(int index)
opcodeExists(QString opcodeName)
```

(Strictly speaking, the opcodeExists() function doesn't interact with the engine, but with the opcode list from the documentation, but they should be in sync, although they might not reflect details of a particular installation. The purpose of this function is more to work with text parsers so that they can identify opcodes against the rest of the text)

There are objects to send score events to any running document, without having to switch to it:

```
sendEvent(int index, QString events)
sendEvent(QString events)
```

There is also a function that can register a Python function as a callback to be executed in between processing blocks for Csound. The first argument should be the text that should be called on every pass. It can include arguments or variables that will be evaluated each time. You can also set a number of periods to skip to avoid.

```
registerProcessCallback(QString func, int skipPeriods
= 0)
```

You can register the python text to be executed on every Csound control block callback, so you can execute a block of code, or call any function that is already defined.

Other

The refresh() function yields to the Qt processing loop. Because Python is run synchronously with the main application, this can be useful in making sure the CsoundQt interface remains responsive even when Python is still running.

Future Work

F-tables

An important function will be to connect f-tables from the running instance to Python. Although not implemented yet, it is hoped they will look like:

```
getTablePointer(fn, index = -1)
copyTableToList(fn, index = -1, offset = 0, number =
-1)
copyListToTable(list, fn, index = -1, offset = 0)
```

The main issue complicating implementation of these is that tables must be accessed at a time when the Csound engine is idle, so these functions must work through a messaging system that sends requests to the performance thread, which will do the work when it should. The messages are stored in a lock-free ring buffer and the caller functions will wait for a done signal from the real-time thread, to read the data and return. This is what SuperCollider does in these cases and some of this has already implemented in the csPerfThread C++ class.

Live Event Sheet Interaction

Although not yet implemented, it is hoped to implement a set of functions which can interact with Live Event Sheets, so they can become a sort of visual matrix, which can be used with the mouse and keyboard or programatically from the API. They will probably look like:

```
QuteSheet* getSheet(int index = -1,
int sheetIndex = -1)
QuteSheet* getSheet(int index, QString sheetName)
```

And they should transparently connect the data so a change in one will affect the other. The QuteSheet object will implement the necessary functionality to query and modify cells.

Conclusions

It is expected that this work will open up new possibilities for control and interaction with Csound.

Some possible uses include:

- A graphical Ftable editor
- Sequencer and notation applications
- Interactive pieces
- Automatic code generation/visualization/transformation
- Design of custom control GUIs and widgets
- Live Coding
- Remote control on mobile devices (e.g. Send the widgets and do the network connections automatically)

COMPOSING CIRCUMSPECTRAL SOUNDS

PEIMAN KHOSRAVI

Abstract

This paper presents a software tool for distributing the spectral content of stereo sounds within an array of 6-8 loudspeakers using Csound's real-time phase vocoder opcodes. The technique is discussed in relation to Smalley's notion of "circumspectral spaces" that refers to acousmatic contexts characterised by the distribution of the spectral content of sounds within listening space. After a general discussion of the concept, the main components of the Csound implementation of the technique are examined. This is followed by an introduction to the graphical interface by means of which the user can interact in real time with the Csound-based instrument. Finally, some examples are provided to demonstrate the practical applications of the technique in a musical context. While remaining focused on the subject, the paper also delves into wider aesthetic considerations about spatiality in acousmatic music in order to highlight the significance of circumspectral states as an inherent aspect of the acousmatic image.

Introduction

While preparing for my first multichannel piece I quickly became aware of the need for software tools which are designed in response to the kind of spatial thinking that grows directly out of interacting with the acousmatic medium. In this respect, one of the least explored areas in spatial audio technology is "circumspectral" sound projection. The term is a combination of "circumspace" and "spectral", and is used by Denis Smalley to describe acousmatic contexts that are characterised by the distribution of the spectral components of a uniform sound around the listener - that is, the circumspatial distribution of spectral energy within listening space (Smalley, 2007). As he elaborates:

> How spectral space in itself is distributed contributes to the sensation of height, depth, and spatial scale and volume. I can create a more vivid sense of the physical volume of space by creating what I shall call circumspectral spaces, where the spectral space of what is perceived as a coherent or unified morphology is split and distributed spatially. (Smalley, 2007, pp. 44–47)

The term "spectral space" refers to the felt spatial character of the frequency domain in some listening contexts: sounds may evoke a sense of height, vertical depth, volume, motion, and texture as a result of the manner in which they 'occupy' and 'move through' the continuum of the audible frequencies (Smalley, 2007). This becomes particularly pertinent when directly-perceived source/cause identities are obscured for the sake of a more abstracted environment in which sonic identities can be felt as visuospatial entities made up of 'spectral matter'. In other words, spectromorphologies themselves can attain a spatial character in listening consciousness and provide the basis for a strongly embodied multi-sensory experience that is invoked by means of sound alone (Smalley, 1997). Consequently, the possibility of sculpting the distribution of spectral matter in listening space significantly contributes towards the establishment of a more integrated compositional relationship between sound and space.

Although with careful mixing one can certainly explore circumspectral configurations, it seems appropriate to take advantage of a purpose-designed computer program that enables a more sophisticated and imaginative approach: my standalone application *Circumspect*, created with Csound's real-time phase vocoder opcodes (see Dobson, et. al.) and a MaxMSP (see Cycling74.com) graphical user-interface, is an attempt towards this. In this paper I will present the basic algorithm implemented in Csound, followed by a description of the program's user-interface. Finally, some examples are provided to demonstrate the practical applications of the technique in a musical context.

Implementation

Circumspect is based on a relatively simple algorithm, which analyses the input audio of a single channel into an FFT signal whose individual bins (each bin can be thought of as a narrow frequency band) are mixed amongst 6-8 output audio channels. The spectral analysis uses Csound's family of *pvs* opcodes which are intended for real-time spectral analysis, transformation, and resynthesis of audio signals. The opcode pvsanal converts an audio signal into a stream of FFT frames stored inside an *f*-

type variable. The data held in an *f-variable* can then be subjected to any number of frequency domain transformations before it is resynthesised back into the time domain using the opcode pvsynth. Here the distribution/mixing of the FFT bins amongst multiple speakers is carried out inside a user-defined opcode that accesses the analysis content via a dynamically updated table (see Csound Code example CSD). A summary of the algorithm for circumspectral resynthesis of a monaural audio signal is provided below (also see Figure 1):

(1) The input audio channel is analysed using pvsanal.
(2) The resulting data for each analysis frame is written to two tables (using pvsftw), one for frequency and one for amplitude. Each table index contains the amplitude or frequency for one analysis bin. The table contents are updated for each new frame.
(3) The amplitude table is then passed on to a user-defined opcode, which divides the amplitude value for each bin amongst 6 tables (one for each loudspeaker) according to a user-defined map stored inside a table: itabpan contains one panning value for each bin.
(4) The resulting 6 tables that contain the amplitude values are then coupled with the original frequency values (we do not alter the frequencies) using the pvsftr opcode. This produces 6 separate *fsig* streams, one for each speaker.
(5) Finally the 6 output *fsig* streams are resynthesised and routed into the appropriate loudspeakers.

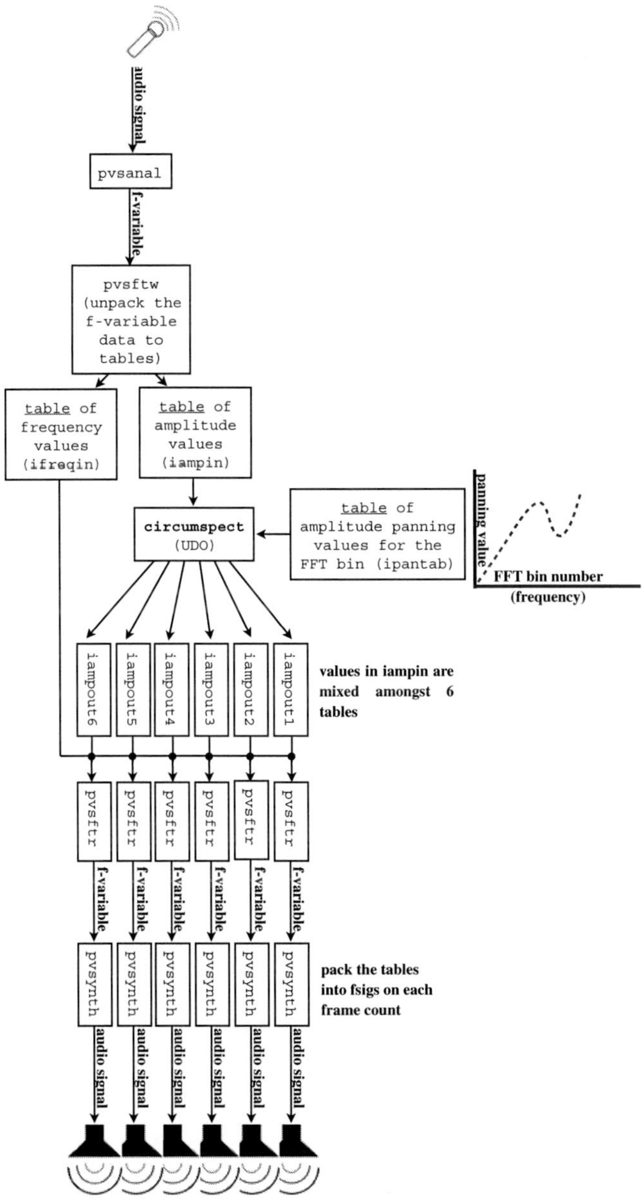
audio signal
pvsanal
f-variable
pvsftw
(unpack the
f-variable
data to
tables)
table of
frequency
values
(ifreqin)
table of
amplitude
values
(iampin)
circumspect
(UDO)
table of
amplitude panning
values for the
FFT bin (ipantab)
panning value
FFT bin number
(frequency)
iampout6
iampout5
iampout4
iampout3
iampout2
iampout1
values in iampin are
mixed amongst 6
tables
pvsftr
f-variable
pvsynth
pack the tables
into fsigs on each
frame count
audio signal

Figure 1.

User Interface

Introducing the Interface

The interface for circumspect was designed in MaxMSP and is available as part of a standalone spectral processing application entitled *FFTools.* The communication between MaxMSP and the Csound api is achieved by means of the MSP external csound~ (Davixology.com). Two instances of csound~ are placed inside a poly~ object in order to enable the 'circumspectralisation' of stereo sound files.

Having discussed the sound engine, it is evident that a more challenging task was the creation of a usable interface for editing the amplitude panning values stored inside ipantab. To enter values bin-by-bin is neither practical nor creatively stimulating. One requires a certain level of interactivity and responsiveness from the system, which can be achieved by providing a higher-level method of controlling the vast number of parameters involved. In *Circumspect* the content of the panning table is visualised as a two-dimensional array where the x axis represents the frequency continuum (i.e. the available FFT bins), and the y axis represents the panning 'position' (figure 2). Moreover, the display table contains a set of two circumspectral panning functions, one for the left- and one for the right-channel content of the input sound - colour-coded as blue and red respectively (white and grey in the images below). Thus, the left and right channels of the input sound can be distributed separately: a quasi-symmetrical relationship will somewhat retain the original stereo width of the image. The panning values range from 0 to 8, making it possible to compose for up to 8-channels. Integer values correspond with single loudspeakers, while fractional values signify mixing between two adjacent speakers. Thus, a value of 0.5 mixes the synthesised bin at a particular frequency equally between channels 0 and 1.

Random Circumspatial Distribution of Frequencies

In order to tackle the problems of low-level control, a weighted random number generator was developed. This enables the user to define circumspectral distribution patterns in terms of tendencies in the circumspatial positioning of the bins. It is possible to choose between *smooth* or *scattered* circumspatial distribution of the frequency bins. The former eliminates large leaps, keeping the adjacent bins relatively close to one-another in terms of their circumspatial 'positioning'. Figures 3 and 4 show a smooth and scattered distribution respectively.

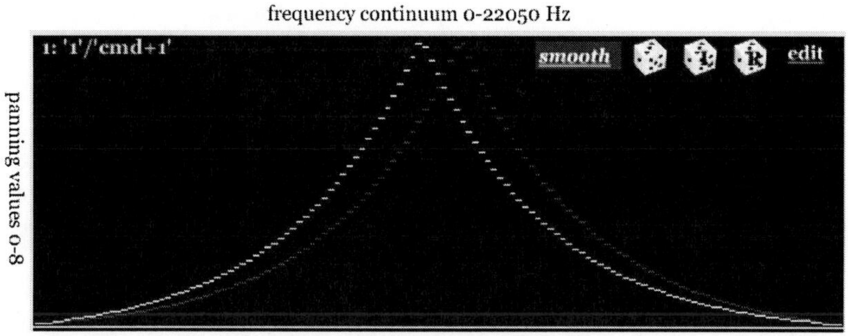

Figure 2. Spectral panning table with an FFT size of 256

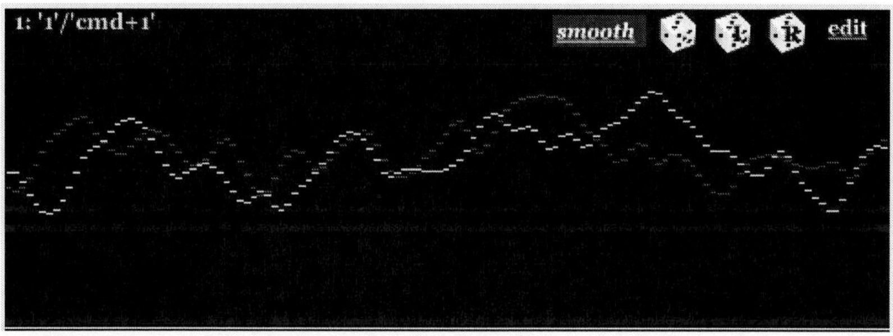

Figure 3. Smooth distribution

Figure 4. Scattered distribution

For instance, one can configure the tendencies so that the bins' circumspatial distribution is biased towards the front and the rear of the loudspeaker array (figure 5). Moreover, the pattern in figure 5 can be further transformed so that the lower frequencies are limited to the front of the loudspeaker array, while the circumspatial distribution of the higher frequencies is more widely scattered (figure 6).

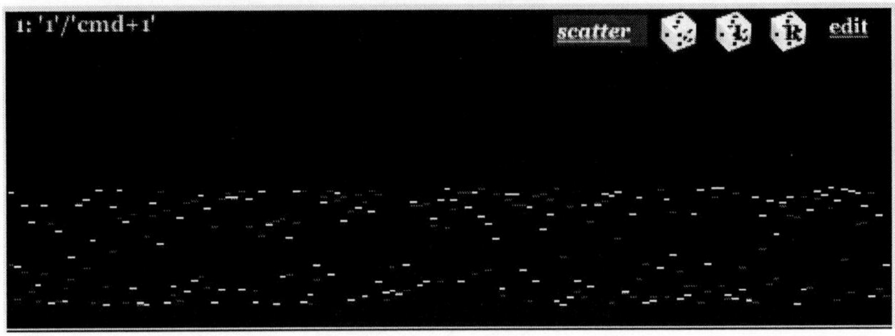

Figure 5. Randomly generated biased panning values

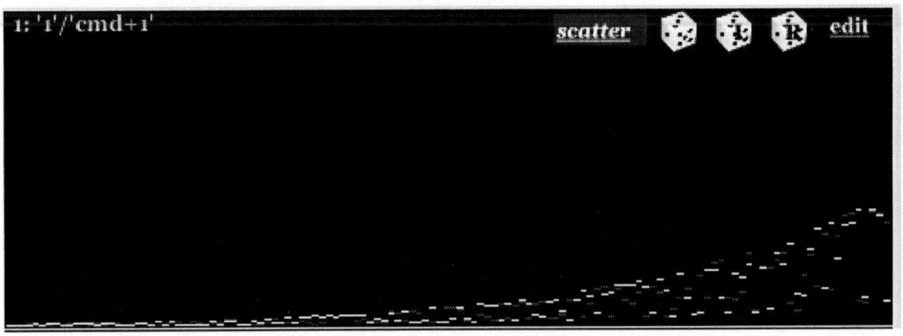

Figure 6. The above further transformed by a masking function

Composing Circumspectral Sounds

General Considerations

Since *Circumspect* is not used to position or move virtual sources around the listener, the conventional notion of 'spatialisation' is not strictly relevant here. To a certain extent the aesthetic attitude that leads to the exploration of circumspectral spaces contradicts the notion of spatial thinking as the positioning and movement of virtual sound sources in a parametric fashion. Here *spatiality* is thought to be inherent in the sound's intrinsic spectral makeup: the apparent spectral matter from which sonic entities emerge. The (re)distribution of spectral matter in listening space, therefore, enables the composer to create a more vivid materialisation of sounds' inherent spatiality by enhancing their apparent sense of physical volume, spread or animation.

Below I have outlined some of the unique characteristics of circumspectral sounds that can be explored by means of the current software tool.

Psychoacoustic Considerations

It is known that distributing the spectral partials of a single sound amongst a loudspeaker array does not by itself lead to the perceptual segregation of the spectral components of that sound (Kendall, 1995). In the absence of decorrelations such as different time delays or micro-modulations amongst the spectral components, the coherence of a circumspectralised sound remains intact - that is, one does not perceive multiple sources but a single source with an enhanced sense of spatial volume and spread. Thus the individual spectral components of a circumspectralised sound are not experienced on a conscious level, unless there is some degree of decorrelation amongst the components themselves, or if the circumspectral image is clearly delineated by separating the low and high frequencies in listening space.

The scattering of spectral energy between the loudspeakers also tends to somewhat enlarge the size of the 'sweet spot'. Multichannel compositions often suffer when transferred from smaller to larger spaces: the integrity of the perspectival image can be less than perfect for listeners in proximity to individual speakers. By spatially redistributing the spectral components of a unified sound one can ensure that no single speaker reproduces the entire signal; rather, the full signal is reconstructed in the listener's mind, which means that physical proximity to a speaker will have a less detrimental impact on the experience of the perspectival image as a whole.

Technological Artifacts

It is essential to bear in mind that FFT bins are not the same as partials: often the combination of two or more bins makes up a single partial, in which case obvious artifacts are produced when the bins are drastically scattered amongst the loudspeakers. One can minimise such artifacts by means of smoother circumspectral distributions where the adjacent bins are not drastically separated from one another in terms of their loudspeaker distribution. The circumspatial scattering of the bins results in highly blurred transients, which may not be noticeable when applied to sustained sounds but will certainly have a drastic effect on more transient materials. This is not to say that the FFT artifacts cannot produce musically interesting results. For instance, using the random generators in *Circumspect*, one can uniformly scatter the bins amongst the loudspeakers as a means of producing spectral decorrelation. In particular, the uniform scattering of the FFT bins of a broadband spectral structure produces a spectrally decorrelated but perceptually identical signal in each loudspeaker. Here the presence of spectrally decorrelated signals in each speaker ensures a more dispersed image that would be impossible to achieve with conventional amplitude panning alone (Kendall, 2010).

Spatial Animation

One can create the impression of an animated spatial texture by more or less contiguously distributing frequency components of a strongly animated spectromorphology. With simpler contiguous configurations (e.g. front-back) I tend to more clearly experience the perspectival expansion of a sound's spectral motion. Imaginative circumspectral textures can be created by coupling complex spectromorphologies with less straightforward circumspatial mapping of the spectral components. I have, for instance, achieved attractive results from noise-based sounds that were preprocessed with numerous filter-sweep-like transformations to create broad spectral undulations. Even more interestingly, one can use stereo sounds where the spectral motion is coupled with panoramic trajectories in the original stereo (possibly inherent in the recording rather than resulting from any amplitude panning). The stereo sound can then be spectrally mapped to the loudspeaker array, thus circumspatially expanding the sense of panoramic and spectral animation in a more organic fashion. In other words, the inherent spectral motion of the sound can be articulated perspectivally in order to create a more distinct sense of spatial texturing.

Spatial Enclosure

Circumspectral sounds can also increase the sense of perspectival 'enclosure' by creating the impression that the listener is placed inside the spectral body of a sound (Kendall & Cabrera, 2012). As an example consider a section from my 6-channel piece *Vertex* (at 02':00"). Here the higher spectral components of the sustained inharmonic material are mixed towards the rear of the listening space, high-pass filtering is then used to gradually expand the upward growth of spectral space: there is a sense that as spectral mass increases, the listener is gradually enclosed within the body of the sound. In this sense, circumspectral configurations help convey a stronger sense of envelopment.[16]

Future Directions

As a final note it must be mentioned that the true power of circumspectral sound design becomes apparent in context, during the mixing stage of composition when different circumspectral sounds are combined to interact in a dynamic manner. For instance, how do circumspectral configurations affect spectral masking, fusion and fission of textural elements? How is the spatial 'feel' of a mix influenced by combining different circumspectral sounds, or even different circumspectral versions of the same sound, with or without small amounts of delay? What happens when this technique is used alongside conventional or per-grain amplitude panning? A full discussion of these questions is beyond the limit of this paper, however, I suspect that many creative possibilities remain to be compositionally explored. No doubt this will imply the creation of new software tools and the development of those currently available. For instance, the addition of per-bin spectral delay and decorrelated amplitude modulation to the current software tool should enable the composer to create interesting ambiguities between textural fusion and fission, as well as enhancing the sense of spatial animation.

Final Remarks

Here I have attempted to encourage the reader to consider the compositional potential of circumspectral spatial design in acousmatic music. *Circumspect* was used to sculpt circumspectral configurations in my 6-channel piece *Vertex* which relies heavily on the spatial character of spectral matter as a basis for the establishment of musical form and meaning. It goes without saying that only firsthand listening experience with a multichannel setup can truly reveal the sonic possibilities. Unfortunately, access to a high fidelity multichannel sound system is not commonplace, which is a limiting factor. On the other hand, it is apparent that we are far from having exhausted the musical potential of spatial audio, and that multichannel technology can have deeper aesthetic implications than the mere positioning and movement of virtual sources in listening space. My ears suspect that with a certain amount of creative imagination one can achieve wonders with a limited number of loudspeakers and without the need for overly elaborate diffusion systems. After all, sounds may be experienced as moving without the presence of directly corresponding multichannel panning 'motion'. This can be easily put to the test by establishing dialogues with nonspecialist listeners (a regular occupation of mine). In such cases one quickly ascertains that these experiences often rely on aspects of source recognition and spectral spatiality. Sounds are pregnant with a certain spatiality that can *suggest* qualia such as physical volume, motion and texture: as a composer I have learned that it is imperative to be guided by this inherent spatiality in order to accomplish a more sophisticated and musically meaningful approach to the composition of space. It is in this context that circumspectral technology plays an essential function in the acousmatic composer's laboratory.

References

Smalley, Denis, "Space-form and the Acousmatic Image," *Organised Sound* 12, no. 1, 2007.

—. "Spectromorphology: Explaining Sound-shapes," *Organised Sound* 2, no. 2, 1997.

"A collection of opcodes developed by Richard Dobson, Victor Lazzarini, & John Ffitch", accessed August 31, 2012, http://www.csounds.com/manual/html/SpectralRealTime.html.

"Cycling74.com" accessed August 31, 2012, http://cycling74.com/.

"Csound code example CSD," The application FFTools were only built and tested on Mac OSX, however, the source patches are available and with simple alterations, it should be possible to build a standalone version on the windows operating system. To obtain the software please contact the author. accessed April 12, 2013, http://www.csounds.com/udo/displayOpcode.php?opcode_id=177.

"Davixology.com," accessed August 31, 2012 http://www.davixology.com/csound~.html.

Kendall, Gary S., "The Decorrelation of Audio Signals and Its Impact on Spatial Imagery," *Computer Music Journal* 19, no. 4, 1995

—. "Spatial Perception in Multichannel Audio for Electroacoustic Music," *Organised Sound* 15, no. 3, 2010

Kendall, Gary S., and Cabrera, Andrés, "Why Things Don't Work: What You Need To Know About Spatial Audio," *Proceedings of the 2011 International Computer Music Conference*, 2011.

CREATING REVERB EFFECTS USING GRANULAR SYNTHESIS

KIM ERVIK AND ØYVIND BRANDTSEGG

Abstract

In this article we will explain how we have used Csound to create a reverb effect with granular synthesis. We will look at some commercial varieties of granular reverb then we will show how to create the same effects using Csound. On account of to the flexibility of Csound it is possible to take this idea even further and expand the concept of a granular reverb effect and we present our own variants of the granular reverb effect.

Introduction

Granular synthesis has long been available as a sound manipulating and sound generating technique, and currently has seen increasing use in commercial music software. Explained briefly, granular synthesis generates sound, based on the additive combination of many very short sonic grains into larger acoustical events. This technique has vast expressive possibilities with its parametric control tied to the time and frequency domain. Some basic examples of granular synthesis parameters are grain rate, grain envelope, grain duration, grain pitch and the waveform inside each grain.

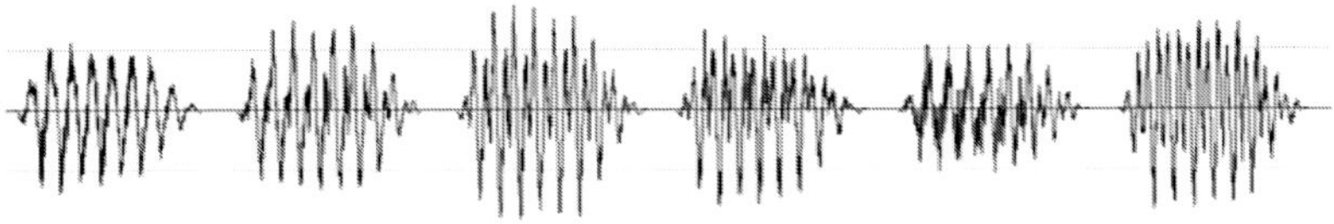

Fig 1: Granular synthesis.

For a long time it has been common to use pre-sampled sound or complex waveforms as source for granular synthesis. In recent years, with the emergence of faster computers, granular synthesis has additionally become available as an audio effect in real time, for instance in a live performance, or as a plug-in in a DAW. A common use of this technique is the "grain delay" effect found, for example, in Ableton Live (Ableton.com). This effect is similar to a classic delay effect in that it delays the incoming signal with the parameters delay time, feedback amount and dry/wet amount. It differs from the classical delay effect in the way that it is possible to chop the delayed signal into grains and use granular synthesis parameters such as grain pitch, grain rate and grain duration. It is also possible to scatter the grains in time with the "spray" parameter, which creates a lush cloud of the repeated signal. If the parameters are tweaked right, this delay effect can sound like a reverb effect.

With Line 6's new stompbox "M" series (M5, M9, and M13) (line6.com) two interesting reverb effects can be found (line6.com). They are called "particle verb" and "octoverb" and generate a lush cloud output, from the audio input signal. Both these effects contain pitch shift as an integrated part of the algorithm. Knowing this and taking the name "particle verb" into account we can assume that granular synthesis constitute a significant part of the reverb algorithm. In "particle verb" one can also hear a kind of grain scattering, which can also indicate that this is a variant of grain delay.

Classic Reverb Algorithms

In the physical world, reverb is generated by reflections from surfaces around the sound source giving the sound object[1] a short tail. In the early days of recorded audio, sounds were played back into an echo chamber and recorded to produce such effects. Later, tape-delay machines could produce the illusion of early reflections by delaying the incoming signal. A combination of allpass and comb filters has been used to create artificial reverb (e.g. Moorer reverb, Gardner reverb, Freeverb) (Smith, 2006). Feedback delay networks constitute another well-known technique (e.g. reverbsc in Csound). Currently, also convolution (Boulanger, 2000) has been used to artificially recreate the response of a physical room or hall. Convolution can also be used to create granular sounding reverb effects. By convoluting a signal with an impulse response created with granular synthesis one get a grainy lush cloud at the end of the input signal (Roads, 1996).

---

[1] A sound object is described as one isolated sound event, for example a note or a drum hit or the sound of a train passing by (Roads, 2001).

Granular Reverb Algorithms

Granular synthesised reverb is similar to the delay effect in the way that it simulates sound reflections by the use of delay, while it resembles reverb in that it also creates reverb-like, lush tails. One could easily term granular reverb more of a special effect than a "realistic" effect.

A granular reverb effect in Csound can be created as a grain delay process, with a delayed signal that is chopped up to smaller grains and treated with granular processing. Scattering of the grains in time creates a cloudy textural tail to the input sound. To facilitate this, audio input is recorded into a table and this table is used as source for granular synthesis. The granular synthesis output is also fed back into the table together with the audio input. This is shown in PartikkelDly.csd (Ervik, Csound example No. 1). To emulate the Line 6 "octaverb", we can use the same example as with the grain delay, but with grain pitch one octave above.

Another way to create a long tail on a sound object is to time stretch it. This is easily done using granular synthesis. In the first track of figure 2, we can see a small sound object. One can "chop" the sound object into grains and stretch the duration of the entire sound object like an accordion, leaving empty space between each grain. This is done in the second and third tracks of the figure. In track four we can see that by filling the empty spaces between the grains with sound from nearby regions, we get a longer sound object with the same structure as the shorter one, still retaining the original pitch.

When performing time stretch using granular synthesis, we must endeavour to minimise artifacts. The most common artifacts are smearing of transients (due to overlapping long grains), and amplitude modulation sidebands (due to high grain rate and periodic grains). With low grain rates (less than 30 Hz), the pitch of the sound object is perceived through transposition of the source audio, as the original source waveform is not distorted by granular amplitude modulation. We can, to some extent, avoid the AM effect at higher grain rates too, by using a small random deviation on the sample position for reading grains. One way to create a smooth time stretch effect is by using a grain rate of about 30 – 40 grains per second, overlapping grains (3 overlaps seems to be OK) and a tiny random offset on the sample position. To achieve a broad stereo image one can double the grain rate and mask every other grain to the left and right stereo channels.

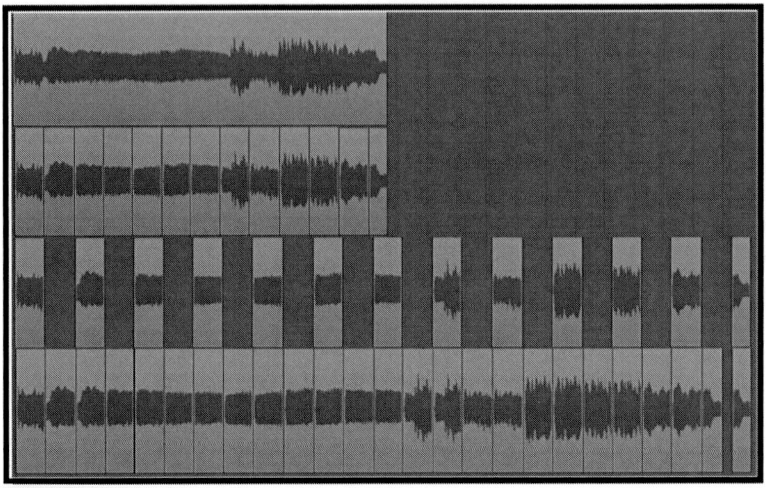

Fig 2: Granular synthesis time stretching.

Time Stretching Real-time Audio

There are obviously some conceptual problems with the idea of time stretching in real time. When a sound is played at its original tempo, at the same time as the same sound is played back at a lower tempo, the lower tempo playback will lag behind the original, and increasingly so over time. In real-time processing this is a problem because shortly after the effect instrument is started, the time between the playback position of the original signal and the playback position of the stretched signal is far to large for it to sound like a reverb effect. Letting the stretching process "skip" some parts of the incoming sound can solve this problem, as this will let us align the two playback positions on a periodic basis. This is not ideal either, because it will be unpredictable which part of the incoming signal which will be skipped and which part will be stretched.

A better approach to real-time time stretch is to use several buffers and several instances of the time stretch instrument simultaneously (Ervik, Csound example No. 2). Using the "schedkwhen" Csound opcode we can trigger a Csound instrument to record incoming sound to a buffer (a Csound table). The same opcode can also be used to start a granulation process of the recorded sound. A metronome and a counter can keep track of which table to write to, and when to start and stop the instances of the recording and playback instruments. In this manner, we can allow several overlapping time stretch instances simultaneously. This can also be seen as a granular process, so we have in effect several crossfading layers of granular synthesis running on top of each other, or nested granular synthesis, if you wish. What we mean with nested granular synthesis here is that we have an inner and an outer granular processing loop. The inner loop does the audio time stretching, while the outer loop performs the skipping and crossfading of time stretch layers, "catching up" with real time. It can also be preferable to let the recording instances overlap each other to allow for the random offset on the sample position.

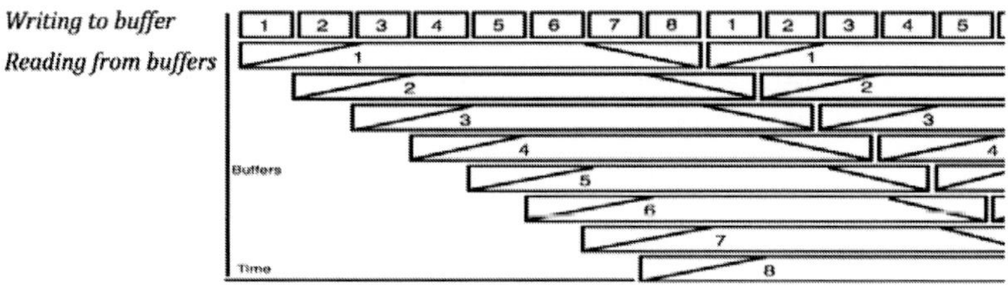

Fig. 3: Writing audio to 8 different buffers, at the same time as they are played back.

In our example we have used 8 buffers, recording 0.5 seconds to each buffer. This fraction of sound is time stretched by a factor of 8 so playback of the sound segment lasts 4 seconds (see figure 1). We have also applied an envelope with a slow attack and a slow release to get all the instances to overlap each other smoothly. The parameter values has been tweaked by empirical adjustments, so that the reverb tail is long enough, and at the same time it is not too unpredictable when an incoming sound "returns" from the audio processing. There will be a small periodically changing pre-delay on the reverb effect due to the moving read position on the time stretched playback. Using more layers of overlapping time stretch would make the effect smoother and the variations in pre delay smaller. The reverberation time can be adjusted by controlling the time stretch ratio. The reverb time can be calculated with the formula:

$$T = \frac{t}{2} - 0.5$$

Fig 4: Where T is the reverb time in seconds and t is the time stretch ratio.

Implementation Considerations

Our granular reverb implementation uses the partikkel opcode (Brandsegg, 2011). This opcode was inspired by Curtis Roads book "Microsound" (Roads, 2001) and is capable of generating all the varieties of granular synthesis described in his book. It is extremely flexible and offers a large set of control parameters.

The "partikkel" opcode is a good choice for implementing granular reverbs, both for its flexibility, and also because one can use up to four sound sources in each opcode instance. A suggestion for optimisation of the reverb algorithm proposed here is to use all the four sound sources of the opcode. This way one could perform the same processing with only two instances of the partikkel opcode instead of eight as we've used here. For the purpose of this paper it was thought that the computationally inefficient implementation might provide a clearer separation of the processing stages involved.

With "partikkel" one has "per grain control" over some of the parameters, meaning that one can, for example, specify the pitch and the amp of each grain. This way one can spectrally compose the "reverb cloud". A neat suggestion is to let every other grain be one octave above the original grains. One could also imagine more exotic variations like pitch sweeping reverbs, and partikkel's "per grain control" can provide a method for spatial scattering of reverb components.

Time Stretch Trigger Instrument

```
; LENGTH OF CHUNK TO BE RECORDED FOR STRETCHING giRecDur
    init 0.5
; PLAYBACK TIME OF THE RECORDED CHUNK
giPlayDdur init 4 ; (0.5 SECONDS STRETCHED TO 4 SECONDS)

instr 1
kmetrotime = 2
ktrig metro kmetronome
; COUNTING TABLE NUMBERS FOR-
; -TIME STRETCH INSTRUMENT
gktablenr = gktablenr + ktrig
if gktablenr > 8 then
gktablenr = 1
endif
; REC TRIG
schedkwhen ktrig,0,3,2,0,giRecDur+0.4,gktablenr
if gkplaytablenr > 0 then
; STRETCH TRIG
schedkwhen ktrig,0,8,3,0,giPlayDdur,gktablenr endif
endin
```

Conclusion

In this paper we have shown how to create reverb-like effects using granular synthesis. We have also explained the concept of a time stretching reverb using nested granular techniques. We have seen how some commercial grain reverb works, and we have shown how to create a grain reverb in Csound. We have also shown that with the flexibility of Csound it is possible to take the idea of a granular reverb even further, creating highly animated and modulated reverb algorithms. Finally, we have suggested some possible optimisations on the provided example implementations.

References

"Ableton Live," accessed December 21, 2012, https://www.ableton.com.

Boulanger, Richard, *The Csound Book*, edited by R. Boulanger. (Cambridge: The MIT Press, 2000), p. 507.

Brandtsegg, Saue, S. and Johansen, T., "Particle synthesis, a unified model for granular synthesis," *Linux Audio Conference*, 2011, http://lac.linuxaudio.org/2011/papers/39.pdf.

Ervik, Kim, "Csound example No.1: PartikkelDly.csd," accessed April 5, 2013, http://folk.ntnu.no/kimer/csoundconference2011/PartikkelDly.csd.

—. "Csound example No. 2: TimeStretchReverb.csd," accessed April 5, 2013, http://folk.ntnu.no/kimer/csoundconference2011/TimeStretchReverb.csd.

"Line 6 Effects," accessed April 5, 2013, http://line6.com/m9/models.html.

Smith, Julius O., *Physical Audio Signal Processing*, 2006, accessed April 5, 2013, http://www.dsprelated.com/dspbooks/pasp/.

Roads, Curtis, *The computer music tutorial*, Cambridge: The MIT Press, 1996.

—. *Microsound*, Cambridge: The MIT Press, 2001.

INTRODUCING CSOUND FOR LIVE

DR. RICHARD BOULANGER

Abstract

CsoundforLive brings virtually all of Csound into the production and performing framework of *Ableton Live*. Through *Max/MSP* and *MaxForLive*, we have been able to make Csound more productive, more intuitive, more playable, more spontaneous, more dynamic, and significantly increased the "user friendliness" and general "usability" of the program. This paper will show you how CsoundForLive makes all of this possible.

Introduction

Ableton Live is the most popular cross-platform music production and performance suite today. Some of its' key features include: Multitrack recording up to 32-bit/192 kHz; Nondestructive editing with unlimited undo; Powerful and creative MIDI sequencing of software and hardware instruments; Advanced warping and real-time time-stretching; Support for AIFF, WAV, MP3, Ogg Vorbis and FLAC files; A comprehensive selection of built-in audio and MIDI effects; Built-in instruments; VST and AU support; automatic plug-in delay compensation; REX file support plus built-in audio to MIDI slicing; Video import and export for scoring, video warping; Simple MIDI mapping plus instant mapping for selected hardware; Full ReWire support; runs as Slave or Master; Single-screen user interface for simple, creativity-focused operation; Multicore and multiprocessor support and much more. It is incredibly powerful, quite intuitive, and promotes great creative flow... when writing and when performing.

Another incredibly powerful and popular computer music program is Cycling '74's *Max/MSP/Jitter* toolkit that empowers musicians to program incredibly sophisticated interactive multimedia systems simply by patching together synthesis, processing, control, and interface modules – called "externals".

Several years ago, all of Csound5 was compiled as a Max/MSP "external" by Matt Ingalls. This work has been continued by Davis Pyon, and today it provides a means for Csounders to integrate the synthesis and signal processing power of Csound into the visually powerful and media-rich world of Max.

Over the past few years, Cycling '74 and Ableton have teamed up to make a version of Max that would run within Live - as and "instrument" or as an "effect". This means that all of Max/MSP, including *csound~* (the Csound5 external) is integrated into Live. CsoundForLive takes full advantage of the unique capabilities and strengths of Max, and Live, and now adds Csound – the world's most powerful synthesis and signal processing system into the mix. With this combination, one is able to hot-swap the most complex Csound instruments and effects in and out of an arrangement or composition on the fly. This is something Csound could never do (and still can't), but CsoundForLive can; the unique capabilities that result from Csound running in this environment makes a huge difference in the playability and the usability of Csound. Let's look at how these pieces all now fit together.

CSound for Live

CsoundForLive today consists of over 150 custom instrument and effect plugins for Ableton Live. These include FM, Granular, Additive, Subtractive, Physical Models, and other Classic Synths; and Samplers, Filters, Reverbs, Time-based Delays, and a unique set of Spectral Processors and Vocoders. One subset of this collection consists of a 12 amazing instruments from Csound masters: Joachim Heintz, Victor Lazzarini, Jacob Joaquin, Jean-Luc Sinclair, Rory Walsh, Hans Mikelson, Oeyvind Brandtsegg, and Iain McCurdy. It also includes a real-time conversion of all of my "classic" 1979 instruments from "Trapped in Convert". (Now anyone can literally "play" them – including me!)

Figure 1. "Additive10" a CsoundForLive adaptation of Iain McCurdy's Additive from his RealTime Collection with a graphical interface that features MIDI mappable drawbars for dynamically changing the strengths of the additive components.

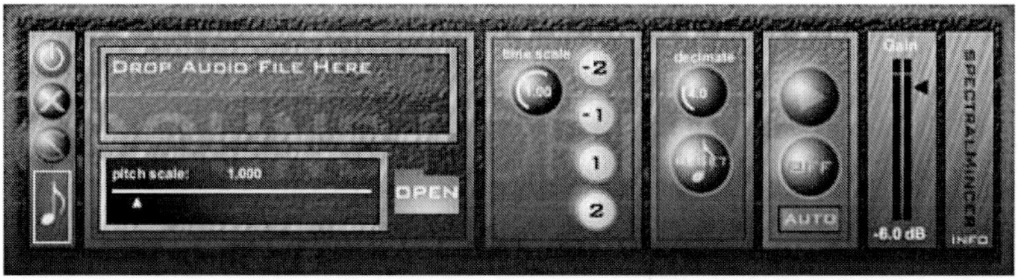

Figure 2. “SpectralMincer” is a CsoundForLive adaptation of one of Victor Lazzarini’s instruments from The Csound Manual. Notice how this GUI features the ability to “Drag and Drop” any audio sample for real-time spectral granularization.

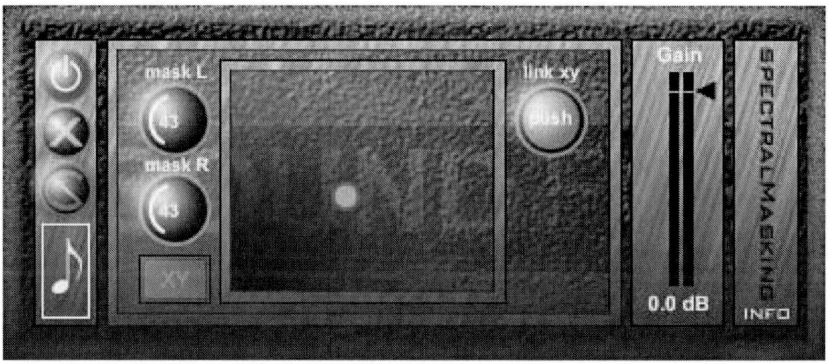

Figure 3. “SpectralMasking” is a CsoundForLive adaptation of one of Joachim Heintz’s instruments from CsoundQt. Notice how this interface features an automatable and MIDI mappable XY control.

Figure 4. “Blue” from Trapped in Convert – converted to a CsoundForLive plugin instrument. In addition to the MIDI mappable ADSR, notice that this “plugin synth” also features a built-in and automatable panning reverb.

Perhaps the most important of the free instruments that are offered with the CsoundForLive collection are the General Purpose *csd* players. These "plugins" allow the user to render any .csd within Ableton Live on the fly. One could very easily then do further processing on the audio as it is being rendered by stringing other plugins into the effects chain. You can hot-swap any CsoundForLive plugin. And, in addition, you can "hot-swap" any Csound piece that is being rendered by a CsoundForLive CSDplayer. And, you can simultaneously, on additional "tracks" render additional compositions.

Figure 5. Drop any .csd file on this "instrument" and it will render the audio in real-time. Note that one can assign a MIDI note to trigger the playback and pausing and re-starting of the rendering process.

It would now be quite possible (easy even) to get on stage with one laptop and do a quick collage combining Steven Yi's "On the Sensation of Tone" (and maybe add some tasteful *SpectralMincing* to the output), with John ffitch's "Different Canons", (and do some *SpectralMasking* on its output), every now and then gate in a little bit of my "Trapped in Convert", and, along the way, on another track, sprinkle in some sound effects and textures by playing and controlling the parameters of the *Blue* instrument from "Trapped in Convert". When it's time for the main "theme", well that's when Iain McCurdy's *Additive10* takes the stage. Working with Csound in this way, quickly mapping MIDI controller to virtually every parameter of this huge library of instruments and effects, and laying the foundation by rendering compositions from The Csound Catalog and The Csound Book and transforming these along the way by dropping other instruments into the chain of effects is a real game changer.

In addition to the collection that was designed and adapted by Colman O'Reilly and myself, a large assortment of very advanced and innovative instruments were developed by Berklee alumni Takahiko Tsuchiya, John Clements, Matthew Hines, and Csound master Giorgio Zucco. These instruments feature more complex interfaces and designs and more sophisticated and advanced synthesis and signal processing algorithms under the hood. Let's look at a few of them.

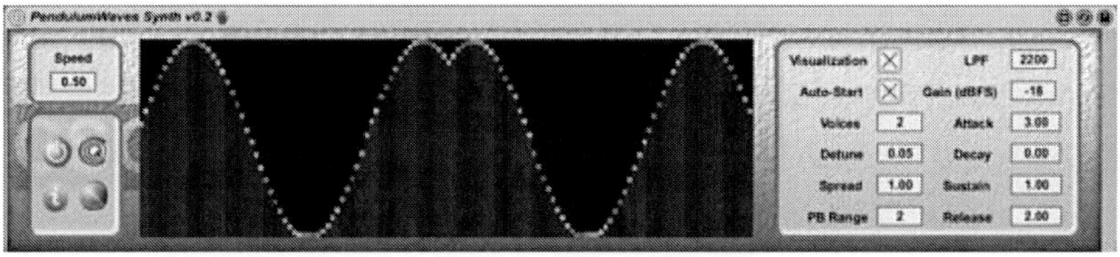

Figure 6. The beautiful "PendulumWaves" synthesizer by Takahiko Tsuchiya was inspired by video footage from Harvard University's "Natural Science Demonstrations". It is not only beautiful to listen to, as the rich and warm sounds evolve over time, but it is also beautiful to watch the ever-changing wave patterns that correspond to this evolving timbres.

Figure 7. Another by Takahiko Tsuchiya, this "DirectConvolution" synthesizer allows the user to draw the waveforms to the left, see the convolved result to the right, and hear them "dynamically intersect", change, and transform – as the user is drawing them on the screen.

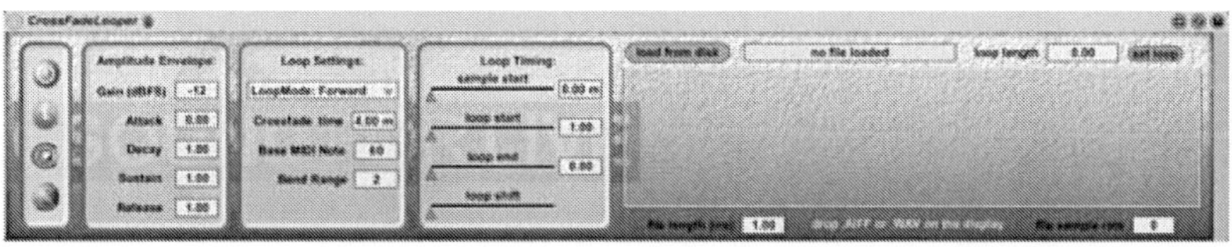

Figure 8. John Clement's "CrossFadeLooper" uses Csound's "flooper2" opcode and allows users to set the fade time between ends of the loop. Once defined, the forward, backward, or back-N-forth loop can be set and shifted using controllers as well as clip envelopes. Sample start and end times can be automated, and with linear interpolation, this sampler allows for some very dynamic looping.

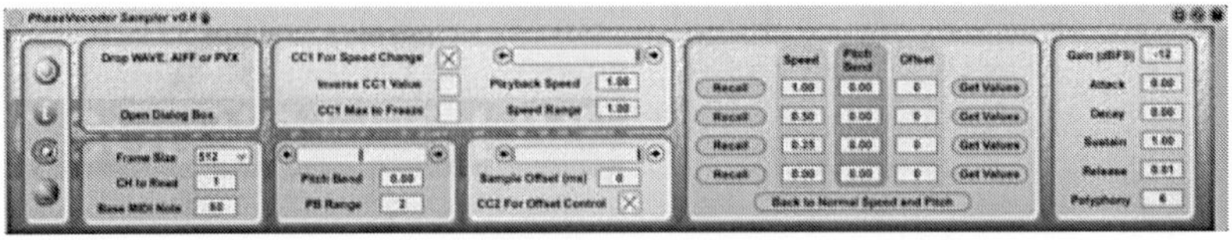

Figure 9. How about a PhaseVocoderSampler? One that does the analysis (extremely quickly) "offline" and then reloads in the .pvx file for the real-time resynthesis!

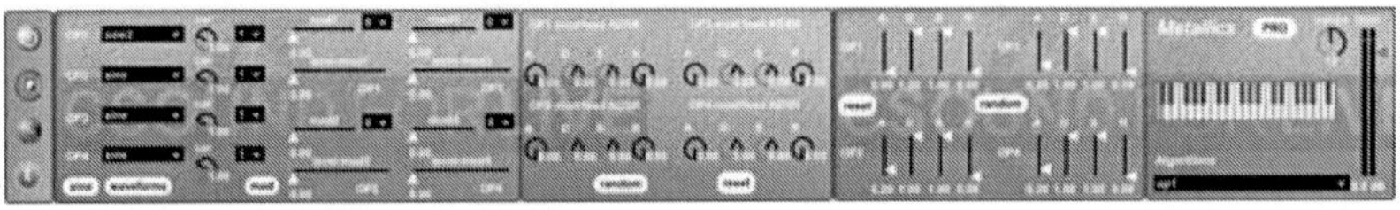

Figure 10. Giorgio Zucco has designed a 4-Operator FM synth modeled on the "classic" Yamaha TX81Z. This amazingly versatile instrument called "Metallics" also includes a button that randomizes all the parameters, leading to some amazingly surprising sounds.

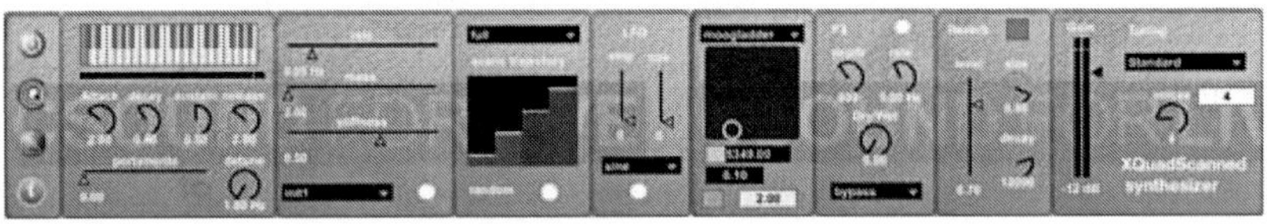

Figure 11. This "XQuadScanned" synthesis instrument by Giorgio Zucco uses Csound's scanned synthesis opcode and follows four pre-defined trajectories around a network of masses which can be unique or identical and can all be used simultaneously.

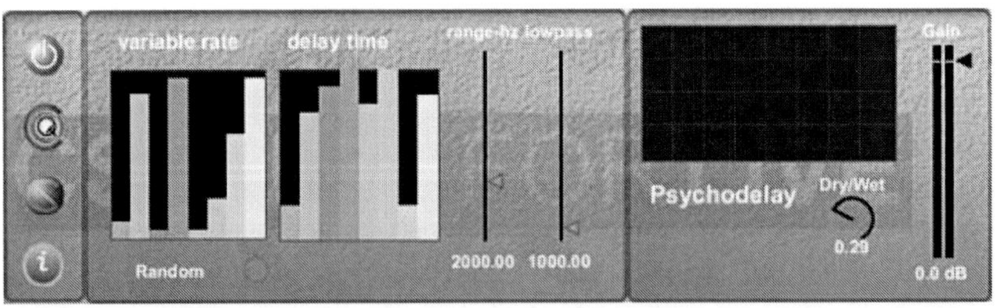

Figure 12. Built with Victor Lazzarini's PVS opcodes, (that allow for real-time "streaming"phase-vocoder-based analysis-resynthesis), Giorgio Zucco's "Psychodelay" creates a complex "cloud" of unique (multiple) delays in different frequency bands.

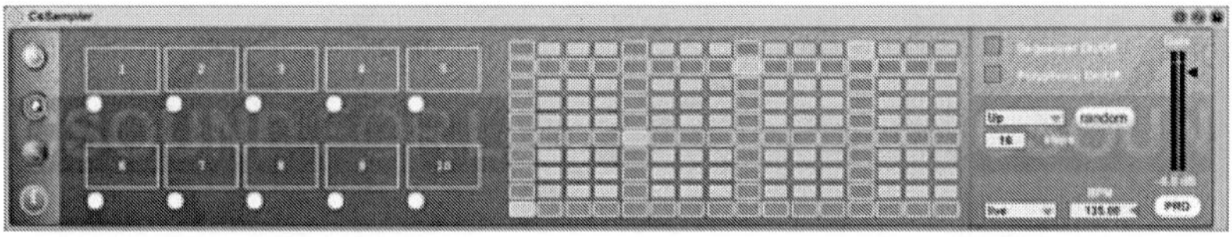

Figure 13. Giorgio Zucco has implemented a fully functional step sequencer that gives you the ability to quickly create clip driven sequences, each with their own internal FX chain. The 10 boxes on the left are "Drop Boxes" where you can drag in any non-mp3 audio clip. These boxes correspond with the rows on the grid to their right. By switching the "Sequencer on/off" (fully MIDI mappable of course), the sequencer will lock to your session's tempo and trigger your clips.

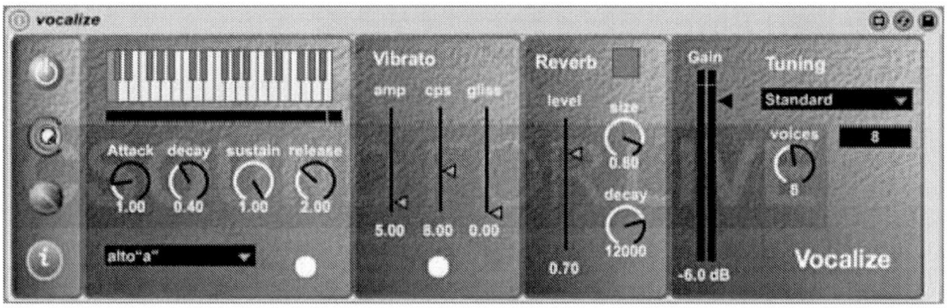

Figure 14. In the "Vocalize" plugin, Giorgio Zucco brings Csound's "fof2" opcode to CsoundForLive. This instrument recreates speech formants and, through the use of a drop down menu, lets you simulate the vowel sounds of a full range of singers – bass, tenor, counter tenor, alto, soprano. For precise control, vibrato has been given fully automatable controls, and Zucco has even added the gorgeous Csound reverb, "reverbsc." Of special note is the "Tuning" option with 14 different scales to choose from – (including my favorite – The Bohlen-Pierce) scale.

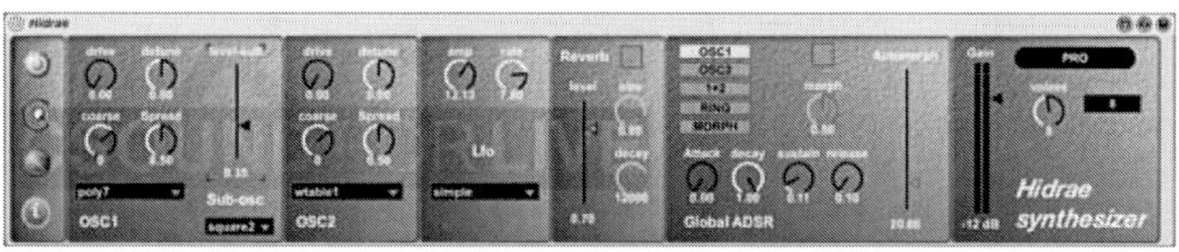

Figure 15. "Hidrae" is a multiple-oscillator morphing synthesizer. One choses from a menu of "oscillator" varieties – actually it is more like choosing between different "classic" synthesis techniques. Once chosen, one has the ability to "morph" between these sound engines – either by a value which the user sets, or automatically, by turning on the "auto morph" switch.

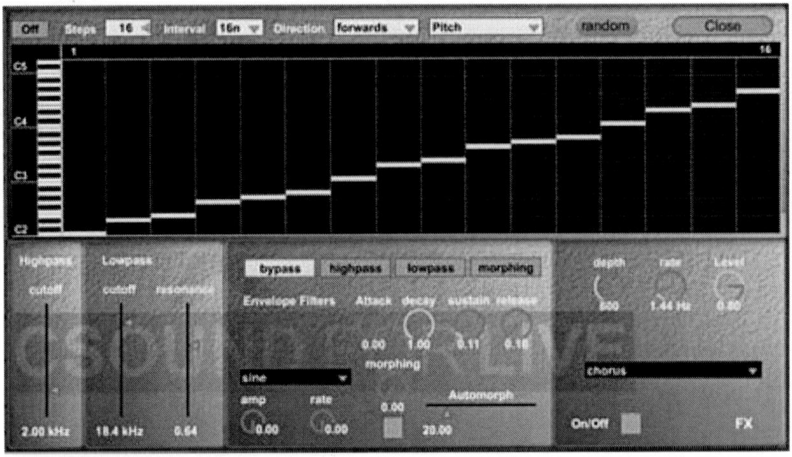

Figure16. Selecting the “PRO” panel in "Hidrae" opens an entire other layer of controls including a fully realized step sequencer with its own built in FX that sync perfectly to your Live set.

What I have attempted to show above is a small sampling of the instruments in the collection (just 15 of the 150+) that have been designed for Ableton Live in MaxForLive using the csound~ Max/MSP external. This combination allows "all" of Csound to be hosted and integrated into these rich and mature cross-platform production and development environments. As you can see, the range of controls, the range of displays, and the diversity of synthesis and signal processing is quite wide and yet, these tools are remarkable intuitive to work with. Incidentally, but by no means insignificantly, to take full advantage of these “plugins” no knowledge of Csound is required. One has only to know how to use Ableton Live. These work like the hundreds of plugins that come with the program. In fact, they work “with” the hundreds of plugins that come with the program. And so, it is nothing to take the output of Hydrae and follow it with Ableton Live’s multiband compressor to puff it up a bit here and there.

But what if you did know Csound, or wanted to learn Csound, or wanted to build CsoundForLive plugins of your own? In the next section we will see how simple this can be.

Under the Hood

Even though one doesn't have to know anything about Csound to use the CsoundForLive plugins, one of the most exciting and informative aspects of these plugins is the fact that Csound is right there running under the hood of every one of them. And in fact, if you click on a button in the interface of each instrument it will open the text file of the working .csd that can be studied, edited, and further refined.

Let's take a look. In figure 17 we see the .csd file for the Blue plugin shown in Figure 4. A push on the little note head button on the left of the panel will open up this file. Those "chnget" commands are receiving values from the knobs and sliders. You might recognize a few of them - att, dec, sus, rel, receive the setting from the ADSR sliders (they are abbreviations for attack, decay, sustain, and release).

```
<CsoundSynthesizer>
<CsInstruments>
sr          =           44100
ksmps       =           128
nchnls      =           2
0dbfs       =           1


garvb       init        0


            turnon      10
            turnon      22


;;;;;;;;;;;;;;;;;;;;;;;;;;;;;;;;;;;;;;;;;;;;;;;;;;;;;;;;;;
;; Global Controller Instrument
;;;;;;;;;;;;;;;;;;;;;;;;;;;;;;;;;;;;;;;;;;;;;;;;;;;;;;;;;;
instr 10
ktrig       metro       100
            if          (ktrig == 1) then


gkcenttmp chnget        "cents"
gksemi      chnget      "semitones"
gkvoices    chnget      "voices"


gkp8        chnget      "shaker"
gkp9        chnget      "harmrange"
gkp10       chnget      "arpspeed"
gkp3        chnget      "dur"


gkp7        chnget      "reverb"
gkpan       chnget      "revpan"


gkatt       chnget      "att"
gkdec       chnget      "dec"
```

```
gksus     chnget     "sus"
gkrel     chnget     "rel"


gkspread  chnget     "spread"
gkdetune  chnget     "detune"


          endif
endin


;;;;;;;;;;;;;;;;;;;;;;;;;;;;;;;;;;;;;;;;;;;;;;;;;;;;;;;;;;
;; Voice "Stealing" Instrument
;;;;;;;;;;;;;;;;;;;;;;;;;;;;;;;;;;;;;;;;;;;;;;;;;;;;;;;;;;
instr 22
kinstr    init 1
kactive   active     kinstr
if        kactive    > gkvoices then
          turnoff2   kinstr, 1, 0
endif
endin


;;;;;;;;;;;;;;;;;;;;;;;;;;;;;;;;;;;;;;;;;;;;;;;;;;;;;;;;;;
;; Blue - From Trapped in Convert
;;;;;;;;;;;;;;;;;;;;;;;;;;;;;;;;;;;;;;;;;;;;;;;;;;;;;;;;;;
instr     1
;Tuning Block:
gkbend    pchbend    0, 2
imidinn   notnum
kcent     =          gkcenttmp * 0.01
kfrq      =          cpsmidinn(imidinn + gksemi + kcent + gkbend)
kfrq2     =          cpsmidinn(imidinn + gksemi + kcent + gkdetune +
gkbend)
iamp      ampmidi    1
iamp      = iamp *  .5


k1        randi     1, 30
k2        linseg    0, i(gkp3) * .5, 1, i(gkp3) * .5, 0
k3        linseg    .005, i(gkp3) * .71, .015, i(gkp3) * .29, .01
k4        oscil     k2, gkp8, 1, .2
k5        =         k4 + 2


ksweep    linseg    i(gkp9), i(gkp3) * i(gkp10), 1, i(gkp3) * (i(gkp3)
- (i(gkp3) * i(gkp10))), 1
kenv      madsr     i(gkatt), i(gkdec), i(gksus), i(gkrel)


aout1     gbuzz     kenv*iamp, kfrq + k3, k5, ksweep, k1, 15
aout2     gbuzz     kenv*iamp, kfrq2 + k3, k5, ksweep, k1, 15


;;Spread Section:
aoutL     =         ((aout1 * gkspread) + (aout2 * (1 - gkspread))) *.5
aoutR     =         ((aout1 * (1-gkspread)) + (aout2 * gkspread))   *.5



          outs      aoutL, aoutR
```

```
amix      =         (aoutL + aoutR)* .5
garvb     =         garvb + (amix * gkp7)
endin


instr     99
k1        oscil     .5, gkpan, 1
k2        =         .5 + k1
k3        =         1 - k2
asig      reverb    garvb, 2.1


asig      dcblock2  asig
          outs      asig * k2*0.25, (asig * k3) * (-1) * 0.25
garvb     =         0
endin

</CsInstruments>


<CsScore>
;=====================================================;
; p6=amp, p7=rvbsnd, p8=lfofrq, p9=num of harmonics, p10=sweeprate
;=====================================================;
; =====================;
; - FUNCTIONS
;=====================;
f1   0  8192  10   1
f15  0  8192  9    1   1   90
i99  0   600000
</CsScore>


</CsoundSynthesizer>
```

Figure17. The score and orchestra for "Blue" from "Trapped in Convert" converted to work with csound~ and MaxForLive.

Not only can you click on a button to edit the Csound instrument, but you can also click on a button and open up the MaxForLive patch.

In Figure 18, you can see how all the controllers in the interface are being sent to Csound with a "s ---toCsound~" external (a global send), and that they are all received and connected to the csound~ object with the "r ---toCsound~" (a global receive) external. If you read some of the words on the blue buttons, you can see that they correspond to the channel names in the .csd. That's how the GUI "connects" and "speaks" to Csound through the interface. Everything here is open to study, ready to modify, all to facilitate your "learning" of Csound by using it at a variety of levels within the same project. Perhaps this will make it possible for you to learn some new algorithms or just sing a new Csong.

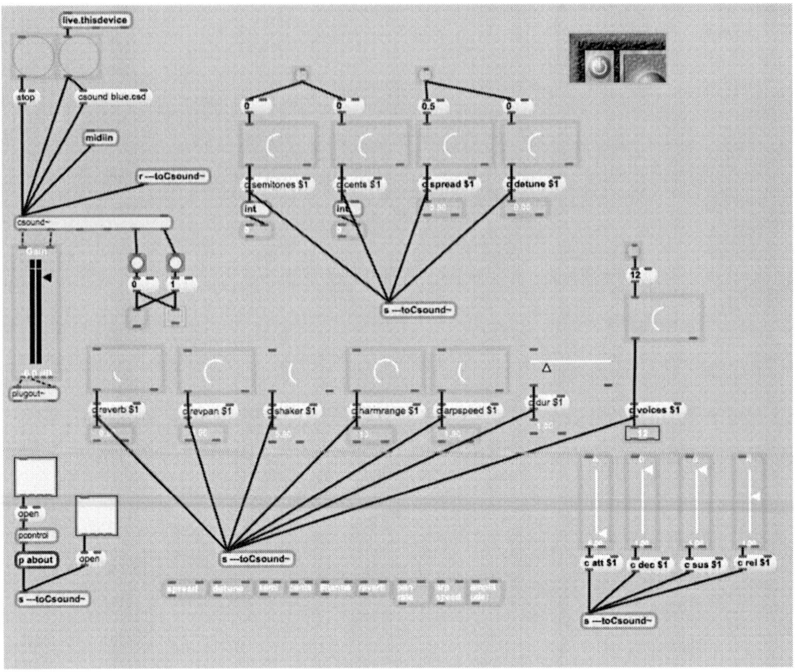

Figure 18. The MaxForLive patch for "Blue". Notice that the .csd in Figure 17 is loaded into the "csound~" external with the command "csound blue.csd" which is remarkably like the command that we would type at the commandline of the Terminal to have Csound render the file there.

Conclusion

There are great tutorials and books on Max/MSP; the documentation embedded right into the program is fabulous. There are excellent tutorials on programming MaxForLive, some of them right in the Max program and some in the Live program. There are many fantastic videos online teaching every aspect of working with Ableton Live; plus, the built-in tutorials that with the program are great. There are some pretty good books on Csound too. All of these will help you learn to put together the pieces should you be interested in pulling these worlds together and mainstreaming some of your work - adapting it to work seamlessly within a powerful and versatile Digital Audio Workstation such at Ableton Live.

The CsoundForLive project began with initial development and composition work done my students Jinku Kim and Enrico de Trizio - it was a “bonus”, “extra-credit” assignment in my Max/MSP class. As they graduated and moved on from Berklee, their work was picked up and expanded on over the following two semesters by my student Colman O'Reilly (who went on to do a preliminary version of the project as his undergraduate thesis in Electronic Production and Design – I was his faculty advisor). After he graduated, Colman and I continued to expand the project and to develop the algorithms and interfaces. Together we turned a homework assignment into a major offering that has a broad appeal and opens the world of Csound to so many new users. CsoundForLive makes Csound a welcome addition to many artistic communities. This is how Audivation was born.

Today, the project continues to thrive; the collection continues to grow; and more "commercial" musicians, producers, composers, players, and DJs are using Csound as a part of their creative work – in the studio, in the club, and on the concert stage. Hopefully you will too. Check out the links below; reward yourself with the time you need to figure it all out; I am sure that you will find a way to use it in your creative work, and with your students too.

My goal was to make it easier for my students and for me to play with, and to improvise with… Csound. CsoundForLive makes it possible. All my students use this program now and Csound is finding its way not only into much of their homework for “my” classes, but also into the assignments that they are doing for their other classes and professors. Hopefully CsoundForLive will make Csound more dynamic, fluid, spontaneous and fun for you, your children, and your students.

References

"Ableton Live," accessed December 21, 2012, https://www.ableton.com.

Boulanger, Richard, *The Csound Book*, edited by R. Boulanger. Cambridge: The MIT Press, 2000.

"Csound~," accessed April 5, 2013, http://davixology.com/csound~.html.

"Csounds.com," accessed April 5, 2013, http://www.csounds.com.

"CsoundForLive.com," accessed April 5, 2013, http://www.csoundforlive.com/.

"Csounds.com," accessed April 5, 2013, http://www.csounds.com.

Cipriani, A., Giri, M., 2009. *Electronic Music And Sound Design: Theory and Practice with Max/MSP - Vol. 1.* Contemponet s.a.s. Rome - Italy

"The CsoundForLive Store," accessed December 21, 2012, http://store.kagi.com/cgi-bin/store.cgi?storeID=6FJCL_LIVE&&.

"The Csound Catalog," accessed December 21, 2012, http://www.csounds.com/shop/csound-catalog.

"Max/MSP," accessed April 5, 2013, http://cycling74.com/products/max/

"MaxForLive," accessed April 5, 2013, http://cycling74.com/products/maxforlive/

COMPOSING WITH BLUE

STEVEN YI

Abstract

I gave a workshop entitled "Composing with Blue" at the 1st International Csound Conference. This article discusses the workshop's goals, the topics I covered, and my overall impressions of the event.

Introduction

This article summarizes a live workshop I gave at the 1st International Csound Conference. I designed the original workshop as an introductory course for Blue[1], a music composition environment for Csound. The audience was expected to have a basic understanding of Csound. Participants were requested to bring laptops to work through examples together with me; I encouraged them to ask questions at any time.

Fundamentals

Understanding Blue's Design and Connection to Csound

Blue is a graphical computer music environment for composition. It is written in Java, and uses Csound as its audio engine. From a high-level view of Blue, Blue's graphical user interface provides a set of tools, and the user decides which of those tools to use. Blue's design allows users to access most of the standard Csound practices and features, and does not try to hide them. Instead, while allowing access to the features and techniques of programming a Csound project, Blue seeks to add additional layers of tools that are available to address possible workflow inefficiencies in working with Csound alone.

---

[1] http://blue.kunstmusik.com

Blue provides tools and abstractions for the user, but does not force the user to use them. This allows a user to do things like use the orchestra manager but skip the score timeline in favor of using a handwritten global score, or vice versa. Also, this allows alternate forms of tools to co-exist in Blue: if a developer wants to create a separate manager for instruments or alternate means to handle signal graph connections, it is possible to build plug-ins to Blue and provide options for the user. Ultimately, the user is in control of what tools to use based on what is best for them and their own individual composition workflow.

Because Blue exposes and adds to Csound, it is important to understand the relationship between the two in terms of their abstractions. In Csound, the primary concepts for organizing and designing a project include:

- ORC
    - Global Variables
    - Instruments
    - User-Defined Opcodes
    - Instr 0 Code
    - Signal Channels
- SCO
    - i-statements (notes)
    - f-statements (function tables)

These abstractions may seem simple but allow for a large variety of musical concepts and ideas to be implemented. The idea of an orchestra/score dichotomy may seem at first to be ingrained with a specific view of music. However, it does not actually limit many other musical ideas to be formed upon them that are not usually associated with an idea of an *orchestra* and *score*. If the ideas are instead generalized into sound generators/processors and events, the possibilities of what can be built upon them may be clearer.

The tools in Blue are built upon precisely these Csound abstractions. In general, the user interacts with Blue, and Blue interacts with Csound. To render audio with Blue, Blue will first generate a CSD file to run with Csound and then may interact with a running instance of Csound (i.e. live updating of values in Csound according to widget modifications). As of the time of the workshop, most users who work with Blue will be fluent in the use of Csound. They will be aware of Csound's abstractions as well as how Blue builds upon them. However, the design of the program allows for a future where there may be users who could create music using only

Blue tools without any understanding of Csound. It will always be the case, though, that users will be able to access and use Csound practices within Blue, so users are encouraged to be familiar with Csound when working with Blue.

Introduction to the Software Environment

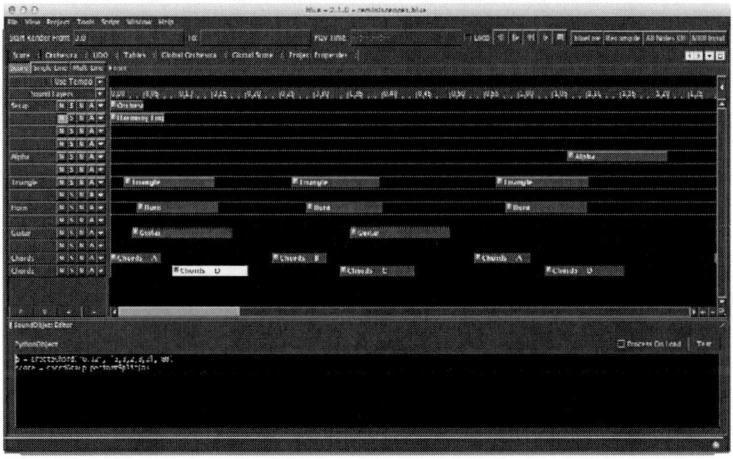

Figure 1. Blue application frame showing Score window and SoundObject Editor window docked into bottom side.

Blue is composed of various main editor tabs for the program (Score, Orchestra, Project Settings, etc.), as well as other supporting tabs. Each component within a tab is called a window. Windows can be opened from the Window menu or by keyboard shortcut. The window system in Blue allows reorganizing the windows by moving them between window groups (sets of tabs), docking and undocking windows into the sides, making window groups sliding, as well as other operations on windows.

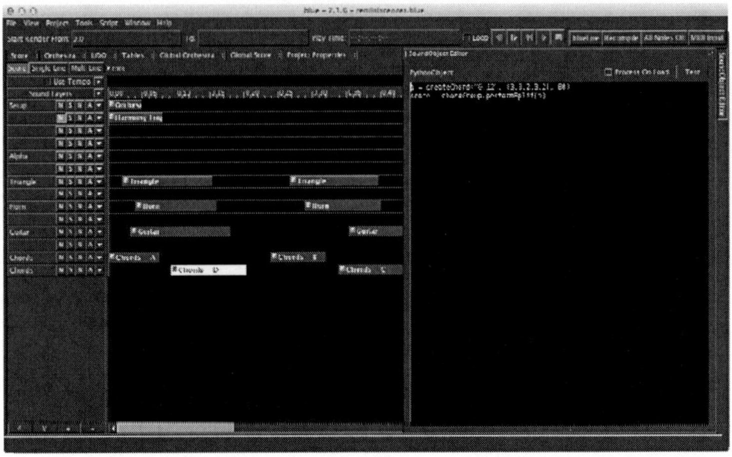

Figure 2. Blue application frame showing SoundObject Editor window docked into right side and made sliding to open above other windows.

Once familiar with the physical layout of the environment, users should look at the Program Options (available from Preferences menu option on Mac OSX, or from the Tools->Options menu on all other platforms). This dialog contains a number of different global settings for configuring the application, including settings to use when rendering in real-time as well as rendering to disk. Blue comes preconfigured with popular settings used by Csound installations on various platforms. Users should consult the Blue manual for further information regarding program settings.

Developing Instruments

From Csound to Blue

A good first exercise to learning Blue is to take a Csound CSD and convert it to use Blue's features. Initially, I recommend using a simple CSD and focussing on the instruments first. Once the user understands Blue's Orchestra Manager and Instrument system, it will be easier to move forward with learning the BlueLive and Score systems for composing. Also, focusing first on Blue's Orchestra system provides an entry point into understanding Blue's tool design and how to integrate them with a previous Csound-only workflow: the user will start to "think in Blue".

One common issue in working with Csound is managing dependencies when reusing instruments. Csound instruments may depend on User-Defined Opcodes (UDO) and f-tables to operate. If you copy an instrument into a new project without the dependencies, it will fail to run. If you copy the UDO and f-tables, you then have to be careful about name clashes and number clashes if you are using other instruments and their dependencies. If an instrument is complex, or very long in terms of lines of code, it is easy to make mistakes when trying to reuse the instrument. While some of these problems are bigger than others, having to deal with them does take time away from other work.

Blue's Orchestra Manager and Instrument system is designed to ease such issues. Converting Csound instruments into Blue GenericInstruments allows them to be easily copied and pasted into new projects. Converting the UDO from text into a Blue UDO object allows it to be packaged directly with the instrument itself. This means when the instrument is copied into a new project, the UDO is already there. The user does not have to worry about name clashes, since Blue automatically renames UDO's and their use in code. Similar features and practices exist for packaging f-tables with instruments.

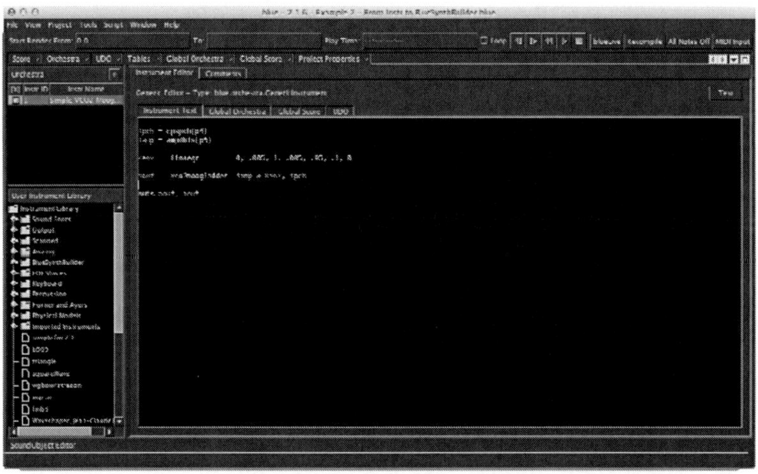

Figure 3. GenericInstrument shown in Orchestra window. The instrument is listed in the upper-left list, and the instrument's editor is shown on the right. The bottom-left shows the application User Instrument Library.

From GenericInstrument to BlueSynthBuilder

The design of Blue's Instrument system does more than ease reuse; it also allows instruments to provide new features and capabilities. I encourage users to learn the BlueSynthBuilder instrument after they have learned the GenericInstrument. BlueSynthBuilder (BSB) builds upon the same system as the GenericInstrument, but adds a few key features: a graphical user interface for modifying values in real-time, a presets system for storing snapshots of widget values, as well as an always-on instrument code section. Also, the widgets used in BSB are "automatable"—they can be automated over time on the score timeline.

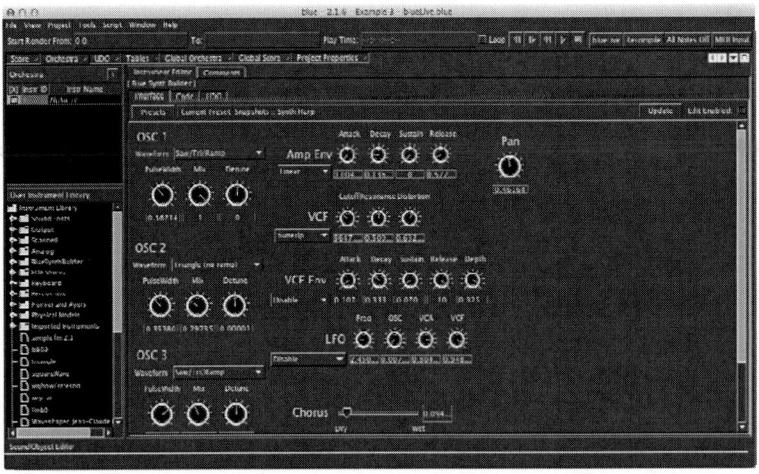

Figure 4. Example BlueSynthBuilder instrument.

After completing the first exercise, a good next step is to convert a GenericInstrument into a BSB instrument. The process involves identifying hard-coded variables within the original instrument, adding widgets for each variable then replacing the variables in the instrument code with the BSB widgets' special variable tags. These steps illustrate a common workflow in Blue: starting with an initial instrument design, then testing, and finally exploring the design by using widgets for displaying and modifying values.

Using BSB brings up more general questions of how tools in Blue might help improve the workflow for users who are familiar with Csound-only practices. For example, with BlueSynthBuilder, one can add a knob for controlling a filter's cutoff frequency as a project renders in real-time. This can improve workflow compared to using a text-only instrument, which requires editing the text and re-rendering to explore a parameter's space. There are some situations where using text alone may be the quickest and most efficient way to work, and others where using a hybrid approach may be more efficient. It is up to the user to choose the tools that best fit their needs.

Another unique feature of BSB instrument design is the "always-on" instrument code section that is encapsulated with the Blue instrument. This feature allows users to write instrument code for continuous processing. Before outputting the end signal, instruments in commercial instrument designs (hardware or software) often have parts of their signal graph that are operated on a per-note instance level, and other parts which then process the combined signals of the notes at a per-instrument level. Examples of always-on code include effects processing such as reverb, delays, filtering and flangers.

Using an always-on block that processes the sum of per-note signals optimizes the amount of processing. Modifying instrument design to use always-on code can enable users to imitate the design of something like a stringed instrument, where a string might be akin to the per-note sound generating block of code, and the resonant body might be akin to the always-on processing code that processes the sound generated by the strings.

BlueLive: Playing Instruments Live

Sketching Music and Using MIDI Input

After learning how to design and build instruments in Blue, users can then explore how to play them. Within Blue, instruments can be played live or directed by a pre-composed score. In this section, we'll look at BlueLive: Blue's tool for real-time instrument performance.

Using the BlueLive tool, users can use either SoundObjects (a score generating object within Blue), the Blue Virtual keyboard, or a MIDI keyboard to play instruments live. When BlueLive is turned on, the project is compiled and run without any score generated from the timeline. In this mode, the instruments and mixer system are all run in real-time and await live input from the user. Using the Virtual Keyboard and MIDI input allows users to play instruments live and this can be useful for experimenting with designing presets as well as general improvisation. Using the SoundObject system with BlueLive is useful for sketching ideas, performing them, and getting immediate feedback. The SoundObjects can later be copied into the Score system for further musical development.

By working with instruments live, users can work more quickly and dynamically than using score text alone and re-rendering projects. At the time of the workshop, the primary foci of BlueLive's design were music sketching and instrument parameter exploration. Its design was limited; it was not a fully featured tool for live performance. Since the workshop, I have continued to develop BlueLive's design. I would like to make BlueLive into a tool that can address requirements for real-time performance and interactive composition, and am currently completing the design of new features in BlueLive to fulfill those requirements.

Score: Composing in Time

The Score system in Blue provides a graphical timeline for composing music in time. The Score in Blue is divided up into a set of layers called SoundLayers, each of which contain SoundObjects (objects that can generate Csound score text). Each SoundLayer can be muted and/or soloed, have automations for widget parameters overlaid for editing, and more.

SoundObjects

The Score system is primarily built upon the concept of SoundObjects: objects that encapsulate a *sonic idea*, such as a note, a phrase, or a gesture. While SoundObjects can be developed to generate instrument code, they are primarily used for generating Csound score text. SoundObjects are plug-ins in Blue, and there are a number of different types. Some are more text-based, such as the GenericScore (uses standard Csound score text) or the PythonObject (uses Python code for generating Csound score), while others are more graphical, such as the PianoRoll and Pattern objects.

I generally categorize SoundObjects into two different types of tools: *Common Practice* tools and *Uncommon Practice* tools. As I define them, these categories are similar to Common Practice and Modern practices in notated music.

In music composition software, a number of software representations of music, such as pattern editors, piano rolls, and audio waveforms, have become similar in their function to what I call Common Practice notation, which uses musical symbols that are widely taught and have a documented history of use. These representations may be found in many different software programs. Users familiar with a tool's form in one program can usually understand the general aspects of the tool as it is implemented in another. There are also many uncommon representations and user interfaces in music software. These unique tools provide ways to create and visualize music that are different from common practice tools. With these Uncommon Practice tools, it is generally understood that reading a manual is required to operate the software, just as reading the definitions of modern notation symbols is necessary to understand their meaning in modern scores.

I have found these categories to be useful as guides when building Blue. It is my desire that common practice tools be available in Blue as well as uncommon ones. It is important for me that the program supports ways that people are used to thinking about music with computer music software, while providing options to explore non-traditional musical ideas.

NoteProcessors

The other major component to the Score system is NoteProcessors. NoteProcessors are objects that can perform additional processing of notes. They can operate on individual SoundObjects, on SoundLayers, or on an entire Score. NoteProcessors are also a plug-in type for Blue, and there are a variety of types for doing different things.

For example, an AddProcessor can be used to add a constant value to p-field 4 for all notes generated by a SoundObject. Another example is using a PchAddProcessor to transpose down all p-field 5 values by 2 steps. NoteProcessors are executed after a SoundObject, SoundLayer, or Score generate their notes, and multiple NoteProcessors can be applied to any of these object types. By using NoteProcessors, users can apply processing to a block of score to achieve things like transposition, crescendos, and humanization of rhythms (i.e., slight randomization of note start times and durations).

SoundObject Library

In addition to working directly with SoundObjects, users can store objects in the SoundObject Library for later reference. Users can make a direct copy of a library object and paste it back into the Score as a unique SoundObject, or instead use "instance copy" and paste Instance objects into the Score. An Instance object can be placed anywhere on a timeline and will render like any other SoundObject, but will generate notes using the SoundObjectLibrary SoundObject that it points to.

If multiple Instances are created, each will generate the same basic score. The unique properties of each instance (start time/duration) will then be applied, as well as their set of NoteProcessors. This enables motivic development, where a single musical idea (the SoundObjectLibrary original) is used in multiple places (the individual Instance objects) and transformed. One benefit of using the SoundObjectLibrary is that if the original SoundObject in the library is modified, changes in the generated score are reflected in all Instances on the timeline. This can be useful if the user wants to work on a piece's structure but is not quite ready to work on the form's individual parts.

Mixer, Effects, and Automation

Blue's graphical mixer system allows signals generated by instruments to be mixed together and further processed by Blue Effects. The GUI follows a paradigm commonly found in music sequencers and digital audio workstations. The mixer UI is divided into channels, sub-channels, and the master channel. Each channel has a fader for applying level adjustments to the channel's signal, as well as bins pre- and post-fader for adding effects. Effects can be created on the mixer, or added from the Effects Library.

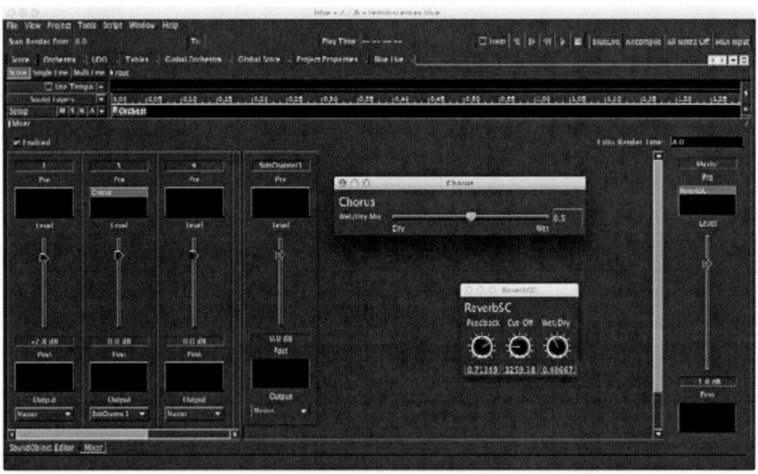

Figure 5. Mixer docked into bottom in sliding mode. Interfaces for Chorus and Reverb effects are shown.

To get a signal from an instrument to the mixer, Blue requires the instrument to use a special **blueMixerOut** pseudo-opcode within the generated Csound instrument code. Once the instrument signals are routed into the mixer, the user is able to further process the signal using Blue Effects.

Effects in Blue use the same GUI editor and code system as BlueSynthBuilder, so the skills and techniques for building graphical instruments transfer to building Effects. Effects can be created and edited when working with the mixer. Pre-created effects can also be added from the Effects Library, which is a tool for storing and organizing effects. Effects can be created in the library as well as copied into the library from a project's mixer. This allows users to easily take an effect from one project, import it into the Effects Library, and then copy it into a new project by selecting it from a popup menu in the mixer user interface.

The signal routing starts from instruments and goes into mixer channels assigned per-instrument. From those channels, signals can then go to either sub-channels or the master channel. Sub-channels themselves can route to other sub-channels (though no feedback is allowed by Blue); ultimately, all signals must end up routing to the master channel. In addition to the standard routing, users can add Sends to the effects bins of a channel and route a separate signal to either a sub-channel or the master channel. This may be useful to send a dry signal as well as an effects-processed signal from a single channel.

The Mixer and Effects work together with the Instrument system to provide an easy-to-modify signal graph in Blue. Users can modify the values of widgets by manipulating them in real-time, but they can also draw automation curves to compose value changes over time. In Blue, most widgets in BlueSynthBuilder and Effects can have automation enabled. Faders in the Mixer can also be automated.

Editing automation is done in the Score timeline. This is done by first selecting a parameter for automation from the SoundLayer's “A” button's popup menu, then selecting the Single Line mode in the Score for editing individual line values. Using Multi-Line mode in the score allows the user to select blocks of SoundObjects and automations and move them as a whole to other parts of the Score.

Other Features

In closing, I will briefly mention two of Blue's other features. The first is blueShare, an online repository for sharing effects and instruments that is accessible both by via the web[2] and directly within Blue. This allows users to directly upload an instrument or effect from the application's Instrument and Effects Library; they can also import directly into those libraries from blueShare.

The second feature is that Blue is designed as *Long-Term Software*, which is to say that it, and its project files can be used long into the future. I have taken the following steps to support this goal:

- Using human-readable XML as the file storage format for Blue
- Developing open-source software using open-source technologies
- Minimizing dependencies for projects

Both the Blue program and project format is designed with backwards compatibility in mind. It is my primary goal that music projects created in Blue today can be opened, used, and referenced in the future. I hope that the program will continue to serve its users for a long time to come.

Conclusion

This workshop was intended as an introductory course for Blue. In my opinion, the format for the workshop—interaction with the audience as its members worked through exercises—worked well. Overall, I think the workshop successfully introduced attendees to Blue. I hope they walked away with both knowledge of Blue's design and experience in how to use it. I would like to thank all of the organizers of the conference as well as the attendees for their participation and contributions to the discussions.

[2] The items available from blueShare are browsable online from the Blue home page: http://blue.kunstmusik.com

THE UDO DATABASE

STEVEN YI AND JOACHIM HEINTZ

A User Defined Opcode (UDO) is the way for a Csound user to write his own extensions to Csound without leaving the Csound language, similar to a collection of „abstractions“ in PD/Max, or a „library“ of functions or classes in any given programming language.

Steven, you are the maintainer of the UDO database at csounds.com. When did you start it, and why?

Steven Yi: I don't remember exactly when, but I think it was 2004 or 2005 when I created the UDO database. I felt there was a need for a place to collect users' UDOs so that as a community we could share our work and learn from each other, as well as help promote the reusing of code. Before UDOs were available in Csound, the only way to create new opcodes was by coding in C or C++. The way most people did any kind of reuse of code was with macros and #includes, but they have some problems in reusability outside of the original project due to possible name clashes. UDOs (and the sub-instruments functionality it was based on) solved a problem of reusability by encapsulation, and has now become a common tool in Csound projects.

How can people contribute to the database?

S.Y.: As it is now, anyone is free to view and download entries from the database. To make a contribution, one needs to register for an account, which is free to do so. After registering and logging in, the user will see an

"Add Opcode" option for creating new entries. For entries that they contributed, they will also see links for editing and removing those.

For adding or editing entries, there are pre-defined fields. These fields correspond mostly with those found in the Csound Manual. Originally, the intent was that the UDO database would look and feel like the HTML version of the Csound Manual, except that it would have the additional field for the UDO code. This was to encourage users, who make contributions, to document their work with the same format as that found in the manual. Also, it was done to create a familiar feel, so that users who have read through the manual could expect the same relevant information for a UDO in the UDO database page.

Are you happy with the number and quality of contributions? Has the UDO database become what you hoped it would?

S.Y.: On the one hand, I'm very happy for every contribution made. I have found a number of the contributed UDOs to be very helpful in my personal work, so in that regard I think it succeeds. On the other hand, I would love to see more people involved with making contributions to the database, as well as helping to make it more useful to everyone with suggestions. I'm always open to hearing new ideas on ways to move forward!

So Joachim, as a contributor to the UDO Database, what are your thoughts on it? What role do you see it having for the community and what have been your experiences of using it?

Joachim Heintz: Let me go back a little into my personal history with Csound to answer these questions. I started to learn Csound in 1995 and my first impression was: it's good for processing sound, but it has a very restricted programming language. So I wrote very simple instruments and all the processes were done with another program such as Lisp which could produce long and complex score files. The more I learned about Csound, however, the more I realised what was actually possible using Csound's (orchestra) language. Sometimes it is not very elegant, sometimes it is, but usually you will have to write your own higher level functions, because the Csound opcodes are usually low-level. More and more I ended up writing UDOs because they give me the ability to write complex instruments in Csound with clean and readable code.

Based on this experience, the UDO database is an extremely important tool for sharing parts of your own library which might be of wider interest to the Csound community. My impression is that the database also offers support to Csound's developers. Not everything users wish for must be coded, as opcodes, in C. Many features can be coded by users like me as UDOs, and these can then be accessible to anyone in a well documented manner. It seems that UDOs are being considered more and more as part of Csound.

Do you have thoughts on how the database could be improved?

J.H.: One issue is the lack of a version control system. I have written many UDOs to which I have later added or removed some parameters. It would be nice to have the different versions of a UDO on the database so that you can revert to an earlier version. I recently started a git repository for my own UDOs to have a better workflow. Certainly git is much too complicated for the UDO database. I don't know whether there is another choice.

Quality control is another issue. We have test suites in the core Csound code but there are no general tests at all for UDOs. It is all up to the authors and it is rare that anyone reports a bug. I think we should have some people who test and check the examples.

Perhaps this group could also assist in finding good names for UDOs. Certainly the final decision should remain with the author/contributor, but some discussions about conventions may help to avoid completely misleading names.

Finally, if the database grows more and more—which we all hope—we might need a greater variety of categories for the UDOs. Most of the UDOs I have contributed are located under „Utilities“, but many of them do very different things: recording to a buffer, converting MIDI to frequency, working with strings as arrays, printing tables etc. If we had good sub-groupings, the user could more easily find what he is looking for, and the contributors could perhaps be inspired to write something which is not yet there.

Steven, as the maintainer, what are your thoughts about this?

S.Y.: Versioning and your other ideas sound very good. I have had the thought in the past that perhaps we should have something like a package manager for UDOs such that users could create packages for the server and they could also use a command line tool for downloading packages. Packages could have versions and other things such as example test CSDs and documentation. I wonder then if we could even extend this further to support binary dependencies such as WAV or AIFF files, or impulse responses. This might be something that the UDO repository could eventually become.

Interview: Alex Hofmann

EDUCATION

USER-DEVELOPER ROUND TABLE II: LEARNING AND TEACHING CSOUND

IAIN MCCURDY

Introduction

This chapter reports on the second round table discussion that took place during the Csound Conference. The over-arching theme was the relationship between Csound's users and its developers. The session was chaired by Dr. Richard Boulanger and the panel consisted of Andrés Cabrera, Victor Lazzarini, Menno Knevel, Steven Yi, Michael Gogins, Peiman Khosravi, Rory Walsh, Iain McCurdy, Joachim Heintz and Øyvind Brandtsegg.

The chair opened this session of discussions by describing his core motivation as being to share Csound with as many users as possible. This is certainly supported by his recent work in opening Csound up to users of Ableton Live by his CsoundForLive project.

Is There Enough Help Available for Those Wishing to Learn Csound?

The primary gateways to learning Csound, such as online list discussions, topical forums and tutorials, were addressed by tireless editor of the Csound Reference Manual examples, Menno Knevel, and conference organiser Joachim Heintz. There are many discussion lists covering different aspects of Csound—most of Csound's front-ends have their own discussion lists—but the main ones are the general discussion list convened by Bath University (and archived by nabble.com) and the similarly hosted developers list. Forums on a variety of topics are hosted on Csound's main website, www.csounds.com. Forums, in contrast to discussion lists, typically address more focused aspects of the software such as "getting started" or "instrument sharing", and interaction with the forum normally takes place within the browser rather than via email. There is no shortage of tutorials for new Csound users (despite occasional grumbles on the discussion list!) but users sometimes have difficulty locating them. As always csounds.com is a good starting point; from there, beginners normally find their way to Richard Boulanger's set of "Toots" tutorials. Whilst the Csound Reference Manual offers little in the way of formal tutorials, the educative value of the examples provided for each opcode is improving constantly. Longtime Csound users notable for their contributions of tutorials or tutorial-leaning example instruments include Jacob Joaquin (The Csound Blog http://codehop.com/), Giorgio Zucco and Iain McCurdy whose "Realtime Collection" is introduced in another chapter in this publication.

Menno Knevel introduced himself as a Csound enthusiast, not a teacher, but someone coming from a background of experimenting with tape recorders for whom the open plan structure of Csound offered similar freedoms. Menno has been single handedly rewriting the examples provided for every opcode in the Csound Reference (and created examples for those that previously lacked them). Menno identified that many of the older examples contained in the manual did little more than demonstrate that the opcode worked but has successfully proved the case for examples that exemplify and educate. Coming very much from the user side of the debate, Menno feels that there is still a sense of separation between the user and the developer. He proposed that greater use be made of the Csound IRC channel (John ffitch pointed out that the channel is more often than not, completely unattended) and Dr. Boulanger followed this with a suggestion of scheduled IRC meetings. It was also suggested that linking to a discussion channel from a front-end like CsoundQt might encourage more users. It has to be accepted however, that younger computer users may view IRC as an old fashioned mode of communication. Since these discussions, a link has been added from Csound's front page at csounds.com to the IRC channel.

Continuing the theme of facilities for community interaction, the relationship between the www.csounds.com website and the Csound site on Source Forge were discussed. www.csounds.com is the front-page gateway established by Richard Boulanger and the Source Forge website at http://sourceforge.net/projects/csound/ is principally where the software source and binaries are stored and maintained. John Clements, who currently maintains csounds.com suggested that the site's content could be mirrored at Source Forge. Victor Lazzarini proposed the creation of a repository of instruments similar in structure to the existing repository for UDOs (User Defined Instruments). Steven Yi reported that work was progressing on a mechanism for sharing and retrieving UDOs and possibly instruments also, not just through a web browser but potentially also from a program such as front-end. This would allow front-ends to reference the newest repository of UDOs and instruments without them having to be stored as part of the program itself. Csound files could address and use UDOs and instruments without the convolution of having to copy-and-paste or download and save online materials. Joachim Heintz pointed out that the main issue with trying to set-up a vast library of UDOs and instruments tends to be in providing an overview of its contents through which the user could easily navigate to what they were looking for. Dr. Boulanger suggested that indications of "featured opcodes", as used already in CsoundForLive might guide users in their research. Use of metadata within the csd might prove the most useful aid to search engines.

At this point in the discussion Michael Gogins asked the group for suggestions as to why Csound was being dropped from many university curricula in favour of programs such as Max and Supercollider. Richard Boulanger suggested that the real-time experience offered by software such as Max might be a factor. Bernt Isak Wærstad suggested that greater use of immediate sound feedback—perhaps from a stock of mp3 files—would improve the user experience when navigating around example libraries. This would certainly remove the need to download and compile the example file before hearing what it could do but a slicker solution proposed by Rory Walsh would be a browser plug-in that could render and played csds using a mechanism that was transparent to the user. John ffitch pointed out the existence the NetCsound utility that allows visitors to upload a csd and then have the result sent to them via email. In respose to the idea of Csound's bewildering expanse of possibilities Øyvind Brandtsegg stated that it was precisely Csound's vast array of opcodes that kept him using it.

Steven Yi suggested that the question of *what is a Csound user?* has become more complex and ambiguous since the development of the Csound API in Csound5 and the program's move away from the paradigm of being purely a text file compiler. In response to this Richard Boulanger proposed a poll of Csound users to ascertain what methods people are using.

Iain McCurdy drew attention to a general lack of knowledge of Csound's capabilities as being something that holds it back from widespread adoption. The notion of Csound being purely a text file driven, non-real-time compiler is still a widely held belief that steers prospective users in other directions away from Csound. Michael Gogins backed this up, describing the public's perception of Csound as being "geeky" and "old fashioned". Peiman Khosravi highlighted Iain McCurdy's sound installation piece *Csound Haiku* as a mode of using of Csound more commonly associated with a program such as Supercollider. Score generating opcodes and secondary languages such as Lua and Python break this tradition of "instrument" and "score" offline rendering.

Michael Gogins suggested that confusion can sometimes arise from the misconception that Csound is an application, instead of a "library". Traditionally this library was accessed via the computer terminal but with the inclusion of Csound's API, access to this library can be made through many other means. It should also be noted that many modern computer users do not know what, or sometimes even where, the terminal is.

In response to Steven's original quastion of *what is Csound?* Richard Boulanger stated: "We are Csound, Csound is its community, backward compatibility is essential… sacred. If we make the community bigger we make Csound bigger."

To provoke some constructive criticism Joachim Heintz asked the session "where does Csound *not* excel?" His own feeling was that a lack of GUI builder-type interfaces, which could potentially offer the user an alternative to raw coding, was an issue. He emphasised however, that he prefers free software and would not consider a move to commercial software such as Max.

The PythonQt functionality in CsoundQt certainly opens a door to more dynamic ways of programming Csound. A discussion ensued concerning the best way of including methods of GUI building with Csound. The case was made for an interface building tool kit being included with the program that did not depend on the appropriate front-end being used. This was balanced with a stated desire to substitute Csound's aging built-in FLTK opcodes—the current built-in GUI—with something more modern. Obviously the FLTK opcodes must remain in order to preserve backwards compatibility but as Øyvind Brandtsegg stated, the desire would be that new users could in future choose a sleeker alternative at the outset. In relation to how the FLTK widgets were implemented within the Csound package, Victor Lazzarini insisted that any new GUI framework must be added as a separate entity from the core Csound program. The manner in which the FLTK opcodes are integrated within Csound's core program account for their uneven performance from platform to platform and for how they can impact negatively upon the real-time audio performance of the program. Victor described a system that could employ different widget frameworks and interpret appropriately but such a general system can cause problems where disparities in functionality between different widget libraries exist. Andrés Cabrera was less optimistic about such an endeavour suggesting that it could prove to be a great deal of work with "too few gains". Some success in integration has been achieved already in the fact that CsoundQt can now export its own widgets as Cabbage widgets.

Peiman Khosravi, who is prominent as a user of the *csound~* external object within Max—Peiman combines Max's GUI programming capabilities with Csound's sound design strengths—laments CsoundQt's convoluted method of setting up a GUI widget and the subsequent necessary creation of a communication link into a Csound orchestra. A channel name must be defined when creating the widget and then the data from that widget can only be used within a Csound instrument once that communication channel is opened in the Csound orchestra using an *invalue* or *chnget* opcode adopting the same channel name. The same procedure must be employed for every widget of the GUI and whilst this may indeed seem convoluted it is the only method possible for GUI frameworks that communicate with Csound through its API. Reducing the problem somewhat, Øyvind Brandtsegg, indicated that the main irritation was having to input the name of each channel twice (and to ensure that the same name was used on both occasions). Perhaps some form of auto-completion or complimentary code generator when creating the widget might be useful here.

As the discussion seemed to be touching upon the user experience of Csound, Richard Boulanger repeated a common request for an integrated table builder. John ffitch pointed out that a table builder using PerlTk already existed as part of the Csound package. Clearly the signposting of some of these options is lacking. Another frequent request that was reiterated here was for an ability to create standalone applications from Csound files. These could be applications that would include the required parts of the Csound engine within themselves and that could be run on a system without a need to install Csound. Progress continues to be made in this direction with CsoundQt and Cabbage leading the way.

An Introduction and Overview of the Different Front-ends Available for Csound

As many of the authors of the principle front-ends for Csound where present at the session, they were each afforded the opportunity to introduce their front-end and to explain how it distinguished itself from the others.

Steven Yi introduced his front-end "Blue". At first glance Blue might resemble a DAW program such as Cubase or Pro-tools and it is indeed an excellent composition environment but it has grown to include many other things such as the integrated editor, Blue instruments and Blue Share for the sharing of those instruments, to name but a few. In some ways Blue can be thought of as the successor to the late lamented Csound front-end "Cecilia" but this does not do Blue justice as it can do so much more than Cecilia ever could.

Next, Rory Walsh introduced Csound's newest front-end, "Cabbage". Admittedly still in its infancy, Cabbage's key innovations are the beautiful GUIs it can create and its ability to export projects as VST or AU (audio unit) plug-ins for use within other programs such as Ableton Live, Audiomulch, Reaper or Garageband. Cabbage can already run on all three of the main platforms: Windows, Mac OSX and Linux. Cabbage offers a pared down user experience when compared to those offered by CsoundQt and Blue but this might enhance the user's workflow if fewer front-end feature are required.

Andrés Cabrera introduced CsoundQt as an "entry level" front-end and perhaps the successor to Matt Ingalls' now abandoned MacCsound. CsoundQt's capabilities are immense however and it is also used by some of Csound's most experienced users. It was at the Csound conference that Andrés was finally coerced into changed the name of his front-end from QuteCsound to its current name.

Mention was made of *csound~*, the Csound object for Max and Pd, originally written by Matt Ingalls and now maintained by David Pyon. Peiman Khosravi endorsed the use *csound~* within Max for creating "sexy looking interfaces and extra functionality".

Stefano Bonetti's "WinXound" was also mentioned. Stefano was not at the conference. WinXound provides a general purpose front-end offering the most typical functionality. As such, it is lightweight and stable across all platforms. WinXound makes no use of the API and is probably not being as actively maintained as the three main front-ends CsoundQt, Blue and Cabbage.

In response to the question as to whether we need all of these front-ends Richard Boulanger responded: "We need 'em all" and this is probably correct as they all offer slightly different feature sets and all users have slightly different needs.

Andrés Cabrera hinted that communication between developers of front-ends was essential in order to see where they could meet and where they can interchange. He went on to say how he had had an intention to create the possibility of an interchange of instruments with Blue. This turned out to be not so easy.

Steven Yi commends the existence of multiple front-ends for Csound but appeals for there to be also a "zipped" version of Csound with no installer (as there was in the past). A discussion of the practicality of this, mainly between Steven and Victor identified possible problems involving Csound Python implementation.

Steven took the opportunity to mention Stéphane Rollandin's innovative front-end "Surmulot". Surmolot make use of the "small talk" language and offers the user a mixture of GUI and typed code. It introduces, as Steven termed it, "real out of the box thinking" but is difficult to use.

Michael Gogins expressed the desire for a decent GUI patcher for Csound orchestras. "Cabel" attempts this but with limited success and the project has been inactive for some time. At this point Rory Walsh makes mention of the existence of a patcher for Cabbage instruments that is currently under development.

Csound and Its Users

Iain McCurdy introduced himself as purely a user and not a developer, and alludes towards the fragile relationship that can sometimes exist between the user and developer. Developers might be deluged with wishes from users but are under no obligation to grant any of these wishes. Users of commercial software have more of right to demand, at the very least, bug fixes. Naturally developers will readily implement new features that reflect their own interests and represent tools that they will actually use themselves but how does a user go about convincing a developer that they should implement *their* wish? How might a user ingratiate themselves into the Csound community such that their voice deserves to be heard? Obviously if a user contributes to the community in some other way, perhaps by sharing music created using Csound, writing tutorials or sharing instruments, it should not be regarded as a purely selfish request. Perhaps the addition of opcodes that implement cutting edge or "Zeitgeist" techniques can be used to tempt in new users.

Richard Boulanger praised the developer response to user requests but criticised the occasional tendency on the list to talk negatively about other competing software. Does this affect the confidence of new users? It is actually a common occurrence to hear these sorts of sentiments expressed on software discussion lists as "team loyalties" are exhibited and it is probably a fairly moderate phenomenon on the Csound list.

Possibilities for User Participation

Is there a formal mechanism for requesting new features? The typical procedure would be to request a new feature is to make a "pitch" on the main Csound discussion list but perhaps there should be a dedicated area on Source Forge for this to take place like the "PYPE" system in python. Steven reminded us that there was already a "request a new feature" mechanism within Blue.

Peiman Khosravi compliments the quality of discussion on the Csound list and how topics sometime extend beyond Csound and into aesthetics.

John suggests that a great way users can contribute is to write good music. Victor broadens this idea by saying that using the software will sustain it and reiterates the importance of bug reports. Embedded links within front-ends to the bug reporting area on Source Forge would streamline this process. John ffitch posts a monthly reminder on the main discussion list reminding list readers that the discussion is open to users of all standards and that "newbies" should not feel intimidated against asking basic questions.

Users' Wish List

Rory Walsh had been informally querying conference attendees during the conference and from this, he had compiled a users wish list. The user wishes that he reported included hierarchical menu code completion as part of an editor, a spectral viewing utility, dynamic loading of UDOs and instruments, cross platform Arduino/serial opcodes, better string manipulation, a Csound debugger that might allow breakpoints within instruments for checking values, a Csound build for Xcode Visual C++, Csound for Android and iOS, the ability to dynamically insert Csound instances within an active signal chain and Open GL support (as was part of CsoundAV).

Richard Boulanger enthusiastically confirmed that porting Csound to Apple's iPad was high on his list. To achieve this Steven Yi explained that Csound would have to be build with less dependence on dynamic loading, essentially it would have to be more monolithic. He accepted that there would be difficulties in removing dependencies but that the first step would be to establish an iOS build file. Michael Gogins felt this would be easier and might only involve a series of *#ifdefs* for dynamically loaded opcodes in the opcode dispatch table. Andrés Cabrera noted that the *system* opcode would have to be removed, as scripting code, with the exception of javascript, is not allowed within apps at the Apple Store. Rory Walsh reminded the group that porting Csound to Android should not be forgotten either. Since the conference Csound has been ported to both iOS and Android.

Should there be a Csound Foundation?

To conclude this second round table session (and to formally conclude the conference) there was some discussion on the possibility of setting up a Csound foundation. The suggestions made ranged from very small initiatives to large multi-million euro proposals.

A foundation (also known as a charitable foundation) is a non-profit organisation or charitable trust most often created for the purpose of generating revenue to fund cultural or educational endeavors. A private foundation would normally be funded by an individual and a public foundation by many sources.

Victor Lazzarini informed the session that a foundation might be able to achieve charitable status (which could prompt tax exemption and possible public support). In the UK a foundation would be regarded as a charity whereas Ireland has no official definition of a foundation. In the US, a foundation must begin with an initial capital of at least $2000. Globally speaking, a foundation is just a fund of money used to back an organisation or group. A Csound foundation could also be used as a more general idea with no specific legal status whose presence might be just a dot-org website.

A foundation could perhaps be used to support the development of Csound in the manner of how the "Google Summer of Code" supports software development. If acquired, this could support 2 to 3 months of intensive development perhaps involving research students or freelancers who could make ideal candidates for code sprints. Victor told us he has already made use of research students to do Csound development work.

Rather than only think on a small scale, Victor Lazzarini pointed out that a major collaborative multi-million euro proposal might be needed to garner major European Union (EU) funds and prizes. Such a project could establish the Csound 6 framework, develop the language and deliver the system that would put the project well ahead of other projects in the field. This might involve 20 researchers and last 3 to 4 years.

Richard Boulanger spoke of how funding could drive forward the move from Csound 5 to Csound 6 and also suggested approaching the semiconductor developers "Analog Devices". As an additional stream of revenue stream he suggested selling Csound related apps on the Apple Store like, for example, a $9.99 Csound front-end app.

Joachim Heintz made the suggestion of providing an opportunity to donate to Csound's development on csounds.com.

Conclusion

This concluding round table session of the Csound conference prompted many ideas on a range of issues. Many of the initiatives that were suggested have already been completed whilst others are now in progress. Naturally other ideas may have been forgotten but hopefully this article will serve as a gathering point for later reference by both people who attended the event and those who were not able to.

A PERSONAL VIEW ON TEACHING CSOUND

GLEB G. ROGOZINSKY

I. Introduction

This paper describes the author's experience of teaching Csound over several years in Saint-Petersburg State University of Film and Television, Russia. The Csound language is given as a part of the course called Computer Music Technologies. This course lasts for two terms and includes several lectures and a practical part. The whole course is new, so that scope for experimentation and research exists.

Saint-Petersburg State University of Film and Television was established in 1918 and during the Soviet period was mainly focused on technical education for the film and television industry. During the modern Russia period after 1991 the University expanded its focus mainly into the field of arts. The Institute of Screen Arts provides specialization in film directing, camera operating and sound production, as well as multimedia production and computer graphics.

I graduated from the Institute of Audiovisual Technics in 2006 and received a masters diploma in radio engineering. My masters thesis was about wavelet-based sound synthesis and processing. In 2010 I completed my candidate work about perceptual audio coding in the wavelet domain and I hold a Candidate of Sciences degree (equivalent to Ph.D.) in Audiovisual Processing Methods.

My first encounter with Csound occurred in 2005 during the course Digital Technologies of Audiovisual Production. Csound was briefly introduced in connection with MPEG-4 SASL (Structured Audio Score Language) and SAOL (Structured Audio Orchestra Language), which are the direct derivatives of Csound. Having a special interest in electronic music, modern composition and synthesizers, I accepted an offer to read lectures for sound producers. I was allowed some degree of freedom so I chose sound synthesis as the main topic of my course using Csound as a language for formal description of different synthesis techniques.

The necessity for specialization and a comparatively conservative attitude from the headmasters means that further practical implementation of achieved skills in sound synthesis and Csound remains uncommon although there are some positive examples. For example, some students ended up using synthesized soundscapes in their sound etudes and even in their diploma film music. The students related to electronic music production were unlikely to use Csound in their everyday jobs, although they admitted that the skills provided in sound synthesis allowed them to expand the resources used in their work from sample libraries to more complex methods of synthesis.

II. Initial Study Problems

After several years of teaching Csound, I could define the following issues that might spring from the initial period of study: background, interface, starting point and language.

To clarify these issues I shall describe the typical format of this course and briefly outline the available equipment. Most students who chose a specialisation such as sound production have already graduated from a music college and sometimes even conservatories of music. This broad cross-section of students arrive primarily wanting to improve their skills in sound recording, mixing and production but are often weaker in physics, mathematics and sound processing. However, these students often have the potential to surpass students from purely technical backgrounds on account of their particular interest in sound synthesis and computer music.

Students from a more technical background might already work at recording studios, in clubs or in post-production and as such might already possess a degree of understanding in the subject but they can sometimes overestimate their skills on account of perhaps having a naïve understanding of sound synthesis theory in conjunction with an overly intuitive approach to the subject.

The last and smallest group of students is those who are, again, from a technical background but who have, for some reason, decided to choose a more artistic specialisation. Quite often such students perform best but with some lack of artistic flair in their projects.

The entire Computer Musical Technologies course lasts for two terms and that includes 14 lectures and 8 practical sessions. For practical sessions the whole group (usually from 18 to 25 students) is divided into subgroups of 3-5 people. The lectures take place in a music studio that is equipped with a video projector and a 5.1 surround sound system. Practical sessions are held in a computer lab with several PCs equipped with multimedia capabilities, however students often prefer to use their own laptops. In addition, there are MIDI interfaces of several types.

Unfortunately the lab is not appointed with hardware synthesizers so I often have to provide my own Access Virus C, Waldorf MicroQ, Clavia Nord Modular G2, Yamaha TX81Z and Roland JP-8000 for demonstrating some classic synthesis sounds.

Background

As has already been highlighted, prior technical knowledge is often lacking in many students with the consequence that many fundamental concepts, such as analog-to-digital conversion, the existence of *a-* and *k-rate* signals, function tables and so on can take a considerable amount of time to explain and clarify. I make extensive use of graphics in my descriptions and avoid formulae such as those associated with the Fourier transform or the Nyquist theorem, preferring instead to discuss them as general concepts. Some useful metaphors might simplify the process: for example, an understanding of *a-rate* or audio-rate signals is quite intuitive for everyone, but the meaning of *k-rate* can sometimes seems quite unclear in the presence of *a-rate* signals. The nature of *k-rate* signals become clearer when related to automation signals such as might be used for volume or pan. One cannot twist a rotary knob of a filter cutoff frequency or mixing console crossfader at a rate equivalent to the rate of amplitude changes in an audio signal so there is no need for a *k-rate* as high as *a-rate*.

Interface

Modern students live in a point and click world so the text-based interface of Csound can seem quite antiquated to students who have never programmed anything beyond changing tag fields in social networks. During lectures, I demonstrated many examples and always encouraged usage of the manual. Csound proves to be an ideal medium for learning sound synthesis on account of its great number of well documented opcodes and examples as well as the simplicity with which instruments can be created and connected. A key factor in Csound's educative strength is in how it allows us to quickly build complex networks from primitive elements, some with input(s), some with output(s) and some with both. I often draw schematics of Csound instruments which might consist of several modules interconnected with lines to illustrate data flows. After these introductions, students begin to become familiar with connecting virtually any module with another just by looking through the syntax given in the manual. In support of this work, I also show students the parallels with other modular systems such as the Clavia Nord Modular.

Starting point: I should give a warning here about 'passive' learning where students mechanically copy the code for example instruments from the projector screen into their workbook or laptop only to forget how they work soon after. To obviate this problem, I ask students to modify the given examples at home but with some simple alterations. For example, they might vary the opcode parameters or use a different GEN routine. Normally I teach Csound using the CsoundQt front-end which has no platform dependence. CsoundQt also simplifies interface building and offers a large number of built-in examples and compositions. Unfortunately CsoundQt sometimes takes time to be set up correctly—buffer sizes, device preferences and so on. Of course this will not present a major problem for technically experienced students but for students more used to using their laptop for checking e-mails and blogging this could prove to be a bewildering task. Furthermore, some hardware configurations do not always provide real-time stability. In such cases I normally recommend that they use WinXsound instead which is solid, stable and clear. In general though they will prefer to persevere with CsoundQt for the opcode colouring, auto-completion and built-in manual it offers.

Language: Whilst many students can speak English competently, most of them struggle to understand the technical language contained within the Csound manual. Sadly this prevents me from being able to give them a list of opcodes for further research. Normally some extra time needs to be set aside for translating syntax and descriptions. There are several Csound resources on the Internet that are in Russian but the variability of the Russian language and differences between programming, musical and acoustics thesauri can often result in an uncertainty of their meaning.

Tasks: I do not provide a demonstration of initial exercises here as they are quite obvious and unsophisticated. As I have mentioned, I ask students to develop instruments provided during lectures by substituting known opcodes with unfamiliar ones. For example, they could change *tone* to *butterlp* or *linseg* to *expseg*. This activity can develop an ability to use and understand the manual. A wide variety of help material can also be found in the first chapter of The Csound Book which is free to download from csounds.com (http://www.csounds.com/chapter1), The FLOSS manual Csound pages (http://en.flossmanuals.net/csound/index/) and Richard Boulanger's TOOTs (http://www.csounds.com/toots/ index.html/).

III. Discussing Modulation

Once this initial groundwork of knowledge has been established, a new set of challenges must be met. In my opinion, the most important thing to be discussed next is the technique of modulation its related issues such as biasing and LFOs.

The principle issue in taking this next step is an understanding of the true nature of modulation. It should be made clear that in the field of sound synthesis, any signal can potentially modulate almost any parameter. When students begin to practice sound synthesis, they often restrict the parameters they modulate to amplitude and frequency. I endeavor to demonstrate and discuss various examples of modulation chains with greater complexity. Some popular software and hardware synthesizers with good modulation matrices can offer great examples of 'source' to 'destination' connections. I use an Access Virus C and a Waldorf MicroQ as well as some software synths to demonstrate the potential in parameter modulation including more unusual examples such as arpeggiator pattern modulation.

Becoming familiar with modulation principles can assist students in creating more interesting algorithms and in achieving a better understanding of the complex presets of virtually any synthesizer through reading their modulation matrices. For one thing, these skills can prove extremely useful in the analysis of multiple operator FM synthesis algorithms.

Tasks: I set a number of special tasks for analysing modulation. They are targeted at discovering what the source(s) and destination(s) of each connection are, what the signals used for modulation are, what the proper biasing should be and what the signal levels are at various points within the network. Figure 1 illustrates three examples of envelopes that should be created in Csound using complex modulation as a part of the signal modulation exercise. The sound signals inside the envelopes are arbitrary, although their generation could have been set as part of an earlier task. Signal A envelope corresponds to series of pulses whose frequency is modulated by a saw wave, signal B envelope corresponds to two-stage amplitude modulation with a biasing offset and signal C envelope corresponds to amplitude modulation using a saw wave whose frequency is modulated by a pulse wave—the same pulse wave changes the left-right balance of a stereo signal. One possible solution for the third example is to use white noise as the enveloped sound signal as shown in figure 2.

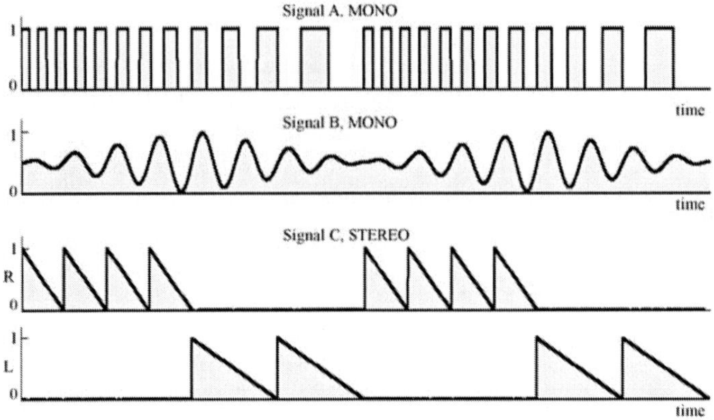

Figure 1. An example of signal envelopes given as a task on modulation practice. Signal A envelope corresponds to series of pulses modulated by frequency using a saw wave, signal B envelope corresponds to two-stage amplitude modulation with a biasing offset and signal C envelope corresponds to amplitude modulation using a saw wave which is modulated by frequency with pulse wave—the same pulse wave changes the left-right balance of a stereo signal.

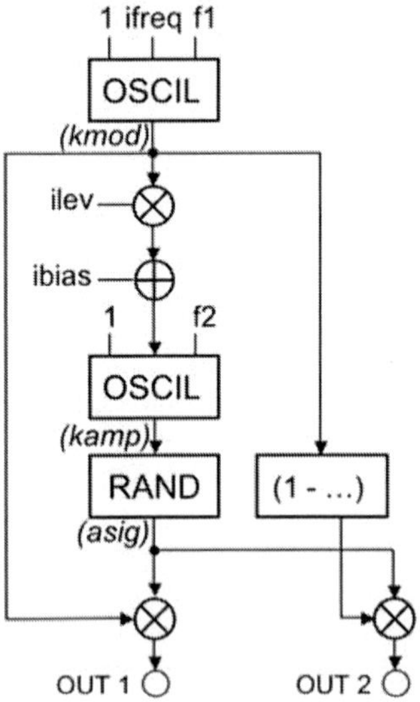

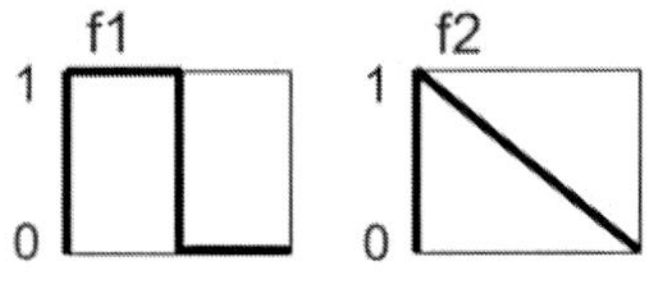


```
      instr 1
ilev  =       4
ibias =       4
ifreq =       1
kmod  oscil  1, ifreq, 1
kamp  oscil  1, ibias + ilev*kmod, 2
asig  rand   kamp
      outs   asig, asig*(1-kmod)
      endin
```

Figure 2. Block diagram and orchestra code for *instr 1* which generates signal C

IV. Visualisation of Signals

I present to the students examples of alternative music score notation, such as that for György Ligeti's *Artikulation* or Karlheinz Stockhausen's *Studie II* to prove that electronic music demands its own language for representation. One of the best solutions for representing synthesized sound with dynamic behavior in the most informative way is the spectrogram (also known as a sonogram). A spectrogram is the result of a time-frequency transform, i.e. a windowed or short-time Fourier transform. It can provide both temporal and spectral information for analyzed signal. Some signals, whose features may appear to be quite elusive within the time domain, can often be more easily analyzed in the time-frequency domain by means of a spectral analysis.

I introduce visualisations of audio signals as an important tool in developing skills for sound design. The proposed approach is to imagine a signal in the time-frequency domain before attempting to synthesize it. When discussing sound design in class, I recommend the following steps: create the desired sound in your imagination, draw a corresponding amplitude envelope (thinking about how fast the attack is, how long does the sound last, does it have a long release, does it have any other notable features) and finally draw its spectrogram in order to understand the dynamics of its frequency components. Once the shape of a sound is established in this way it becomes easier to select an appropriate technique for realisation.

Almost any music editing program provides a means for displaying a signal's spectrogram. Whilst Csound and CsoundQt also include some means for signal visualisation, most of my students prefer to use the freeware Audacity (or some other commercial software) for deriving waveforms and spectrograms. It is worth mentioning that some students begin their electronic compositions from graphic scores, which are in most cases relate in some way to the time-frequency domain. Figure 3 presents a spectrogram of one of my student's granular synthesis compositions which was in turn based on a graphical score.

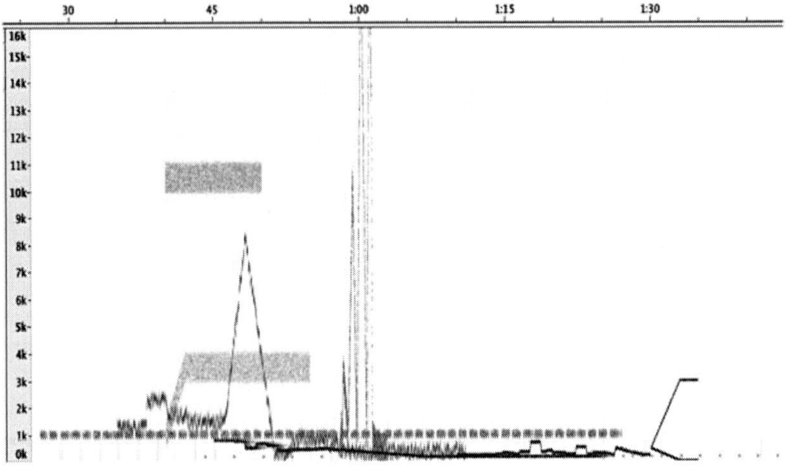

Figure 3. An Audacity spectrogram of a student's work that was originally based on a graphic notation score.

Tasks: Figure 4 illustrates an example where two synthesis tasks should be combined into one audio file. The two signals are simple and contain frequency domain dynamics. The student should create similar signals in Csound using the waveforms and spectrograms provided. These graphs should be analysed to uncover what kind of modulation was used, what the source of modulation was and whether any kind of filtering was used.

V. Expanding the Boundaries

I now propose several directions into which the basic knowledge of sound synthesis can be expanded: an improvment of opcode vocabulary, electronic composition analysis and exploring the world of commercial synthesizers and other modular systems.

Improving opcode vocabulary: Each lesson should provide students with an expanding set of options depending on what topic was discussed, e.g. *rand* opcode, *GEN07* with a few words about Gibbs phenomenon, different Csound filter opcodes when discussing subtractive synthesis, and *GEN01*, *soundin*, *poscil*, soundfont format opcodes when discussing sampling. As a part of a control task, each student must explore some opcodes or modules that were not discussed in lectures and build several examples exemplifying how they might be used.

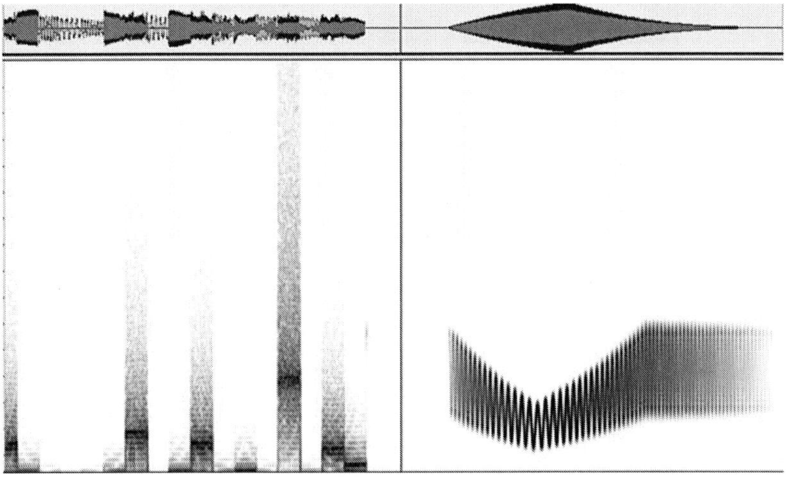

Figure 4. An example of two signals and their corresponding spectrograms which must then to be synthesized using Csound by the student. The signal on the left is white noise filtered by a low-pass filter with its cutoff frequency modulated by a sample-and-hold shaped LFO. The signal on the right is a harmonic signal with an exponential AR(attack-release)-envelope, which modulates frequencies of the signal.

Analysing electronic music: To learn more about the world of electronic music, I encourage my students to listen to modern electronic music compositions and to match them to known classes of synthesized timbres. This allows them to define typical sounds and common functions of synthesized instruments. There are several electronic compositions included in CsoundQt, such as Terry Riley's *In C*, John Chowning's *Stria* and Richard Boulanger's *Trapped in Convert*, which are ready for performance by Csound.

Exploring commercial synthesizers: Discussions of classic synthesis techniques become more relevant and colourful when specific existing instruments are described, modeled, and analysed. Examples of this might be the Hammond organ, the Moog synthesizer, the Yamaha DX7 and the Mellotron. As an example, an indisputable cornerstone of acid house-related music is the Roland TB-303, but even with its few control parameters, modelling their subtle interaction can be a challenge. Sometimes students begin by analysing the rate of the filter cutoff variation, the result of a note being accented and so on, before creating a block diagram of the model and then attempting to recreate it using Csound. Another good example for such a task is the ‘supersaw’ oscillator on the Roland Juno synthesizer, which gave birth to the famous 'hoover' sound still popular today. A benefit of using Csound here is the existence of The Csound Catalogue which includes a lot of models of commercial synthesizers. Some instruments from this catalog can be found on the data CD that accompanies The Csound Book (Boulanger, 2000). Other useful sources of information are the Csound Journal (http://www.csounds.com/journal/) and the earlier Csound Ezine (http://csounds.com/ezine/).

Tasks: The task of modelling classic synthesizers can be done in a sequence of tasks, the number of which will probably depend on the complexity of original algorithm. For example, a basic emulation of a Hammond organ could be achieved with just 9 harmonic oscillators tuned to the appropriate frequencies. The next step might be to emulate the volume envelopes of the Hammond. The next stage of complexity could be achieved by modelling the Leslie speaker and tone-wheel 'leakage'. Ability levels may vary from student to student so the complexity of emulation they attempt might depend on this fact.

Usually this kind of practical task takes place in the computer lab with a subgroup of students and students will be provided with a lot of information about the device, its front panel layout, examples of its typical sounds, and sometimes an example of an existing VST/AU emulation. I do not demand that they finish the task at all costs. It is more important that they understand every line of the code they write and every link in the modulation chain.

VI. Beyond the Horizon

In the final part of the Csound course, by which stage students are able to understand syntax and create their own sounds, I stress the need for students to broaden their knowledge. An overview might be given of more complex synthesis techniques. This then offers students who have already excelled the opportunity to make further exploration of synthesis, supported by their own research. Granular synthesis techniques (and related techniques such as FoF, trainlet, pulsar and wavelet synthesis) are always intriguing for students. Compositions that highlight granulation techniques such as those by Iannis Xenakis, Barry Truax and Curtis Roads can provide excellent examples of their expressive potential. The work of Curtis Roads (Roads, 2001) also provides essential information on granular synthesis, beginning with its historical context and building to its practical realisation.

Table 1 provides an example of a week-by-week schedule. All lectures last for four academic hours. The name of the lecture describes the main topic that will be discussed during the first half. In the second half of the lecture I normally demonstrate some new Csound opcodes with corresponding examples and engage in a discussion with the students based on what they have learned.

No lectures are devoted solely to the use of Csound for DSP techniques such as reverberation or vocoding, instead they are discussed during practical work and some examples are provided during lectures. It is worth mentioning that the University offers other modules devoted exclusively to signal processing.

To successfully pass the course students must complete several projects alongside their weekly homework tasks. During the first term every student must create a soundscape etude with a duration of a few minutes. This etude must be created only using Csound and should include several instruments that make use of modulation, filtering and well known synthesis methods. The main course project should normally be completed by the end of the second term. In order that students will not feel forced to work on a project they are not so interested in, they are always offered a choice of projects. Students are free to organise their own group for undertaking one task or another, although the size of each group will be limited. Typical project tasks are:

- *Recreate an electronic composition that makes use of distinctive electronic timbres.* Usually this task requires the student to take an instrumental electronic composition or soundtrack and deconstruct it into separate Csound instruments. The instruments created during this work should be described and discussed in class.

- *Translate a classical music excerpt into the electronic music domain.* The student can take a classical work of their own choosing, for example *Elsa's Procession to the Cathedral* from Wagner's *Lohengrin* or Shostakovich's Violin Concerto and create an electronic orchestra of Csound instruments to perform it. The emphasis here falls on the dramatic role of each instrument. The instruments themselves are not required to sound exactly like the real ones, but should instead reflect their dramatic relationships within the original composition.

Table 1. A week-by-week schedule of a typical Csound course

Term	Part	Week	Lectures and practice
First term (Spring)	Initial Study	1	Lecture 1A. Introduction to sound synthesis and Csound
		2	Lecture 2A. Simple work in Csound
		3	Lecture 3A. Modulation
		4	Lecture 4A. Additive synthesis Practice 1A. First steps in Csound. Making simple instruments.
		5	Lecture 5A. Subtractive synthesis Practice 2A. Exploring modulation and filtering.
	Intermediate Study	6	Lecture 6A. FM synthesis Practice 3A. Discovering FM synthesis
		7	Lecture 7A. MIDI, OSC and real-time work with Csound Practice 4A. Real-time work with Csound. Using MIDI and OSC in Csound.
		8	Lecture 8A. Sampling
		9-10	End-of-term Testing

Term	Part	Week	Lectures and practice
Second term (Autumn)	Advanced Study	1	Lecture 1B. Commercial synthesizers Practice 1B. Building a commercial synth model I
		2	Lecture 2B. Physical modelling Practice 2B. Building a commercial synth model II
		3	Lecture 3B. Granular synthesis I Practice 3B. Working with Granular Synthesis
		4	Lecture 4B. Granular synthesis II Practice 4B. Project discussion
		5	Lecture 5B. Algorithmic composition
		6	Lecture 6B. The world of modular systems
		7-10	End-of-term testing. Projects

- *Create an inter-computer performance using OSC-based message transportation.* Students who are focused on technical aspects or performance art often take this task. At least one computer of the network should use Csound. This task could be performed in real-time using a controller or controllers such as iPhones. It is up to the students discretion as to what controls what and how. Sound design is not necessarily the primary goal here.

- *Create an algorithmic composition or total serial composition along with a description and a short score.* This is a task intended for those who did not take to Csound as much as the others. Sometimes conservatory graduates prefer this task.

During a final concert and presentation—which is open for all comers to attend—students have to also present block diagrams of their Csound instruments, graphical scores or any other material they might have used while working on their projects. They accompany these materials with a brief analysis.

Most students interested in specialisation tend to have musical and artistic backgrounds so the final part of the course is always the most interesting. Unlike other Western universities, it is uncommon for Russian universities to allow students to select subjects according to their own interests so that once the Csound module is completed students do not have the possibility to choose something closely related to it. At the same time though, they all go on to do a course entitled 'Synthesized Sound in Film Production'. This course is not purely technical but also includes a lot of artistic content, focussing on the use of electro-acoustic sound in film production supported by an analysis of a number of well-known Russian and Western movies that feature a notable use of electronic sound.

VII. Conclusion

The principal aims of the discussed course are to provide an introduction to sound synthesis techniques and to Csound programming. During the course students have to undertake several tasks, some of which have been described. These tasks include a final class concert.

I should mention that some students do not pass this module. On the other hand, most of such students systematically fail the other subjects too so their poor progress seems to be behind the Csound-specific difficulties. I would like to suggest that providing a variety of projects from which the students can choose can result in higher pass rates as students are then able to select a project that matches their own particular strengths and interests.

To conclude, I hope that the approaches discussed in this chapter might prove useful for anyone who teaches and learns Csound. Having both a technical and musical education, I understand that occasional difficulties might discourage students from delving deeper into Csound (and the wider world of sound synthesis), but if some of the factors discussed above are addressed, the barriers will begin to fall.

References

Boulanger, Richard, *The Csound Book*, edited by R. Boulanger. Cambridge: The MIT Press, 2000.

"Csounds.com," Richard Boulanger's Introduction to Sound Design in Csound, accessed December 21, 2012, http://www.csounds.com/chapter1.

"Csound FLOSS Manual," accessed December 21, 2012, http://en.flossmanuals.net/csound/.

Boulanger, Richard, "An Instrument Design TOOTorial," accessed December 21, 2012, http://www.csounds.com/toots/index.html

"The Csound Catalog," accessed December 21, 2012, http://www.csounds.com/shop/csound-catalog.

"The Csound journal," accessed December 21, 2012, http://www.csounds.com/journal.

"The Csound Magazine," accessed December 21, 2012, http://csounds.com/ezine.

Roads, Curtis, *Microsound*, Cambridge: The MIT Press, 2001.

PWGL:
A Score Editor for Csound

MASSIMO AVANTAGGIATO

Abstract

PWGL has stood out, since its introduction in Electronic Music classes, as an important tool for the development of the musical creativity of students at the "Giuseppe Verdi" Conservatoire[1].

The uses of PWGL are manifold: other than being a great teaching aid for rebuilding the composition of historical pieces, it offers new opportunities in the creation of original pieces and the application of several techniques of sound synthesis. I have concentrated on the need to create functional links between PWGL and Csound in order to integrate the processes of algorithmic composition with those of sound synthesis.

Introduction

A piece is usually written with using thousands of lines of instructions, however, most musicians do not compose pieces writing note by note, but use programs to produce scores.

Such programs, known as score generators[2], aim at relieving the composer of the repetitive task of typing many lines of code.

PWGL, a program for algorithmic composition based on Common Lisp[3], can be employed as a score generator and can be interfaced with

---

[1] "PWGL could be seen as an attempt to fill the gap between several different aspects of music tuition. It is our belief that PWGL could be established as a pedagogical tool for academia" (M. Kuuskankare, M. Laurson, 2010).

[2] Score Generators have been written in several languages: C, C++, Java, Lisp, Lua and Python. In one of his writings Gogins makes a list of different types of Score Generators and Composing Environments, including AthenaCl, Blue, Common Music, Pure Data. (M. Gogins, 2006).

[3] For an in-depth study see: G.L. Steele (1990), "Association of Lisp Users (A.L.U)"

Csound, a widely used sound renderer based on the C language; it can also become a powerful driving force for synthesis[4].

PWGL enables an unskilled programmer, without the support of external libraries, to do the following:

- produce electronic gestures with full control of sound parameters involved in the sound "composing" process: instrument, attack time, note, amplitude, frequency, pan, reverb, delay etc.
- create a quick rendering directly with Csound, to repeat processes and correct PWGL patches; implement, by using simple algorithms, several techniques of synthesis.

Additive Synthesis and Karplus

First of all consider the synthesis of Karplus and Strong: the patch I am going to show, allows us to choose between spectra which will undergo a process of acceleration or deceleration.

The resulting gesture will be synthesized in Csound by means of the following opcode[5]:

```
ar pluck kamp, kcps, icps, ifn, imeth[iparm1,iparm2]
```
[6]

[4] It is an option for the use of PWGLSynth, which PWGL is already equipped with (M. Kuuskankare, M. Laurson, 2010).

[5] See references for an in-depth study of Karplus and Strong's synthesis techniques (K. Karplus, A. Strong, 1983; D. Jaffe, J.O. Smith, 1983).

[6] kamp = sound amplitude; kcps = target frequency.; icps = value (hertz) setting out the length of the table. It usually equals kcps, but can be increased or decreased to get special timbre effects. ifn = number of the function to initialize the table. When ifn = 0, the table is filled with a random sequence of values (original algorithm of Karplus and Strong) imeth = method used to change the values of the table during the sound-producing process. There are six of them (R. Bianchini, A. Cipriani, 2007).

First of all, the instrument is written:

```
        instr  1
idur    =      p3
iamp    =      p4
ifrq    =      p5
ipanl =        sqrt (p6)
ipanr =        sqrt (1-p6)
kenv    linseg 1, p3*.50, 1, p3*.25, 0
a1      pluck  iamp, ifreq, ifreq, 0, 6
        outs   a1*kenv*ipanl, a1*kenv*ipanr
        endin
```

Secondly, the patch is produced (see figure 2):

- in (1) the starting sequence of notes is singled out;
- in (2) the abstract- box is made. Its function is to produce the data for the synthesis and, if necessary, go on with the acceleration or deceleration of the material;
- in (3) the data is collected in a text-box to implement the Csound synthesis.

The abstract-box, seen from the outside, consists of a series of sliders linked with the inputs (see figure 1-2).

Each parameter-field can be matched by one or more inputs (see figure 3):

1) **INSTRUMENT (p1):** the values given to the instruments are repeated as many times as the frequencies composing the spectrum.
2) **CREATION TIME (p2):** the attacks of the original sequence are rescaled (or not) by means of a parabolic function in order to bring about the acceleration or deceleration of the starting material;
3) **LENGTH OF NOTES (p3):** the lengths of notes, ranging between a minimum and maximum value, are defined by using g-scaling and taking into account the distance between the creation times previously defined;
4) **AMPLITUDE (p4):** it can be expressed using absolute values or can be defined in dB;
5) **FREQUENCIES (p5):** they are the frequencies of the starting spectra; if midi values are employed it will be necessary to convert them using the function "Patchwork Midi to Frequencies";

6) **STEREO PANNING**[7] **(p6):** following a parabolic function it ranges from 1 (all the sound in the left channel) to 0 (all the sound in the right channel).

As for the parameters relating to creation time, length, amplitude and pan, the type of interpolation applied is based on a concave/convex curve, even if it is not the only type of interpolation available.

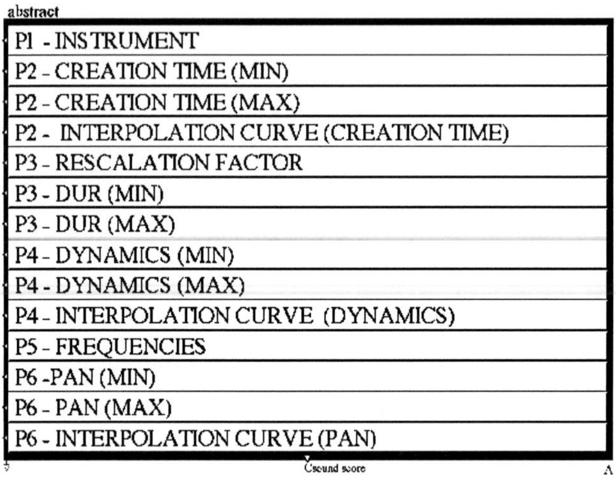

Figure 1: The sliders of the abstract-box employed to transfer data to Csound.

[7] "The most popular spatial illusions are horizontal panning—lateral sound movement from speaker to speaker—and reverberation—adding a dense and diffuse pattern of echoes to a sound in order to situate it in a larger space. Vertical panning (up and down and overhead) can also create striking effects in electronic music" (C. Roads, 1996). Mickelson mentions strategies for panning and offers a grading of some basic strategies: Simple Pan; Square Root Pan; Sine Pan; Equal Power Pan; Delay and Filtered Panning (H. Mickelson, 1999).

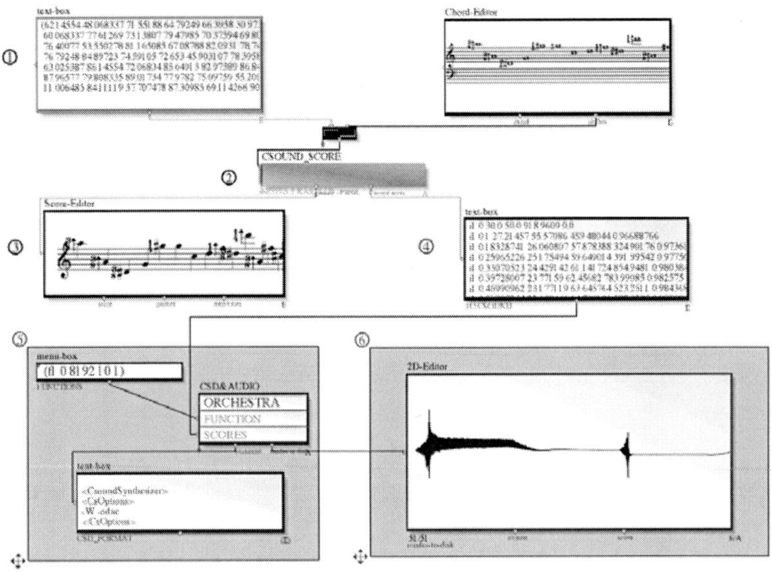

Figure 2: The PWGL patch enables the transfer of data in Csound. In (1) the starting (harmonic or inharmonic) spectra can be chosen; in (2) the abstract- box can be seen. The detail is provided by figure 1. In (3) you can see the score related to the spectrum chosen in (1); in 4) you can see the score; in (5) you can choose function from a ‘menu - box’, which can be used to define custom menus: here we select our function. All information regarding orchestra and score is combined in the last Abstract Box, which has the task of rendering using Csound, whose result is shown in a 2-d editor (6).

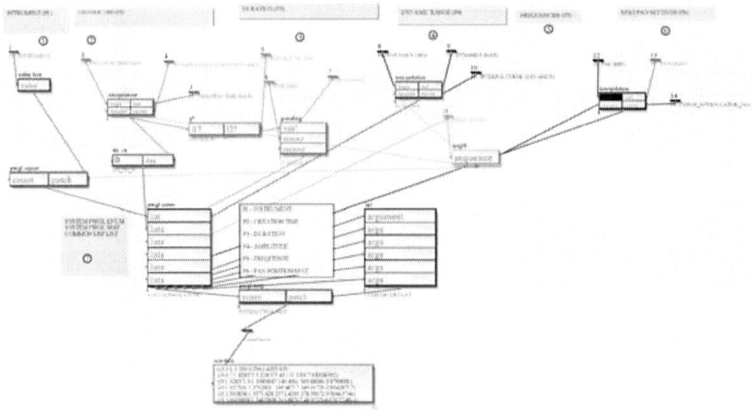

Figure 3: The abstract- box is seen from the inside. You can see the entries concerning: (1) instrument; (2) attack; (3) length; (4) amplitude; (5) frequency; (6) pan. In (7) the PWGL-enum box is linked with the first entry of the PWGL-map: if combined, they can create loops and they can simultaneously process several links of values, that is to say those concerning parameter-fields. The result is placed in a text-box for every interaction. The text-box serves as "result-list": that is the Csound score.

Once the sequence of the first notes is set, the patch for the synthesis of Karplus I have just described can be substituted with an additive patch and we can move from one synthesis technique to another[8] by using, for instance, the following instrument:

```
giamp_fact =       16               ; Amplitude factor
           instr   2
idur       =       1/p3
iamp       =       p4 * giamp_fact
ifreq      =       p5
ipanl      =       sqrt(p6)          ; Pan left
ipanr      =       sqrt(1-p6)        ; Pan right
aamp       oscili  iamp, idur,  2
aout       oscili  aamp, ifreq, 1
           outs    aout*ipanl, aout*ipanr
           endin
```

[8] For an in-depth study of the additive synthesis techniques see Lorrain (1980), Mathews (1969), Moore (1985), Moorer (1985) and Risset (1969, 1989a, 1989b).

From these examples it follows that the instruments, after being created, can be employed again in other circumstances, apart from the initial material and the algorithmic composing material (see figures 9-10).

Additive Synthesis

PWGL offers the opportunity to repeat the compositional process of piece from history and to rediscover its conceptual idea by singling out the rules of composition and any exceptions.

Of the works I have personally rebuilt, my attention has focused on pieces such as Studie II by Karlheinz Stockhausen. In this study the German composer used 81 frequencies starting from a base frequency of 100 hertz.

From this base frequency he obtains a scale of 80 subsequent frequencies, a scale of 25 identical intervals, from harmonic 1 to harmonic 5, whereas the frequency rate in equal temperament is the twelfth root of two.

Stockhausen employs intervals that are wider than a semitone, with a frequency rate that is the twenty-fifth root of five: each subsequent frequency was obtained by multiplying the previous one by 1.066494.

Five is a recurring number in the piece: 5 notes make up a sequence; 5 sequences make up a set or "sequenzgruppe". After singling out the frequencies, the lengths in relation to the length of the tape (2.5 centimetres is equal to 0.039 seconds) and the loudness, the different sections of the piece can be rebuilt for each sequence or group: 5 parts plus the final coda[9], as you can see in figure 6 concerning the rebuilding of the first section of the piece.

PWGL enables not only the rebuilding of historical pieces but also the reinterpretation of sounds from the past: this task can prove worthwhile, particularly for those approaching Csound for the first time.

In the second example, proposed by composer H. Torres Maldonado, we create micro-polyphonic textures of a spectral nature starting from an instrument designed by Jean-Claude Risset[10] and create, as usual, a patch to transfer the result in Csound.

---

[9] It is fundamental to read about the score (K. Stockhausen, 1954 [22]) and the analysis of H. Silberhorn (H. Silberhorn, 1980).

[10] The instrument, created by the French composer Jean-Claude Risset (1969) for the piece "Mutation", is included in The Amsterdam Catalogue of Csound Computer Instruments, available on the website:
http://www.music.buffalo.edu/hiller/accci/02/02_43_1.txt.html

This lovely sound, similar to the Tibetan harmonic chant, produces an arpeggio with the series of harmonics: you can clearly hear the fundamental and the partial ones from 5 to 9.

Risset's score was modified by using a starting pitch of C2=65.41Hz instead of the original frequency of 96Hz.

The notes which weren't present in the arpeggio will be used to produce new spectra. From the starting frequency of 65.41Hz the new set of pitches obtained is (see figure 5): 69.3; 77.78; 87.31; 92.5; 103.83; 110.0; 123.47Hz.

These pitches, along with the starting frequency, will be the fundamentals of the new spectra of the micropolyphonic texture.

Even in such circumstances, the abstract (see figure 8) will collect the music information from the Csound score: instrument; start time, defined by Fibonacci series; length, derived from the retrograde of the series; frequency, amplitude; offset.

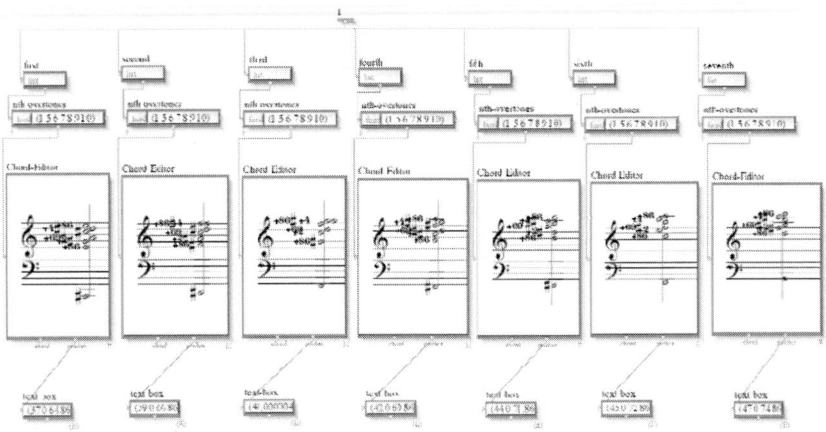

Figure 4: Production of new spectra with fundamental 69.3; 77.78; 87.31; 92.5; 103.83; 110.0; 123.47.

```
f1 0 1024 10 1 0 0 0 .7 .7 .7 .7 .7 .7
;       start    dur     freq     amp      offset
i1      1        68      65.41    1500      .03
i1      2        42      69.3     1500      .03
i1      3        26      77.78    1500      .03
i1      5        16      87.31    1500      .03
i1      8        10      92.5     1500      .03
i1      13        6      103.83   1500      .03
i1      21        4      110      1500      .03
i1      34        2      123.47   1500      .03
```

Figure 5: Musical information contained in the Csound score.

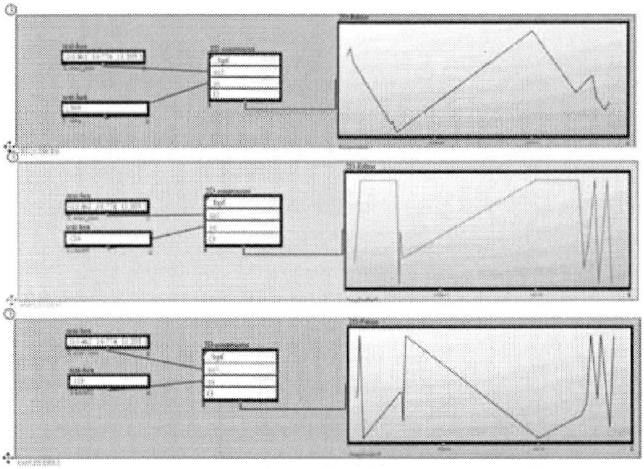

Figure 6: First section of Studie II - Instrument one: graphic representation through a 2d editor of amplitudes and frequencies. 2d- editor is a generic editor box for objects that have data in 2 dimensions: x (creation times) and y values (amplitudes/frequencies).

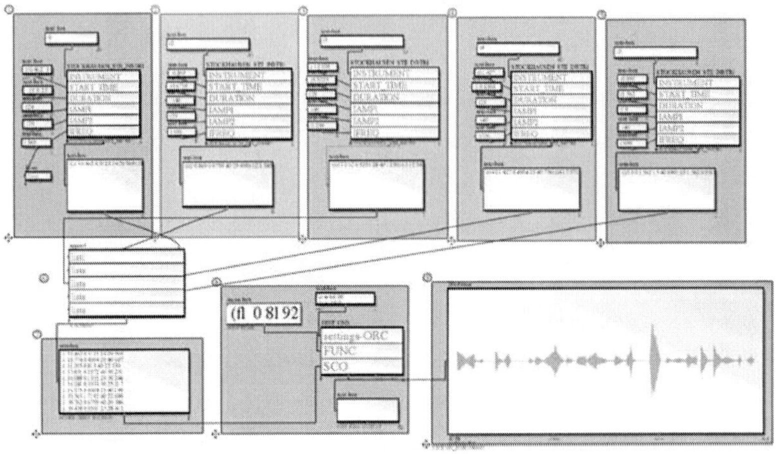

Figure 7: First section of Studio II. In (1-5) you can see the material for the five instruments or "mixture" composing the "gruppen". In the result list (7) you can see the final score achieved by gathering the x-append of the score for each instrument (6). In (8) you can choose function from a 'menu box', All information regarding orchestra and score is combined in the last Abstract Box which has the task of rendering using Csound (9).

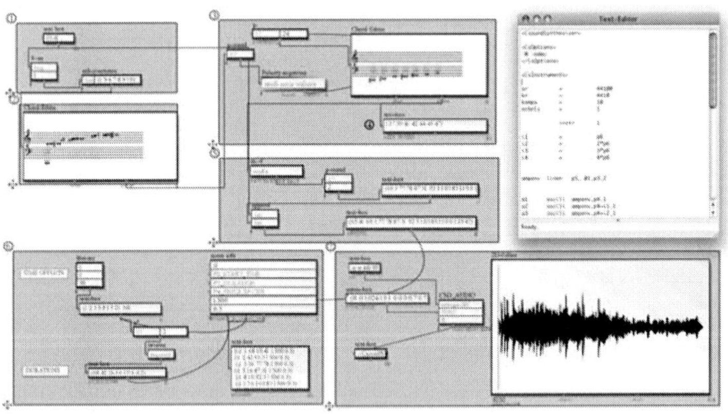

Figure 8: In (1) you can see the fundamental frequency of the arpeggio (65, 41 Hertz) and relative harmonics (2). In (3) the spectrum is made "negative" by obtaining a set of frequencies that will pave the way for new arpeggios (4). In (5) the fundamental frequency is added to the resulting frequencies, which brings about the abstract- box (6). In (7) the result of rendering is shown.

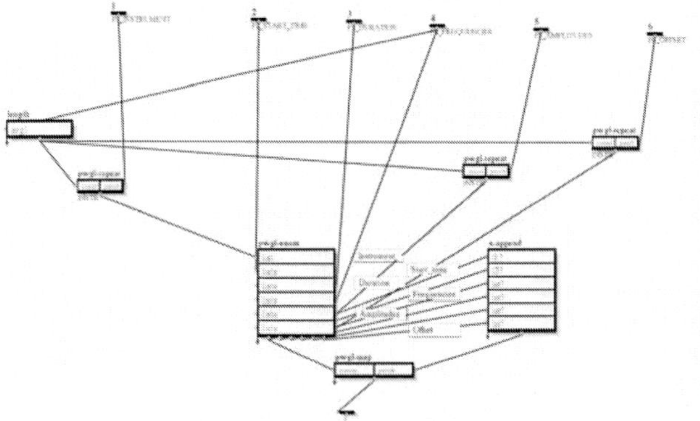

Figure 9: Detail of the abstract-box in figure 6: all the music data to be transferred to Csound can be seen.

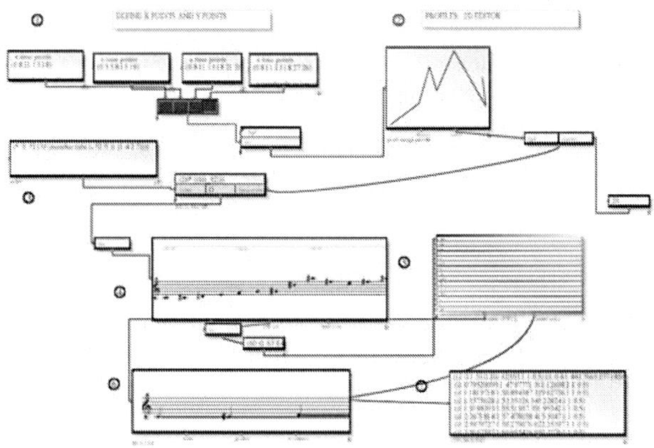

Figure 10: A sequence of midi notes between the extremes follows a melodic profile chosen among the ones available (2). The melodic profile is made through Cartesian values (x,y) in a text-box (1). The type of interval chosen influences the result by using the heuristic rules defined in (3). The resulting sequence is accelerated or decelerated and provides a sequence in (6) with the relevant score in Csound (7).

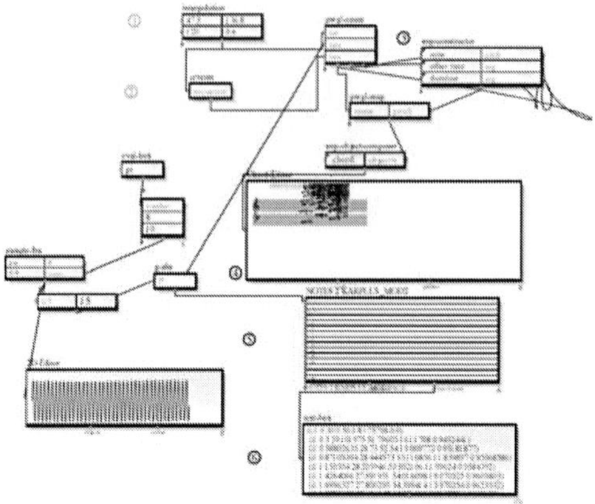

Figure 11: A sequence of notes defined between two extremes follows a sinusoidal harmonic profile combined with a concave/convex curve. In (1) the extreme notes of the sequence are defined; in (2) a sinusoidal function is used to deliver the notes; in (3) we interpolate, by using PATCH-WORK INTERPOLATION, between the two. In (3) all the information (note, offset time, duration etc.) is channelled, making it possible to see the information in the "Chord Editor" ; in 4) we can check the result of the sinusoidal delivery process. In (6) we get the result to be transferred to Csound by means of an abstract-box (5).

Conclusion

In this article I have described how to combine PWGL with Csound in order to make a collection of Csound instruments. By doing so, musicians can avoid using expensive programs and libraries, which are often influenced by the ideas and approaches–even compositional ones–of their creators, and they can make their own.

Thanks to these modest suggestions, musicians can create their own libraries for sound synthesis and can modify them, on the basis of their needs as these present themselves.

I have described the first result of a work in progress, which will lead to a suite of synthesizers or a virtual synthesizer to conduct orchestras and Csound synthesis; such instruments will come up alongside the existing PWGLSynth modules. PWGL will become an environment for the design and graphical display of the instruments.

It is easy to envisage that PWGL will have an increasingly important role in algorithmic composition and sound synthesis, thanks to the support of an ever widening community of developers and end users.

References

"Association of Lisp Users (A.L.U)," accessed April 12, 2013, http://www.alu.org/alu/home.

Boulanger, Richard, *The Csound Book*, edited by R. Boulanger. Cambridge: The MIT Press, 2000.

Bianchini, R., A. Cipriani, *Il suono virtuale - Sintesi ed elaborazione del Suono – Teoria e pratica con Csound.*: ConTempoNet Ed. pp. 343–362, 2007.

Gogins, M., *A Csound Tutorial*, pp. 54–55, accessed April 12, 2013, http://michaelgogins.tumblr.com/CsoundVST, 2006.

Jaffe, D. and Smith, J.O., "Extensions of the Karplus-Strong Plucked-String Algorithm," *Computer Music Journal* 7, no. 2, 1983. Reprinted in C.Roads, *The Music Machine.* MIT Press, pp. 481–494, 1989.

Karplus, K., Strong, A., "Digital Synthesis of plucked string and drum timbres," *Computer Music Journal* 7 , no 2, pp. 43–55, 1983.

Kuuskankare, M., Laurson, M., "PWGL, Towards an Open and Intelligent Learning Environment for Higher Music Education," *Proceedings of the 5*th *European Conference on Technology Enhanced Learning.*: EC.-TEL 2010, 2010.

Kuuskankare, M., Laurson, M., Norilo, V., "PWGLSynth, A Visual Synthesis Language for Virtual Instrument Design and Control," *Computer Music Journal* 29, no. 3, pp. 29–41, 2005.

Laurson, M. and Norilo, V., "Copy-synth-patch: A Tool for Visual Instrument Design," *Proceedings of ICMC04*, 2004.

Laurson, M. and Norilo, V., "Recent Developments in PWGLSynth," *Proceedings of DAFx 2003*, pp. 69–72, 2003.

Lorrain, D., "Inharmonique, Analyse de la Bande de l'Oeuvre de Jean-Claude Risset," *Rapports IRCAM* 26, 1980.

Mathews, M., Risset, J.-C. "Analysis of Instrument Tones," *Physics Today* 22, no. 2, pp. 23–30, 1969.

Moore, F.R., "Table Lookup Noise for Sinusoidal Digital Oscillators," *Computer Music Journal* 1, no. 2, pp. 26–29, 1977. Reprinted in C. Roads and J. Strawn, *Foundations of Computer Music.* MIT Press, pp. 326–334, 1985.

Moorer, J.A. "Analysis-based Additive Synthesis," ed. Strawn J. *Digital AudioSignal Processing: An Anthology.*: A-R Editions, pp. 160–177, 1985.

Mickelson, H., "Panorama," *Csound Magazine*, Autumn, 1999.

Risset, J.-C., *An Introductory Catalogue of Computer Synthesized Sounds*, reprinted in *The Historical CD of Digital Sound Synthesis.*: Computer Music Currents nº 13, Wergo, Germany, 1969.

Risset, J.-C., "Additive Synthesis of Inharmonic Tones, " ed. M.V. Mathews and J.R. Pierce, *Current Directions in Computer Music Research,* MIT Press, pp. 159–163, 1989a.

Risset, J.-C., "Computer Music Experiments 1964-...," eds. C. Roads, *The Music Machine*, Cambridge:MIT Press, pp. 67–74, 1989b.

Roads, C., *Computer Music Tutorial*, Cambridge:MIT Press, p. 452, 1996.

Silberhorn, H., *Die Reihentechnik in Stockhausens Studie II*, 1980.

Steele, G.L., *Common Lisp: The Language*. Digital Press, 1990.

Stockhausen, K., *Nr.3 Elektronische Studien, Studie II, Partitur.*: Universal Edition, 1954.

Stroppa,M., "Paradigms for the high-level musical control of digital signal Processing," *Proceedings of the International Conference on Digital Audio Effects (DAFx-00),* 2000.

QUINCE:
A MODULAR APPROACH TO MUSIC EDITING

MAXIMILIAN MARCOLL

Abstract

This paper is an introduction to the basic concepts of the software "quince" as well as to some fundamental ideas that lead to its development. Quince is a modular, non-media-centric, open source editor that presents time-based data in a very flexible way that enables quince to be used for a multitude of applications. Since one of the modules that quince uses to process sound in realtime is Csound, quince can be used as a front end for Csound.

Because of its open and extensible structure quince can be interesting for all those who want to perform a variety of nonstandard operations on different types of time-based data in a single project.

This text is not intended to cover all the functionality of quince, or serve as a tutorial or user guide. For a more comprehensive discussion of features, please refer to the documentation provided on the quince website (http://quince.maximilianmarcoll.de).

I. Introduction

Almost all artists, working with digital media, at some point ask themselves, "What tools fit my needs best?" The problem that one encounters very often is that computer programs do not only carry out tasks and give us options and possibilities, but also determine the ways in which we use them. In order to find out what tools we need, we first have to find out what we actually want to do. This is not as easy as it might seem. We tend to do what technology suggests to and sometimes we even confuse those suggestions with our own ideas. In order to find out what we really want, it is necessary to critically reflect on our use of technology and to overcome the tendency to do what our tools were made for, what is easy and convenient. Sir Ken Robinson put it this way:

> "Being creative means challenging what you take for granted."

but:

> "The problem in challenging what you take for granted is, that you don't know what it is, because you take it for granted." (Robinson, 2009)

There are many excellent programs available, for all kinds of specialised tasks. Usually, they are solutions to one particular problem. Quince, however, is not. The process of composing music, as I understand it, is a complex network of many interconnected tasks which have to be carried out in ever changing orders on different stages of various kinds of data. Quince's structure corresponds to this nonlinear approach to the working process and is not bound to any traditional working paradigm. Its flat hierarchy and flexible modular structure offer full responsibility and control about the working process and the "treatment" of data. Moreover, quince was designed to carry out operations not anticipated at the time of its development.

The fundamental concept of quince is a genuinely digital approach that breaks with some traditional paradigms in order to help users find suitable workflows for their respective situations. As a result, the structure and working paradigm are very different from those of traditional editors, digital audio work stations or sequencers.

Just like the fruit, the usage of the program quince requires quite some knowledge about its features, its strengths and weaknesses as well as some getting used to. Once one knows how to deal with it though, the results can be delicious.

II. General Structure

Working Paradigm

Quince breaks with the classic "tape recorder & mixing board" paradigm. Every digital audio work station presents audio data in tracks that can be mixed using a digital simulation of a mixing board. The only aspect of these models that quince does implement is the timeline. Quince does not represent data arranged in tracks and since there are no tracks, there also is no mixer to mix them. Instead, data is hosted by "Strips": Vertically aligned areas containing Layers in which data can be displayed and edited. There can be virtually any number of Layers in a Strip, which are displayed on top of each other (see Figures 1 and 2).

Modularity

Almost everything that does carry out significant tasks in quince is a plug-in. The views that display data, the components that play back sequences as well as functions which manipulate data all are external bundles loaded at runtime. It is not necessary to rebuild the entire program to add new functionality.

Media Types

Quince is not media centric. The only constraint about data is that it has to be time-based if it should be edited in quince. Whether an event represents an audio or video file, a note in a score or the execution of a shell script - it does not matter as long as the data being represented somehow happens in time. However, in order to be drawn and played back appropriately, there need to be plug-ins that can understand the respective media types.

Hierarchy

Almost every piece of software is designed in a hierarchical way, so that some functions are easier to reach and some tasks are easier to achieve than others, depending on the judgement of the programer(s). As stated earlier, it is my belief that a program's structure determines the ways in which we use it. In this sense, the design of the program - its hierarchy of functionality - has a great impact on the supposedly creative and original choices that artists or composers make while using it.

To strengthen the decisions of the user and to give her or him more freedom, quince implements a flat hierarchy in which all functionality is directly in one's grasp. Nothing is hidden in complicated drop-down menu trees and no function is considered to be more important than any other. Of course there are always tasks and workflows that are complicated and involve multiple steps. Quince does however offer a way to combine multiple operations into one single step in order to create more powerful tools and to simplify the utilisation of complicated operations. (See the sections on Functions and FunctionGraphs for an explanation.) Of course Quince is not neutral; on the contrary, my convictions are reflected in the software in a way that is far from subtle. The design of the program does however address the issues mentioned above and seeks to offer an alternative solution.

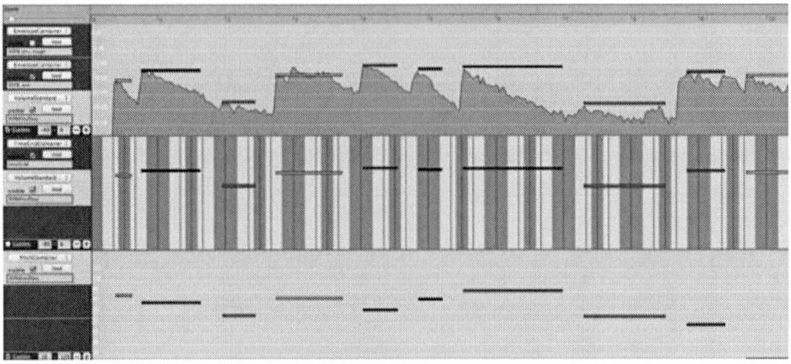

Figure 1: Project window with three strips containing multiple layers.

III. Data Representations

Events

An event in quince simply is a set of parameters. A parameter is a combination of a keyword (e.g. “volume”) and a value (e.g. 0 dB). Every event is created with a basic set of parameters like ”start”, ”duration” and ”description” that can be extended to virtually any number. Apart from a few reserved words, any string can be used as the keyword of a parameter.

Sequences

There actually is no difference between an event and a sequence in quince. Every event can contain an arbitrary number of sub-events. If an event contains sub-events, it may be regarded as a sequence. Hence, it is a question of perspective whether something is an event or a sequence, which is why the term “object“ is used instead. A selection of objects (events) can always be folded into a super-object (sequence) by the push of a button. Accordingly, a sequence can always be unfolded in a similar manner.

Data Types

For a better understanding of how data is being represented it might be helpful to know about a few internal data types used to distinguish between different kinds of objects:

- *QuinceObject*, the most basic type of object, used for events and sequences, also the supertype of all other types.
- *DataFile*, a reference to any kind of file.
- *AudioFile*, a reference to an audio file.
- *Envelope*, a representation of a volume envelope, typically extracted from an audio file.
- *PitchCurve*, a progression of frequency values.

Visual Representations

ContainerViews

ContainerViews are plug-ins that display data and provide interfaces for the editing and arrangement of objects. There are different ContainerViews available for different types of data and for the display of different parameters. While the time-related parameters ("start" and “duration”) are always assigned to the x-axis of the ContainerView, the parameter that is displayed on the y-axis is determined by the view. Every Layer contains exactly one ContainerView to show its contents.

ChildViews

While ContainerViews display the contents of objects, ChildViews are plug-ins used to graphically represent the sub-events of the object loaded by the surrounding ContainerView.

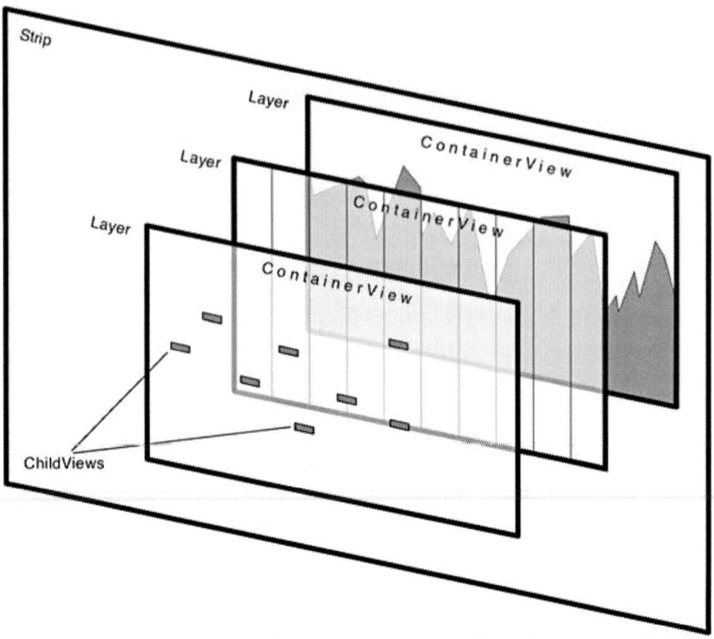

Figure 2: View Hierarchy. Schematic representation of a strip containing three layers with ContainerViews, one of which uses ChildViews to display data.

IV. Manipulating Data

Functions

Functions are plug-ins that perform operations on objects. The result of the execution of a function can either be

- a new object,
- a change in the object the function operated on, or
- the export of data into an external file.

There already is a great variety of functions available. By the time of the publication of this book, there were 43 Functions available for

- Alignment of objects
- Mapping data onto objects
- Peak detection

- Data conversion and extraction
- Creating grids
- Data reduction
- Equal distribution of objects
- Context sensitive corrections
- Sorting (automated folding)
- Importing data from external programs, including Praat (Boersma and Weenink, 1992) and SPEAR (Klingbeil, 2003)
- Exporting data to external programs, including LilyPond (Nienhuys and Nieuwenhuizen, 1997)
- Quantisation (time and pitch)
- Set operations
- Transposition (time and pitch)

If a function requires one or more input objects to operate (as opposed to functions which create objects without manipulating existing data), it needs an object of the correct type in each of its input slots. For example, if a function maps a *PitchCurve* onto a Sequence it will have two input slots: the first expecting an object of type *PitchCurve* and the second expecting an object of type *QuinceObject* to map the *PitchCurve* on to.

Function Graphs

There is a way to create powerful customised tools right within quince: Functions can be combined, very similarly to the way in which events can be folded into sequences. Using the FunctionComposer, two Functions can be combined into a bigger unit, called FunctionGraph. Not all combinations of functions are possible, though. Two functions are compatible if the output object of the first is of the same type as one of the input objects of the second. For example, if the output of the first function is an envelope (an object of type *Envelope*), and the second expects a sequence (an object of type *QuinceObject*), they cannot be combined. Although only two functions can be joined together at a time, much more complex FunctionGraphs can be built: FunctionGraphs behave just like functions, so you can combine them both with one another.

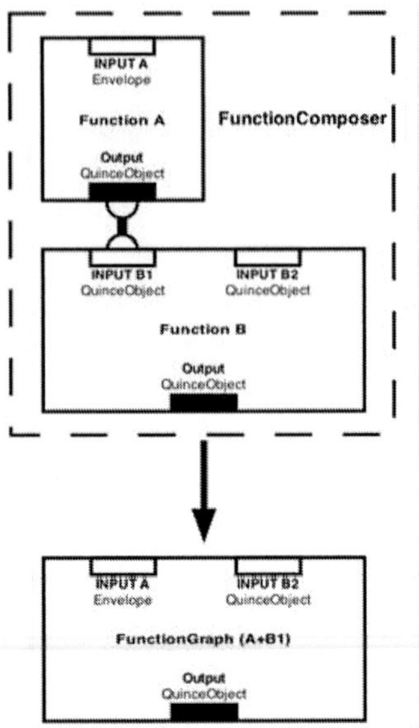

Figure 3: FunctionComposer Example.

V. Playback

Objects are played back using "Players": that is, plug-ins which interpret an object's parameters in a certain way and produce output in real time. During playback quince sends all the data to the currently active player plug-in. How the player reacts to the incoming data is dependent on its implementation.

There are currently two players available:

- The *AudioFilePlayer* that interprets events as references to audio files and
- The *CsoundPlayer*, an actual instance of Csound that converts events into Csound score lines and performs the resulting Csound score in realtime using one of the built-in Csound instruments or a custom orchestra written by the user. (The orchestra files used for the playback of sequences using the *CsoundPlayer* can be written directly in quince, too. Thus, quince can serve as a front end for Csound.)

VI. Expandability

Quince is released under the GNU Public License. It is written in Objective-C and can easily be extended by writing plug-ins (also in Objective-C). The QuinceApi is lightweight and simple to use. It was designed in such a way that in order to create a new plug-in, only a minimum of administrative code has to be written. Players, Views and Functions can all be added by users to customise quince to their respective needs.

VII. Conclusion

It is a well known fact that new technologies can have a great influence on the works of artists. This is of course also true the other way around: Whenever art changes in respect of content and aesthetics, new tools may be required. Quince was developed to implement a new working paradigm that corresponds to new ways of composing music. Its aim is to open up mewpossibilities for decision making where many other programs only offer black-box solutions.

VIII. Future Work

Although there already are a variety of plug-ins available, there are still many more to be written: FFT and pitch detection plug-ins, export and import to and from various formats (Midi, SDIF, MusicXML, to name a few), players that support video, OSC, amongst others. So far quince only runs on Mac OS X but it will be ported to Linux/Unix and Windows using the GNUStep framework in the future.

References

Boersma, Paul and Weenink, David, “Praat” (1992) , accessed August 24, 2012, http://www.fon.hum.uva.nl/praat/.

Klingbeil, Michael, “Spear” (2003) accessed August 24, 2012 http://www.klingbeil.com/spear/.

Nienhuys, Han-Wen and Nieuwenhuizen, "LilyPond" (1997), accessed August 24, 2012, http://lilypond.org/.

Robinson, Sir Ken, Commencement Address at the Rhode Island School of Design, (2009) accessed August 24, 2012, http://youtu.be/ELLLocSXy0Y.

CSOUND AT HMTM HANNOVER

AN INTERVIEW WITH JOACHIM HEINTZ AND ALEX HOFMANN

Joachim Heintz is a composer and is head of the Incontri electronic music studio at the HMTM Hannover. He lectures in composition and computer music programming at the HMTM Hannover and at the HfK Bremen.

Alex Hofmann is an improvisor and former student at the HMTM Hannover and is currently working on his PhD thesis in Music Acoustics at the University of Music and Performing Arts Vienna.

Joachim, you are teaching electronic composition and live-electronics at a music university. What tends to be the background of your students?

J.H.: My job is teaching the composition students. So they have a good knowledge of composition in contemporary music and experiences with their own way of working. Usually they have very little, or even no knowledge about the technical side of electronic music.

How would you rate the willingness of the students to get into computer programming and use tools like Csound?

J.H.: I would make the distinction here between willingness and interest in general, and whether the students are using programming tools for their own work. When I explain methods of sound synthesis or sound modification, I usually explain it with Csound and PD, and I experience the students as being interested in understanding what is happening, and how it sounds. Whether the students use tools like Csound or PD for their own work, depends on many things: their creative nature, their knowledge, and what they need for realising their compositional ideas. There are so many ways of working in electronic music and programming is not always the right way to go for everyone. But to give you a number, I would say that at least half of the students use programming tools to realise their ideas.

Alex, you studied at the HMTM Hannover some years ago. How did you first get interested in audio programming?

A.H.: I was fascinated by synthetic sounds since my early childhood. I must have been around 6 or 7 years old, at this time in school, after nap time, the educator woke us up with some "outta space" music. I was very impressed by the wideness of the sounds and couldn't identify the instruments, which made me curious. I asked for a copy on cassette, which I got, but with no label on it. Then in Berlin in the 90s the electronic dance music scene was very big and I was again taken by the artificial sounds of synthesisers. I did a bit of DJing but nevertheless I passed traditional music education and learnt to play flute, saxophone and piano. Around 2002 I had the idea to combine saxophone improvisation and electronic sounds for a solo-performance, but didn't know exactly how to do it. I used commercial software sequencers and VST plugins to generate MIDI backings and improvised over them, but I wanted to interact with sounds in real-time. Then I came to Hannover to study saxophone with Matthias Schubert and soon after I started, I met Kostia Rapoport and Damian Marhulets from Johannes Schöllhorn's composition class. They told me about a course on electronic composition and that Joachim Heintz was teaching how to write crazy code snippets, so that the computer generates and modifies every sound you can think of. At this time I was already experimenting with the Clavia Nord Modular, but this was more a keyboard instrument you had to play, so the interaction with the sound-engine was limited on the controller interface of keyboard and knobs. I wanted an interface to sound-synthesis, which was controlled by other sounds, in my case by the improvisation on the saxophone. In Joachim's class I realised quite soon that learning an audio programming-language like Csound, Max/MSP or SuperCollider would be a good tool for that. At this time Max/MSP came with a lot of demo-patches, which seemed to solve all separate problems and I just had to "copy/paste" them together in the right way to build the interactive music system I had in mind. But you can imagine what a mess of virtual-cables this ended up in. That was the time I saw some slim lines of SuperCollider code during a workshop of Nikolai Zinke and thought, I should translate everything into it. So I learnt programming SuperCollider and built a lot of little tools and patches for several live-performances.

I.M.: *Why did you then start to experiment with Csound?*

A.H.: In SuperCollider I always got stuck with programming interactivity because of the need for OSC communication between language and server. Analysis of audio-input (e.g. pitch and beat-tracking) has to be done on the server side, processing the obtained high-level data has to be done in the language and sound synthesis is on the server again. I never got used to it and things got complicated very soon. So I was still using my old Max/MSP patch to play "Me against myself". Then I talked to Joachim and he pointed me to Csound and asked me if I'd like to learn it by my own and document the learning-process.

Joachim, what was your idea behind that?

J.H.: Well, my core intention was to improve the learning process of Csound. So I thought: at first we need a kind of diagnosis. What is good when you start learning Csound, what is missing? What can Csound learn from other Open Source software like SuperCollider or PureData. I thought it might be ideal to have someone like Alex, who has a lot of experience in this area, knowing Max, PD, SC and more. What are the pros and cons of Csound in this comparision?

Alex, what, in detail, was your diagnosis?

A.H.: I started to learn Csound with Richard Boulanger's introduction examples (toots), which are available in the CsoundQt menu. But they covered just the basics so I started to read the "Canonical Csound Reference Manual", but this was too much, because it's really a reference. What I was missing at this point was a simple introduction to CsoundQt, explaining the language of Csound, together with the possibilities of GUI "widgets" and how to setup your preferences, just to have a quick-start into creating music.

What I really liked about Csound compared to other environments was the score. Thinking about sound events in time strikes me as being a very musical idea. On the other hand, you are not forced to use the score, you can also work with live-electronics. So I made notes about every little step during my learning process: questions I had in mind, and the answers I got from the manual, Joachim, or from the mailing list.

Then Joachim and I showed this protocol to Andres Cabrera in the winter of 2009 and together we decided to add an "Examples -> Getting started" menu point to CsoundQT. There, we demonstrated issues from the topics “Basics”, “Real-time interaction”, and “Language features”. Which will hopefully make beginning with Csound a little easier. Joachim also provided useful instruments like an “Audio Input Test” and a “Multi-Channel Soundfile Player”.

Joachim, you started several activities involving open source software. What do you like about the idea of open source software and how far can institutions like universities support open source software?

J.H.: Let me start with the latter; universities, at least most universities in Germany, like the Hannover Hochschule, are actually part of the public domain. Their aim is to offer services to everyone, independent of whether you can pay for them or not. At least this should be the case, although in the past few decades many elements have been introduced which compromise this “for everyone” ideology.

So, being part of the public domain, a school or university should actually have a proper interest to work with open source software, and help the development of this software. This can be done in several ways: donating towards the development, inviting developers for workshops, contributing examples. Many things are easy to do if you are in an institution, which are hard, or even impossible to do if you are not. Doing this, the institution gets a lot back, and so do the students. They can work with software that is free in many senses, they can be a part of its development, and they can share their patches with their friends in Chile, China or Iran.

For the more personal aspect of your question: I like to collaborate with other people beyond any commercial interests. Put simply, the removal of money from the equation creates an atmosphere that offers a counterbalance to a society driven mainly by buying and selling. Moreover, I have met such nice people and gained such good and valuable friends in this community.

Interview: Iain McCurdy

THE CSOUND REAL-TIME COLLECTION

IAIN MCCURDY

Abstract

The Csound Real-time Collection is a popular collection of examples written by Iain McCurdy.

Begun in 2006 as an online resource, the collection has been continuously built upon since its inception until, as of January 2013, it holds over 350 examples. These examples range from simple demonstrations of individual opcodes to more elaborate demonstrations of synthesis and DSP techniques. Some examples exemplify techniques specific to working with the Csound language and some examples offer implementations of classic electronic instruments. The collection is hosted on the authors own website at www.iainmccurdy.org/csound.html and receives an average of 250 visitors per day.

This article serves as an introduction to the collection.

Introduction

In the early 2000s Csound was still predominantly used as an environment for offline rendering and whilst facilities for real-time performance existed they tended to be unstable or incomplete. Prior to the implementation of Csound's API, options for GUI were pretty much non-existent. Prior to the release of Csound version 5, the project was becoming increasingly fragmented with a variety of developers having each released their own 'flavour' of Csound to suit their own requirements. One of these was DirectCsound (which later became CsoundAV) written by Gabriel Maldonado. It made the running of Csound in real time a practical reality through its use of the Window's Direct X system and later Steinberg's ASIO protocol. Another of Maldonado's additions, which defined the approach of the Real-time Collection, was the inclusion of GUI widget opcodes that made use of the Fast Light Tool Kit (FLTK). All of the early examples made use of these FLTK GUI building widgets (fig.1).

The opcode examples in the Canonical Csound Reference Manual at this time would prove that the opcode worked but tended to do little to exemplify its capabilities. (The examples in the Csound Reference Manual have improved immensely in recent years due to the tireless work of Menno Knevel.) The Real-time Collection attempts to provide examples that allow the user to explore the hidden recesses of an opcode or technique through a real time exploration of its critical parameters. This is aided through on-screen controls, MIDI control and an incorporated instruction panel with every example (fig.2). Many of the examples have been employed by other Csound users as finished instruments but it has always been my desire that once the user has got the flavour of an example and the opcodes it employs through real-time tinkering that they delve deeper into the code and make changes. The point of using Csound is surely to provide users with the power to work at a code level. In fact, the Real-time Collection grew out of examples that I wrote while teaching a course on Csound, the students were still restricted to rendering their Csound orchestras and scores in non-real time but I used the real-time examples as a demonstration of the sonic possibilities of the techniques they were learning.

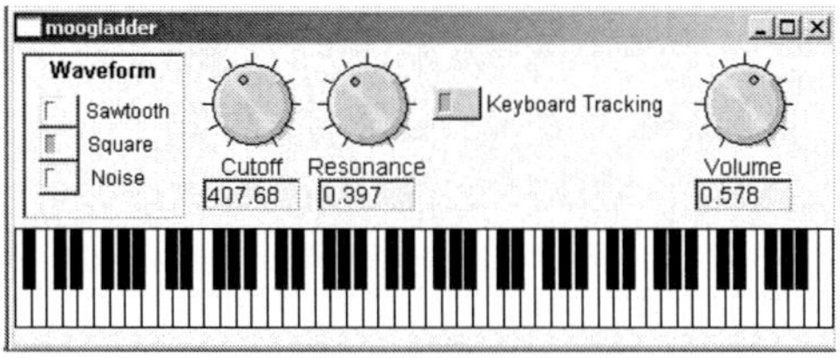

Figure 1. Main control panel for an FLTK GUI example that deonstrates Victor Lazzarini's moogladder filter emulation.

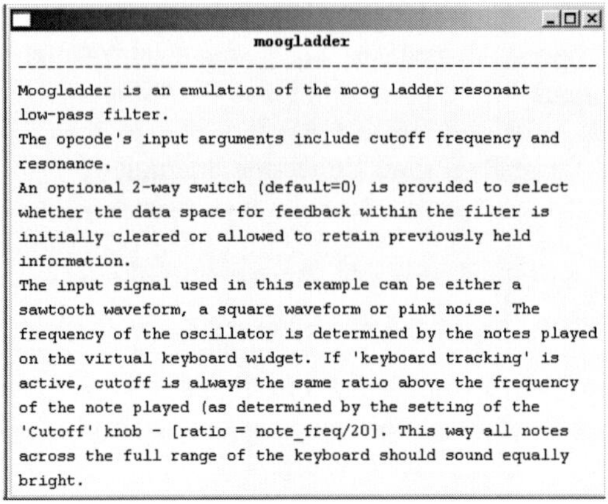

Figure 2. The corresponding instructions panel for the GUI panel shown in figure 1.

Csound now offers many other options for building GUIs—this has come about mainly thanks to the API (application programming interface) —but the Real-time Collection, for the sake of continuity, cross-platform uniformity and front-end independence, continues to make use of Csound's built in FLTK widgets.

CSoundQt

CsoundQt is now the front-end where most people begin their journey with Csound; it is the front-end that comes packaged with the Csound installers. CsoundQt possesses its own set of GUI widgets (employing the Qt framework) and to reflect this, Rene Jopi has ported most of the examples to CsoundQt (fig. 3). These examples are accessible through CsoundQt's built-in examples menu so there is no need for a separate download. Some of the CsoundQt examples are also able to capitalise upon features unique to it such as the GUI file browsers.

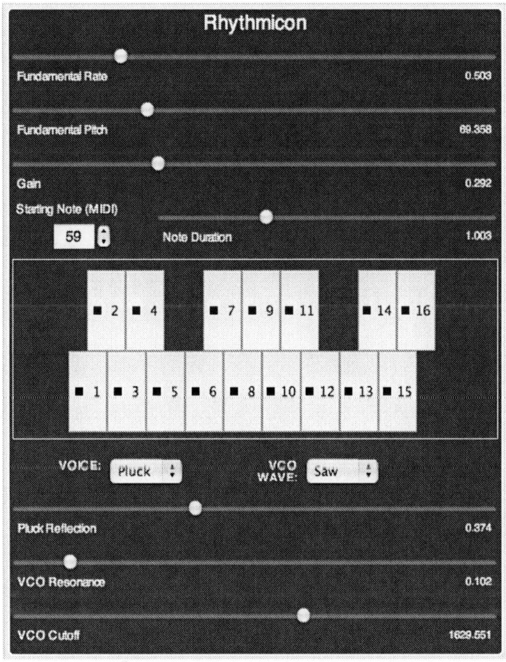

Figure 3. A CsoundQt example that emulates the historical electronic instrument invented by the composer Henry Cowell, the 'Rhythmicon'.

Cabbage

There is now also a growing section of examples that have been written specifically for Rory Walsh's "Cabbage" front-end for Csound. These examples are available either from the collection's main website or from Cabbage's own website. Cabbage can render much more modern looking GUIs than FLTK (using the Juce framework) and the code needed to do so is much sleeker. It also offers users the possibility of exporting examples as VST or AU plug-ins for use in other software such as Ableton Live or Garageband.

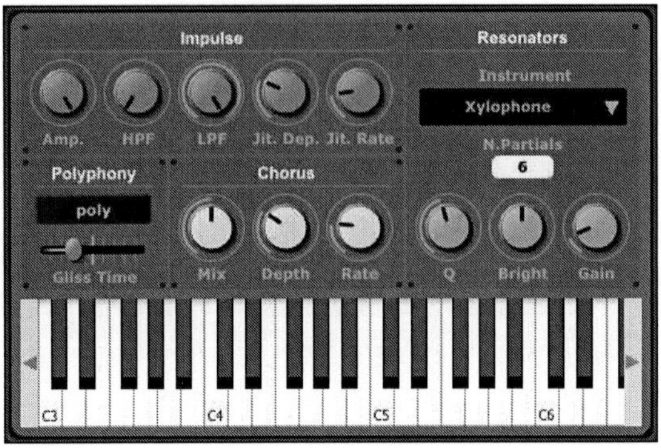

Figure 5. A modal synthesis example that utilises the more modern looking Cabbage front-end.

Method

The didactic nature of the examples is reflected in their extensive use of commenting within their code. Users are encouraged to delve into the code and to edit, explore and experiment, but even before this stage, an instruction panel will provide users with an example overview to help users get started. I regularly receive emails from users from around the world requesting further assistance and I normally do my best to offer that help. Were it not for user feedback, I would probably have abandoned my work on this online resource some time ago.

Conclusion

The Csound Real-time collection continues to be added to but at a much slower rate than in its initial stages. Newer examples tend to be larger and more complex and as Csound has diversified, with the emergence of the front-ends Cabbage and CsoundQt, the medium for examples has broadened beyond the use of Csound's built-in FLTK opcodes. In order to constrain the number of examples and prevent the collection from becoming too unwieldy, disparate smaller examples are being gathered into larger single amalgamations to facilitate quicker comparison of opcodes and techniques. Many instruments have also been transplanted into UDOs (user defined opcodes) in order to facilitate easier transplantation in other Csound projects.

References

Boulanger, Richard, *The Csound Book*, edited by R. Boulanger. Cambridge: The MIT Press, 2000.

TEACHING WITH CSOUND

INTERVIEW WITH PEIMAN KHOSRAVI AND RORY WALSH

Rory Walsh lectures in music at DkIT (Dundalk Institute of Technology) in Ireland and Peiman Khosravi lectures at City University London.

Pictures: Rory Walsh (left), Peiman Khosravi (right)

How long have you both been using Csound?

Peiman Khosravi: I started learning it with the aid of the Csound Book about 10 years ago, when I was an undergraduate music student. Then I was using it on and off, mostly to do the odd sound transformation. I took it up more seriously about 6 years ago or so and started to make more elaborate instrument designs.

Rory Walsh: No books for me, I started learning Csound in 2000 with the help of Victor Lazzarini. As it turns out, it was one of the very first audio programs I ever used.

Please briefly describe the area in which you teach and the subject/module(s) titles?

PK: I teach music technology to undergraduate music students. This includes conventional recording, editing, and mixing, as well as electroacoustic composition and software programming.

RW: Like Peiman, most of my teaching is focused in the area of music technology. I teach subjects such as sound synthesis, acoustics, interactive systems, and computer programming for audio applications.

What other software do you use in your teaching?

PK: Protools, MaxMSP, Audacity, CDP (composers desktop project), Audiosculpt, and Spear.

RW: Pure Data, Reaper, Audacity, Renoise, Processing, various screen-casting software depending on the OS, and a host of different compilers for various languages.

How do you use Csound in your teaching?

PK: I teach Csound as the main music programming language for the composition technology module. Students are first introduced to its power by using FFTools, my Csound/MaxMSP program for advanced sound processing. At a later stage they are introduced to the Csound programming language in order to produce sound materials and transformations for their composition projects. Students are also required to submit three sound synthesis/processing instruments.

RW: I'm very in that I get to work with a single class of students over the course of 4 semesters so my students probably get more long-term exposure to Csound than Peiman's. The sound synthesis modules which I teach all use Csound as the implementation language for various processing algorithms, and all assignments must be submitted in Csound code. In semester 3, which is the student's first introduction to Csound we work on basic additive synthesis and modulation techniques using WinXound/CsoundQT. Following on from this, in semester 4, we start looking at time-domain audio processing techniques like chorus, flanging, reverb etc. At this stage I introduce csLADSPA so students can apply their processes to audio tracks within Audacity. At the start of the following semester we move on to MIDI driven instruments and I get them to try modelling basic hardware synths using whatever schematic flowcharts we can find. For their final Csound module the students start developing VST plugins using Cabbage and Csound. It's a nice way to close out their time with Csound as it means they can package what they've learned over the two years into distributable software. Apart from the modules in which I teach Csound, I also use it in my acoustics lectures to demonstrate things like wave-shapes, harmonics, and different tuning systems.

How does Csound compare with other software, as a tool for teaching?

PK: I can only answer this question on the basis of my own experience, which is limited to Csound and MaxMSP insofar as music programming languages are concerned. It seems to me that students usually grasp Csound more readily than Max. I suspect this is because in the case of Max one not only has to learn the basic concepts of programming and DSP, but also the graphical user-interface which has its own quirks. When teaching MaxMSP I do not introduce basic DSP until the second or third class, whereas with Csound we start playing with additive synthesis by the end of the first session. Moreover, the score language makes Csound readily usable as a note-based composition tool, which appeals to students who come from the instrumental music background. However, it could just be that I am better at teaching Csound!

RW: It's the same for me. I find that using Csound forces the students to learn some very important principles of digital audio without having to get bogged down in understanding a GUI. It's impossible to teach Csound and avoid things like sampling rates, control-rates, vectors, aliasing, table look-up oscillators, etc. Other systems provide out-of-the-box solutions to various synthesis techniques, but students are often left wondering what exactly happens 'in-the-box'. Learning Csound is a time-consuming endeavour, but because progress is that little bit slower I find that it helps students to be more inquisitive about what they are learning.

In your opinion, what features are lacking and what improvements could be made within Csound to enhance it a teaching tool?

PK: A few years ago the answer to this question would have been the absence of a simple graphical user-interface builder. However, now we have CsoundQT as well as Cabbage, so I have nothing to complain about. As these two programs are rapidly improving I feel that in the near future,

Csound can easily be the number one choice for teaching DSP and creative sound synthesis/processing. Perhaps one element currently lacking is a better display of table contents as well as a spectrogram.

RW: I agree, things are getting a lot better. However, I think better integration of UDOs would be a great. There are many UDOs that help make things more accessible for beginners, but using UDOs can be a little off-putting because of the often complex nature of the code. It has been discussed on the Csound mailing list, but I think that all current UDOs should be shipped with Csound, and placed into a default directory that Csound knows about. This would allow students to use UDOs without having to include the code in-line which clutters orchestras. I think this would have a big impact on teaching Csound, as teachers could develop suites of UDOs for particular modules. Students could also start to deconstruct UDOs over the course of a semester in a type of reverse engineering approach. I think the idea of abstraction is something that works very well in teaching and it's one of the reasons I continue to use Pure Data with my interactive systems students. The mechanisms are already there in Csound, it's just a matter of putting them in place.

For which synthesis or DSP tasks do you see Csound as superior to other platforms?

RW: Probably the vast array of phase vocoder streaming tools?

PK: As far as sound quality is concerned Csound is in my experience superior in spectral processing in comparison with other open-source programming languages that I have used, as well as most commercial software packages I know. Of course, unlike commercial software tools, Csound gives low-level control over the FFT data: the possibilities are endless. I am of course referring to the amazing set of PVS opcodes.
In addition, the Partikkel opcode is without a doubt the most powerful granular synthesis tool that I have ever come across.

How would you assess students' initial response to Csound?

PK: They can become very excited by it. They begin to see the possibilities and the kind of sonic malleability that Csound offers. But more importantly, as soon as they have grasped the basic concepts of the language such as the difference between i-rate, k-rate and a-rate variables, the simplicity of the syntax means that students can quickly start using Csound for composing.

RW: I think excited might be too strong a word, but curiosity, and intimidation are two responses that come to mind!

How many of your students subsequently adopt Csound as their main music software?

PK: It is too soon for me to judge since I only started teaching Csound last september but so far at least one of my current students is working on a piece entirely composed in Csound/Blue and an ex-student is designing MaxMSP/Csound patches for his live performances.

RW: Well I've been lucky enough to be teaching with Csound for about 8 years or so, but even still, I wouldn't imagine that any of my former students have now adopted Csound as their main music software. Many continue to use Csound, but within the context of a larger set-up. Some pipe audio to and from Csound to other software using Jack and Soundflower, while others are using Cabbage to create Csound plugins which they can then use within their preferred workstations. But I don't think any of them have made a complete change-over.

What aspects of Csound prevent them from doing this?

PK: I think using Csound as an algorithmic composition tool is somewhat more cumbersome in comparison with Supercollider. Moreover, the ease with which one can build complex and polished interfaces in MaxMSP is another reason why some may be more attracted to Max. On the other hand, no single software tool offers everything and that is where the power of the Csound api becomes apparent. We can use Csound inside MaxMSP, Pd and Python, as well as inside commercial DAWs such as Ableton Live and hopefully soon Logic when Cabbage has better support for creating AU plug-ins.

RW: Up until recently I would have said it was because it is so difficult to integrate Csound with other audio systems but, as Peiman alluded to, this is changing. Many of our students come to us with a good working knowledge of today's most popular DAWs and I see little point in trying to get them to give up what they know in order to learn a system like Csound. I think a better approach is to enable the students to use Csound with, or within, their preferred software, in a hope that they will start to appreciate just how powerful it is. I think we are currently on the cusp of something big in the life-cycle of Csound and there are two main developments which I see as being significant in this. One is the emergence of fully functional, standalone Csound software such as Boulanger's csGrain, Partikkel Audio's amazing Hadron plugin and not to mention a host of mobile applications, all of which use Csound as a back-end. All these systems allow users to take advantage of Csound's incredible power and versatility without having to write any Csound code at all. Next we have systems like Cabbage and CsoundQT which provide a two-tiered approach. Users who don't know Csound can just use the various high-end instruments provided by the systems to carry out their sound design. Those users who do know Csound can use their skills to develop more high-end instruments for other users. The beauty of these systems is that they provide an entry point for students. Finally we have the emergence of a growing number of interfaces to the Csound core library. Csound can now be run on virtually any device, ranging from phones to tablets, and most recently users have successfully run Csound on the new Raspberry PI. I believe all these developments will help to ensure that Csound stops being a purely academic endeavor for students, and starts becoming the first tool they turn to when it comes to making crazy sounds!

Thank you both for taking the time to talk to me!

Interview: Iain McCurdy

COLLABORATIVE DOCUMENTATION OF OPEN SOURCE MUSIC SOFTWARE: THE CSOUND FLOSS MANUAL

ALEX HOFMANN, IAIN MCCURDY
AND JOACHIM HEINTZ

Abstract

Csound, like most Open Source Music Software, is developed by a group of volunteers. Often developers are also users and their dual role can enhance the project through the addition of unique and idiosyncratic features that reflect a particular developer's area of specialism. Documentation for proprietary software normally closely follows the development of new features for that software but the plethora of documentation for widely used open source software can frequently be found scattered across a range of locations and media, both printed and online, and for this reason it is often difficult for beginners to locate the materials best suited to their needs.

In this article we describe the benefits of the FLOSS manuals platform for the collaborative documentation of free software. Specifically we describe the Csound FLOSS Manual project: an endeavor to produce a concise yet reasonably comprehensive textbook for Csound users. The Csound FLOSS manual is written by the Csound community so that it can be contributed to by experts in the various fields it covers.

Introduction

Open Source Software Development

Collaborative development of open source music software is based on the voluntary work of enthusiastic programmers and musicians. The capacity that various individual developers have to devote themselves to the project often dictates the number of contributions that are made and how quickly the software improves. New features (or feature improvements) are sometimes requested by users while they are realising a new piece of music using Csound. These feature requests are frequently discussed on mailing lists first.

In some cases these discussions lead to collaborations between composers and programmers and sometimes even the composers themselves are able to program the required extensions. Ultimately a successfully developed feature might get added to the software. In most cases the development process is completed by a short entry about its functionality being added to the Csound Reference Manual.

Since Csound's inception in 1986 its documentation has evolved far beyond the scope of the original manual written by Barry Vercoe. Repositories of examples and tutorials have sprung up across the Internet. Many books reference Csound and several books have been devoted entirely to Csound. With all of this, one may very well question the need for yet another addition to this canon of literature. On investigation of the Csound FLOSS Manual's remit, it becomes clear that its intention was not to replicate existing literature but to address an area of instruction that was previously missing (Csound, Flossmanuals.net). Critically this endeavor would employ the new possibilities offered by the Internet to write, distribute and maintain such a textbook.

In the case of Csound, the signal processing units (opcodes) are written in the C programming language (ffitch, 2011). A combination of a number of opcodes, written in the Csound language, can define an instrument that generates or manipulates sounds (Boulanger, 2000). To enrich Csound's signal processing potential, more than 1500 opcodes have been coded and added to the Csound package. Developments in the signal processing and synthesis worlds have led to improvements in existing opcodes, often with subtly different characteristics. To ensure backwards compatibility, older opcodes remain within the Csound package even if newer ones added might supersede them. For example, there are currently eighteen resonant lowpass filters documented in the Csound reference manual (Csound 5.18, 2012). For a beginner the natural question is: Which one do I try first?

Open Source Software Documentation

Documentation is an important part of making software attractive to users.

There is an ongoing discussion about whether proprietary or open source software should be taught in schools and universities (Heintz, 2011). Obviously there are pros and cons regarding both. Commercial software companies are keen to ensure that their software looks user-friendly and that the workflow it exhibits is efficient. To achieve this a great effort is made to provide adequate tutorials, documentation, instructional videos and online support. Software companies are very often keen to offer cut-price versions of their software for schools and teachers and are will equip computer labs with their programs at a fraction of the commercial price in order to win over future customers.

In contrast open source software is easy to install in a computer laboratory because no copy protection will exist. Students who learn the software as part of a course can make a copy of the program (or download it) and transfer it to any other computer without violating copyright. Mailing lists and forum discussions are used to establish an exchange of knowledge between users and developers. Students who are interested in delving deeper can look into the source code and learn about the mechanisms within the software. Users and developers are normally enthusiastic about sharing their knowledge about the software.

A number of questions from Csound newcomers recur on the Csound mailing list: How do we use MIDI in Csound? How do we record and play sound files? How do we to implement FM? It can take a lot of time for a beginner to find answers to these questions on their own whereas when working with commercial software they can usually find a lot of well-ordered examples and instructions close to hand.

In summary, one key disadvantage of Open Source Software can be its diffusion of documentation.

Method

Collaborative Documentation of Community Developed Software

The FLOSS Manuals project was started in 2005 by digital artist Adam Hyde in order to collate knowledge about free software (Flossmanuals.net). FLOSS is an abbreviation for "Free (Libre) Open Source Software". FLOSS Manuals is a non-profit foundation and community creating free manuals and tutorials for free software. Through Adam Hyde's connections with other digital artists, manuals for software like Audacity, Gimp, Blender and PureData were written in the early years. The FLOSS Manuals platform is also interested in hosting translations of existing manuals.

The FLOSS online platform is based on the "booki" engine that–as a descendant of a Wiki–supports collaborative writing and parallel editing of different chapters using a web front-end. A version tracking system logs all contributions with their authors being attributed. Anyone interested in contributing can create a free FLOSS Manuals account and immediately begin writing their own chapters or edit and improve existing ones.

Organisation of Collaborative Writing

In early 2010 Joachim Heintz proposed the idea of a Csound textbook to a number of members of the Csound community. Immediately prior to this proposition there had been some discussion on the Csound list regarding the extent of Csound's existing documentation and an identification of possible gaps. It was felt that while the Csound Reference Manual provided comprehensive documentation of all of its opcodes and features, this was, as its name suggested, best used as a reference rather than as a book from which one might read an entire chapter. The experience of beginners seemed to be that, in the interests of brevity, the manual would often assume some degree of prior knowledge of synthesis principles, mathematics, DSP, computer music or programming concepts.

The Csound Book (Boulanger, 2000), first published in 2000, has promoted Csound to a new and wider audience and has become an essential part of libraries in music departments around the world but since its publication, many new and exciting developments have taken place within Csound and it was hoped that a Csound textbook might provide an update to *The Csound Book* filling in some of the gaps that had appeared since it publication. The Csound textbook could potentially provide more than just a "bridge" until the publication of the next *Csound Book*. *The Csound Book* is essentially a printed publication and in contrast the Csound textbook would be a free online publication, which could be freely added to or edited by any member of the community. It was eventually suggested by Rory Walsh of Dundalk Institute of Technology that the Csound textbook could become part of the FLOSS Manuals project, providing online production tools for creating an online book as well as the facility to publish the finished document through Lulu.com self publishing. Finally, The Csound textbook became the Csound FLOSS Manual.

Results

An initial discussion with several members of the Csound community, amongst them Andrés Cabrera, Richard Boulanger, Rory Walsh, Oeyvind Brandtsegg and the authors of this chapter, resulted in the establishing of a book outline covering a wide variety of topics. A so-called book sprint, in which writers meet for several days to push a project forward, can provide the impetus to drive it towards publication. This can prove to be a particularly potent method if there is no contract, and therefore no deadline with a publisher. This also turned out to be the case for the Csound FLOSS Manual, which finally saw its first publication following a book sprint in Berlin in the spring of 2011. The first hard copy prints of the Csound FLOSS Manual were unveiled at the 2011 Csound Conference in Hannover and in this state it reflected the work of thirteen different contributors.

The Content

The Csound FLOSS manual's first section provides an overview and tutorial of Csound's principle mechanisms. Here a new Csound user will be guided through setting up Csound and to writing their first Csound orchestra and score.

Some later sections of the Csound FLOSS Manual mirror the structure of the Canonical Csound Reference Manual, as in the sections which introduce various methods of sound synthesis and sound modification, but unlike the reference manual, it introduces the concepts behind these techniques beyond their implementation in Csound and each technique is further illustrated with several examples, often progressing gradually in complexity. The FLOSS manual does not attempt to replicate the comprehensive coverage of all opcodes that the Csound Reference Manual achieves but instead selects one or two example opcodes of that technique that are best suited to introducing the new user to that technique. For example, Csound offers fifteen different opcodes for granular synthesis but the relevant FLOSS manual chapters focus upon just the *sndwarp*, *fof* and *granule* opcodes, which provide an adequate insight into the overarching concepts behind the technique.

The focus of the Csound FLOSS manual on Csound's use in typical situations, results in there being chapters specifically about using MIDI and OSC and working with samples. The manual also offers tutorials and introductions on subjects related to Csound that will hardly be found elsewhere: chapters introducing Csound's main front-ends, CsoundQt, Blue, WinXound and Cabbage are written by the authors of those front-ends. Useful tutorials on, for example, using Csound within Pd using the csoundapi~ external object. More esoteric uses of Csound are introduced in chapters on the Csound API, on Python in Csound and CsoundQt, and on using Csound as a VST plug-in or within Ableton Live.

A unique section of the Csound FLOSS manual is the *Opcode Overview*, which offers the new user a digested selection of essential opcodes chosen from Csound's enormous catalogue of over 1500 opcodes.

The Csound FLOSS manual is now in its second edition and it continues to evolve, reflecting Csound's own evolution and, as more and more Csound users discover the project, it welcomes new contributors thereby communicating with the reader from a wider base of expertise.

The online version offers a well-structured interface and is easy to navigate. An advantage of the online version is that it always holds the latest version. The second publication of the Csound FLOSS Manual, made in March 2012, is currently only available as an online version.

Discussion

The Csound FLOSS manual displays some characteristics typical for collaboratively written documentation for free software. These idiosyncrasies become clear when it is compared to printed books like *The Csound Book* (Boulanger, 2000) or the recently published introduction to Csound, *Csound Power!* by Jim Aikin (2012).

As already discussed, a strength of an online book is that it has the unique ability to reform itself continually but a disadvantage can be that the diversity of contributions from a variety of contributors can lead to an unevenness in style and quality. The only way to prevent this might be to employ a dedicated editor who could contact the relevant authors if required to suggest improvements and fixes. In the case of the Csound FLOSS Manual, this could very easily become a full-time job but the reality is that all manual contributors do their work as volunteers alongside their full-time occupations.

The quality of the Csound FLOSS Manual is dependent upon the willingness of the best-qualified people to get involved in the project. Well-informed feedback from users of the manual will also ensure improvements. If these practices are implemented then collectively written documentation for open-source software has the potential to match or even surpass the quality of that supplied with commercial software.

References

Aikin, Jim, *Csound Power!* The Comprehensive Guide. Boston: Course Technology, 2012.

Boulanger, Richard, *The Csound Book*, edited by R. Boulanger. Cambridge: The MIT Press, 2000.

"Csound FLOSS Manual," accessed December 21, 2012, http://en.flossmanuals.net/csound/.

ffitch, John, *The Audio Programming Book*, edited by R. Boulanger and V. Lazzarini. Cambridge: The MIT Press, 2011.

"FLOSS (free/libre/open-source software) Manuals was set up as a central gathering point and publishing house for community written manuals for open-source software," accessed December 21, 2012, http://booki-dev.flossmanuals.net/.

Heintz, Joachim, "Mitentwicklung Freier Audio-Software durch Studierende und ihre Institutionen. Für eine offene Plattform aller Studios zum Austausch von Beispielen," *kunsttexte.de/ auditive_perspektiven,* no. 4, 2011, accessed December 21, 2012, http://www.kunsttexte.de/index.php?id=711&idartikel=38902&ausgabe=38844&zu=907&L=0 .

"Lulu – Self Publishing Platform," accessed December 21, 2012 http://www.lulu.com/ .

Vercoe, Barry, et. al., "Canonical Csound Reference Manual," accessed December 21, 2012, http://www.csounds.com/manual/html/index.html.

IMPRESSIONS OF THE FIRST INTERNATIONAL CSOUND CONFERENCE

Wolfgang Motz, Sigurd Saue, Kita Toshihiro, Tarmo Johannes, unidentified, Andreas Möllenkamp, Michael Gogins, Oeyvind Brandtsegg, Jan Jacob Hofmann, John ffitch, Francois Pinot, Victor Lazzarini, Stefan Thomas, Menno Knevel, Johannes Schütt, Max Marcoll, Iain McCurdy; Jedrzej Tymchuk, Kim Ervik, Joachim Heintz, Rory Walsh, Gleb Rogozinsky, Richard Boulanger, Steven Yi, Bernt Isak Waerstad, John Clements, Peiman Khoshravi, Takahiko Tsuchiya. Missing (al least): Alex Hofmann, Massimo Avantaggiato, Reza Payami, Luis Antunes Pena, Giacomo Grassi, Nicola Monopoli, Andrés Cabrera, Damian Marhulets, Torsten Fischer, Clemens von Reusner

Richard Boulangers Csound Conference Opening Concert: 30. September 2011 (John Clements, Richard Boulanger, John Ffitch, Takahiko Tsuchiya)

John Clements performing: Fingers in the Waves

User-Developer Round Table II

Steven Yi's Workshop on Blue

Damian Marhulets, Alex Hofmann, Joachim Heintz, Kita Toshihiro

Richard Boulanger, Alex Hofmann, John ffitch, Victor Lazzarini

Iain McCurdy and Rory Walsh

Victor Lazzarini and Richard Boulanger

SCHEDULE OF THE FIRST INTERNATIONAL CSOUND CONFERENCE

hmtmh hochschule für musik theater und medien hannover [Incontri – Institut für neue Musik] **30 September - 2 October, 2011**

C-Sound conference

Friday, September 30	17:00 Welcome 17:15 Richard Boulanger: Csound yesterday, today and tomorrow 19:30 Concert session with Richard Boulanger and friends
Saturday, October 1	09:00 - 11:00 Papers 11:30 - 14:00 Workshops 15:00 - 18:00 Developer-User-Roundtable I: Technology 19:30 Concert (Kammermusiksaal Plathnerstr. 35)
Sunday, October 2	09:00 - 11:00 Papers 11:30 - 14:00 Workshops 15:00 - 18:00 Developer-User-Roundtable II: Community

FRIDAY, September 30

Location: HMTM Hannover, Emmichplatz 1, 30175 Hannover **[1]***

			Room
17:00 - 17:15	**Welcome** (Joachim Heintz)		E 15 [1]*
17:15 - 18:30	Sound installations from Iain McCurdy, Clemens von Reusner and others in the Foyer.	**Csound yesterday, today and tomorrow** (Richard Boulanger)	
18:30 - 19:30		**Reception**	
19:30		**Concert session** Richard Boulanger and friends playing with Csound and Wiimotes, iPads, iPhones, p5 gloves and other stuff.	

* *The numbers in brackets in this schedule refer to the numbers on the city map in the appendix.*

2 hmtmh hochschule für musik theater und medien hannover [Incontri – Institut für neue Musik] C-Sound conference, 30 September - 2 October 2011

SATURDAY, October 1

Locations: HMTM Hannover, Emmichplatz 1, 30175 Hannover **[1]**

and

Kammermusiksaal, Plathnerstr. 35, 30175 Hannover **[4]**

Concert hall, Plathnerstr. 35 **[4]**

Time		Programme			Room
09:00 - 11:00	Sound installations from Iain McCurdy, Clemens von Reusner and others in the Foyer during the whole day.	**PAPERS**			E 15 [1]
09:00 - 09:40		**Python Scripting in QuteCsound** (Andrés Cabrera)			
09:40 - 10:20		**Csound and Object-orientation: Designing and implementing Cellular Automata for Algorithmic Composition** (Reza Payami)			
10:20 - 11:00		**A Personal View on Teaching Csound** (Gleb G. Rogozinsky)			
11:00 - 11:30		**Break**			
11:30 - 13:45		**WORKSHOPS** Most of the Workshops are repeated twice to give the attendees the chance to visit two of three workshops.			
11:30 - 12:30 (Slot I)		**Writing Csound Opcodes in Lua - Part I: Conception** (Michael Gogins) Room: **130 [1]**	**Csound - Max/MSP translation: Implementing a framework for Serial Composition and Frequency Modulation** (Reza Payami) Room: **315 [1]**	**Composing with blue - Part 1** (Steven Yi) Room: **Z 40 [1]**	
12:30 - 12:45		**Break**			
12:45 - 13:45 (Slot II)		**Writing Csound Opcodes in Lua - Part II: Examples** (Michael Gogins) Room: **130 [1]**	**Csound - Max/MSP translation: Implementing a framework for Serial Composition and Frequency Modulation** (Reza Payami) Room: **315 [1]**	**Composing with blue - Part 2** (Steven Yi) Room: **Z 40 [1]**	
13:45 - 15:00		**Break**			

hmtmh Hochschule für Musik Theater und Medien Hannover [Incontri – Institut für neue Musik] C-Sound conference, 30 September - 2 October 2011

15:00 - 18:00		**DEVELOPER-USER-ROUNDTABLE I: TECHNOLOGY** The discussions between developers, users and the audience are initiated by a short statement (aka init-pass). The chair of this roundtable is Victor Lazzarini	
15:00 - 15:20		**New Parser and Multithreading** What's the state of development, what will be possible when it's finished. init-pass: John ffitch	E 15 [1]
15:20 - 15:40		**New Language Features: Csound5 or Csound6?** Arrays, control structures and more: What can be included now; what is for Csound6. init-pass: Michael Gogins	
15:40 - 16:00		**Performance Improvements** Realtime safe memory allocation. How to improve performance and optimization. What kind of compiler optimizations or vectorizing is possible. Inlining functions, introspection. debugging. init-pass: Andrés Cabrera and Michael Gogins	
16:00 - 16:20		**The Csound API** Functionality, Problems and further Development init-pass: François Pinot	
16:20 - 16:30		Break	
16:30 - 17:00		**Csound's design philosophy** Individual developer motivation and a clear direction of development with a common sense of purpose init-pass: Steven Yi	E 15 [1]
17:00 - 18:00		**Towards Csound6** Which decisions to take to the next major version of Csound init-pass: Andrés Cabrera and Jacob Joaquin	
19:30		CONCERT	Kammermusiksaal, Plathnerstr. 35, 30175 Hannover Concert hall, Plathnerstr. 35 [4]

hmtmh Hochschule für Musik Theater und Medien Hannover [Incontri – Institut für neue Musik] C-Sound conference, 30 September - 2 October 2011

SUNDAY, October 2

Location: HMTM Hannover, Emmichplatz 1, 30175 Hannover **[1]**

Time				Room
09:00 - 11:00	**PAPERS**			
09:00 - 09:40	**Circumspectral Sound Diffusion** (Peiman Khoshravi)			E 15 [1]
09:40 - 10:20	**Creating reverb effects using granular synthesis** (Kim Ervik and Oeyvind Brandtsegg)			E 15 [1]
10:20 - 11:00	**PWGL: A Score Editor for Csound** (Massimo Avantaggiato)			E 15 [1]
11:00 - 11:30	**Break**			
11:30 - 13:45	**WORKSHOPS** Most of the Workshops are repeated twice to give the attendees the chance to visit two of three workshops.			
11:30 - 12:30 (Slot I)	**quince: new ways of modular musical editing** (Maximilian Marcoll) Room: **130 [1]**	**Csound for Live** (Richard Boulanger) Room: **315 [1]**	**Developing Csound Plugins with Cabbage** (Rory Walsh) Room: **Z 40 [1]**	
12:30 - 12:45	**Break**			
12:45 - 13:45 (Slot II)	**quince: new ways of modular musical editing** (Maximilian Marcoll) Room: **130 [1]**	**Csound for Live** (Richard Boulanger) Room: **315 [1]**	**Developing Csound Plugins with Cabbage** (Rory Walsh) Room: **Z 40 [1]**	
13:45 - 15:00	**Break**			
15:00 - 18:00	**DEVELOPER-USER-ROUNDTABLE I:** **COMMUNITY** The discussions between developers, users and the audience are initiated by a short statement (aka init-pass). The chair of this roundtable is Richard Boulanger.			
15:00 - 15:30	**Lists, Forum, Tutorials: Is there enough help for learning Csound?** Analysis of the current state and suggestions for further improvements. init-pass: Joachim Heintz and Menno Knevel			E 15 [1]
15:30 - 16:00	**Confusion or prosperity: Different frontends for Csound** QuteCsound, WinXound, MacCsound, Blue, Cabbage - should there be any unification? init-pass: Andrés Cabrera, Steven Yi, Rory Walsh			E 15 [1]
16:00 - 16:30	**Csound and its users** Where does it excel, what role does it play in users' music making, and where are areas to further grow. init-pass: Steven Yi and Oeyvind Brandtsegg			E 15 [1]

Sound installations from Iain McCurdy, Clemens von Reusner and others in the Foyer during the whole day.

hmtmh Hochschule für Musik Theater und Medien Hannover [Incontri – Institut für neue Musik] C-Sound conference, 30 September - 2 October 2011

SUNDAY, October 2

Location: HMTM Hannover, Emmichplatz 1, 30175 Hannover **[1]**

<table>
<tr><th></th><th></th><th colspan="3"></th><th>Room</th></tr>
<tr><td>09:00 - 11:00</td><td rowspan="16">Sound installations from Iain McCurdy, Clemens von Reusner and others in the Foyer during the whole day.</td><td colspan="4">PAPERS</td></tr>
<tr><td>09:00 - 09:40</td><td colspan="3">Circumspectral Sound Diffusion (Peiman Khoshravi)</td><td rowspan="3">E 15 [1]</td></tr>
<tr><td>09:40 - 10:20</td><td colspan="3">Creating reverb effects using granular synthesis (Kim Ervik and Oeyvind Brandtsegg)</td></tr>
<tr><td>10:20 - 11:00</td><td colspan="3">PWGL: A Score Editor for Csound (Massimo Avantaggiato)</td></tr>
<tr><td>11:00 - 11:30</td><td colspan="4">Break</td></tr>
<tr><td>11:30 - 13:45</td><td colspan="4">WORKSHOPS
Most of the Workshops are repeated twice to give the attendees the chance to visit two of three workshops.</td></tr>
<tr><td>11:30 - 12:30
(Slot I)</td><td>quince: new ways of modular musical editing (Maximilian Marcoll)
Room: 130 [1]</td><td>Csound for Live (Richard Boulanger)
Room: 315 [1]</td><td colspan="2">Developing Csound Plugins with Cabbage (Rory Walsh)
Room: Z 40 [1]</td></tr>
<tr><td>12:30 - 12:45</td><td colspan="4">Break</td></tr>
<tr><td>12:45 - 13:45
(Slot II)</td><td>quince: new ways of modular musical editing (Maximilian Marcoll)
Room: 130 [1]</td><td>Csound for Live (Richard Boulanger)
Room: 315 [1]</td><td colspan="2">Developing Csound Plugins with Cabbage (Rory Walsh)
Room: Z 40 [1]</td></tr>
<tr><td>13:45 -15:00</td><td colspan="4">Break</td></tr>
<tr><td>15:00 - 18:00</td><td colspan="3">DEVELOPER-USER-ROUNDTABLE I:
COMMUNITY
The discussions between developers, users and the audience are initiated by a short statement (aka init-pass). The chair of this roundtable is Richard Boulanger.</td><td rowspan="4">E 15 [1]</td></tr>
<tr><td>15:00-15:30</td><td colspan="3">Lists, Forum, Tutorials: Is there enough help for learning Csound?
Analysis of the current state and suggestions for further improvements.
init-pass: Joachim Heintz and Menno Knevel</td></tr>
<tr><td>15:30 - 16:00</td><td colspan="3">Confusion or prosperity: Different frontends for Csound
QuteCsound, WinXound, MacCsound, Blue, Cabbage - should there be any unification?
init-pass: Andrés Cabrera, Steven Yi, Rory Walsh</td></tr>
<tr><td>16:00 - 16:30</td><td colspan="3">Csound and its users
Where does it excel, what role does it play in users' music making, and where are areas to further grow.
init-pass: Steven Yi and Oeyvind Brandtsegg</td></tr>
</table>

5 hmtmh Hochschule für Musik Theater und Medien Hannover [Incontri – Institut für neue Musik] C-Sound conference, 30 September - 2 October 2011

16:30 - 16:40		**Break**	
16:40 - 17:10		**Ways of user participation** What can users do (bug reports, sharing examples, uploading UDO's). Which participation do users look for. What is the optimal workflow between users and developers. init-pass: Iain McCurdy, Peiman Khoshravi	**E 15 [1]**
17:10 - 17:30		**User's wish list** A collection and discussion of features users like to see in Csound. init-pass: Rory Walsh	
17:30 - 18:00		**Do we need a Csound Foundation?** Csound development between volutariness and the lack of money. init-pass: Victor Lazzarini	
18:00	**Farewell** (Joachim Heintz)		

EDITORS

Joachim Heintz after studying Literature and Art History, began his composition studies with Younghi Pagh-Paan and Guenter Steinke in Bremen in 1995 at the Hochschule Fuer Kuenste. He is the head of the electronic studio Incontri at the HMTM in Hannover (Hanover University of Music, Drama and Media), teaches Audio-Programming at the HfK Bremen and is a member of the Theater der Versammlung in Bremen. As a composer, he works for instruments as well as for electronic media. www.joachimheintz.de

Alex Hofmann (*1980) is a former student at the HMTM Hannover. His studies focused on saxophone playing, improvisation, computer music and development of interactive music systems. He is currently (2013) working on his PhD thesis in Music Acoustics (IWK) at the University of Music and Performing Arts Vienna.

Iain McCurdy is a composer of electroacoustic music and sound art originally from Belfast and currently based in Berlin. Having come from a background of writing for fixed medium, more recent work has focussed on sound installation, exploring physical metaphors of compositional structures through the creative use of electronic sensors and innovative human interface design. Physical designs are minimalistic, using primary shapes and colours and utilising instinctive user inputs.
www.iainmccurdy.org